IF YOU DON'T MIND MY Saying So:

SOME IMPERTINENT THOUGHTS ON EDUCATION & POLITICS IN THE AGE OF POLITICAL CORRECTNESS

JOHN CALVERT

IF YOU DON'T MIND MY Saying So:

SOME IMPERTINENT THOUGHTS ON EDUCATION & POLITICS IN THE AGE OF POLITICAL CORRECTNESS

JOHN CALVERT

Gotham Books

30 N Gould St.
Ste. 20820, Sheridan, WY 82801
https://gothambooksinc.com/

Phone: 1 (307) 464-7800

Published by Gotham Books (June 20, 2023)

  ISBN: 979-8-88775-323-2 (P)
  ISBN: 979-8-88775-324-9 (E)

TABLE OF CONTENTS

For my big brother Harold, who didn't
teach me everything I know … just the
important things.

I am grateful to my wife, Nellie Branch,
for her forbearance with a man
who never seems to finish anything.

But the peculiar evil of silencing the expression of an opinion is that it is robbing the human race, posterity as well as the existing generation, those who dissent from the opinion, still more than those who hold it. If the opinion is right, they are deprived of the opportunity of exchanging error for truth; if wrong, they lose, what is almost as great a benefit, the clearer perception of truth, produced by its collision with error.

John Stuart Mill, On Liberty

FOREWORD

The essays herein were written as op-ed pieces for the Fargo Forum newspaper over several years. They are concerned mostly with education and with politics, though in either case they reflect the view of a skeptic with an innate suspicion of the received wisdom, that is, of what "everyone knows."

My views of education have been shaped by many years of experience as a teacher in higher education where I, and most of my colleagues, have found the preparation of entering freshmen to be visibly declining almost by the year. I found myself in agreement with prominent critics and reformers like E.D. Hirsch, Jr., Dianne Ravitch, Chester Finn, William Bennett, Mortimer Adler and many other whose views of elementary and secondary education represent a radical departure from current practice and most especially from the ideas prevailing in the schools of education.

Decades of "progressivism" – an ideology of near-anarchy – in the teacher colleges has resulted in the erosion of the core of curriculum in the public schools and its replacement by what the 1983 *A Nation at Risk Report* call the "smorgasbord curriculum," i.e., a random assortment of electives intended to appeal to the impulses of juveniles. In part this is because the educational establishment has followed a romantic philosophy that assumes students are the best judges of what they need to know, and also because that same philosophy reflects an anti-intellectual strain that is widely shared in the culture.

The campuses are also, of course, straight jacketed by an ideological conformity that is immune to internal criticism and opposition. For these reasons, substantial reform has so far proven to be impossible.

The decline of talent among college students has its counterpart among the faculty. "Contingent" or "adjunct" teachers, a proletariat of part-time and temporary substitutes who resemble day laborers more than member of a profession, have largely replaced the core of full-time professional scholars. Although this has largely escaped public notice, it is a revolution in higher education that has lowered the quality of teaching and is an admission by the education establishment that it no longer regards higher education as a serious undertaking. What matters today is not quality teaching but the status that supposedly accrues to the institution from research and from sheer institutional growth.

My interest in politics goes back to my youth and from thence to a here-and-there career as a college teacher of political science. There is of course much overlap between educational topics and political ones – such as fights over affirmative action and the damage wrought by the ideology of multiculturalism in both spheres – as the essays herein will try to show. One difference between education and politics is that failings in the political system are widely acknowledged and properly resented even if, as with education, they also defy reform.

Even so, some of the essays on politics deal with ideas that are not commonplace and are even counter intuitive. These include seemingly bizarre possibilities such as the threat of artificial intelligence to the economy and the culture and some unexpected consequences of government regulation and subsidies.

On Main Street my political views would likely be seen as somewhat left of center, but on almost any college campus they would be regarded as far to the right of most of the faculty. In any case I have tried to present each topic, whether academic or political, on its own merits and to give the devil his due.

A Liberal Pundit
Discovers Political Correctness

Were syndicated columnist Ellen Goodman in the habit of studying politics before presuming to instruct others in them, she might have spared herself the embarrassment of her recent essay on the subject of "political correctness." As it is, she endorses a doctrine that is anything but liberal.

Goodman thinks PC is a "progressive campus virtue," and an "idealism that was at worst excessive." She has discovered forces, however, which despise virtue and idealism. For conservatives, the campuses have become "a juicy target for conservatives … another way of trashing idealism, putting a lid on change, pushing back … humanistic values."

Never mind Goodman's need for self-flattery (we liberals have ideals, conservatives don't). By equating PC with idealism, and the opposition to it with the off-campus Right, she trivializes the value of academic freedom and minimizes the threat to it from the on-campus Left.

Conservatives, portrayed as the sole opponents of PC, ought to feel honored, but it's an honor they must decline. The fact is that most of the opposition comes from principled liberals. Much to their credit, conservative publications have joined the attack, but so have *Newsweek, The New York Times Magazine, The New York Review of Books,*

The Progressive, The New Republic (which recently devoted an entire issue to the subject) and several other liberal publications.

Eugene Genovese, writing in *The New Republic,* notes that "as one who saw his professors fired during the McCarthy era and who had to fight, as a pro-Communist Marxist, for the right to teach, I fear that our conservative colleagues are today facing a new McCarthyism in some ways more effective and vicious than the old."

Perhaps Goodman is pleased to believe that PC is merely a threat to conservatives, who are more or less extinct on the campuses anyway. But it is not just conservatives whose academic freedom is at risk. It is everyone's.

PC is not idealism. It is born of what Prof. James S. Coleman has called "conspicuous benevolence" – the academic equivalent of what Thorstein Veblen called conspicuous consumption among the rich – though in the former one suspects motives far more sinister. While it masquerades as a noble defense of minority groups against the insensitivities of white middle class students and faculties, it is in fact a systematic assault upon the whole idea of academic freedom.

Goodman says she has "counted now a half-dozen cover stories" on PC. Had she actually read them, she would found dozens of stories like these:

The University of Delaware announces its "right to set priorities for support of scholarly activity" – and then exercises that right by aborting a research project, already well advanced, because it involved the touchy issue of the heritability of intelligence.

At the University of Washington, a male student enrolled in a women's studies course asks for evidence for his teacher's assertion that the nuclear family is "dysfunctional" and that lesbians make the best parents. The next day he is barred from the classroom by campus police.

And at Clark University a philosophy professor is required to explain how a proposed course will incorporate "pluralistic views." When she refuses to politicize the course, she is denounced by her dean as a threat to academic freedom and a campus rally is organized against her.

The Modern Language Association, whose conventions once dealt with the likes of Shakespeare and Marlowe, now offers panels with titles like "The Lesbian Phallus – or does Heterosexuality exist?" and "Strategies for Feminist Team Teaching of Hispanic Women Writers." Where scholarship is not suppressed under PC it is made derisory.

At Smith, Haverford, Tulane and elsewhere, Mao-style re-education courses and sensitivity seminars have become mandatory. Conversely, substantive courses which make appropriate use of historical documents are being dropped on charges that they contain racist language. History in particular is being sanitized and falsified in order to avoid giving offense to ethnic minorities.

So also, is language. New linguistic sins are being discovered at so prodigious a rate that a new vocabulary is being invented to catalog them. Along with the old standbys of racism and sexism, we now have "ableism" ("the oppression of the differently abled by the temporarily abled"), "looksism" ("the oppression of the unattractive by the attractive"), and other parallel oppressions like "ageism," "heterosexism," "classism," and even "speciesism" – prejudice against non-human life. One of the worst sins today is "Eurocentrism," which oppresses almost everyone with its vile conceit that Aristotle is weightier than Alice Walker.

Woe to those who fall, however innocently, into this tangled nest of evils. At the University of Pennsylvania, memos using the word "individual" are sent back with a warning that it is a "red flag phrase today which is considered by some to be racist." "Girl," "kid," and "old people" are out too. When you are on a campus, watch yourself, always; a moment's carelessness can bring a mob to your door. A slip of the tongue and you are sent straightaway to a sensitivity seminar. The smart scholar keeps his thoughts to himself.

PC demands equal rights for all minorities, but some minorities are more equal than others. It rightly condemns racism directed against blacks, but racism *by* blacks is defined away as a theoretical impossibility. Stereotypes of Jews are often patronized as normal and even proper, so long as it is disguised as anti-Zionism. And at selective universities, admissions preferences for black and Hispanic students have led to a very low glass ceiling for both Jews and Asians. The latter groups tend to have strong families, embrace the work ethic, and arrive academically well-prepared, all of which unambiguously identifies them as members of the oppressor class.

Of her liberal campuses, Goodman says, "Nowhere else in America do people believe so passionately in the power of ideas." Absolutely right. No one understands better than academics that ideas are dangerous – and that is exactly why so much energy is devoted to suppressing them. Much teaching, and much research, threatens the conspicuous benevolence of politically correct faculties and the egalitarian interests of their clientele groups. Teaching and research must therefore be rigorously monitored and, where necessary, squelched.

One of academia's most cherished legends is that threats to its freedom come overwhelmingly from the proles, hillbillies, and rednecks in the surrounding community, those drooling and half-drunk knuckle-draggers who are always on the verge of forming lynch mobs in retaliation for some rumor they've heard about on the campuses. Hence, academic freedom necessarily requires the protection of tenure. But the legend of professorial insecurity is cultivated strictly for external consumption. Otherwise, it is sheer self-serving nonsense, and every academician knows it to be nonsense.

The strongest pressures for conformity come now, not from the outside but from within the academy itself. "The greatest enemy of academic freedom, writes James S. Coleman, "is the norms that exist about what kinds of questions may be raised – there are taboos … which if broken lead to sanctions not primarily from … the general public, but from one's own colleagues."

PC will pass, as the previous McCarthyism did. It will be beaten, however, not alone by conservatives, but also by principled liberals, of whom Ellen Goodman is not one.

Not Everyone
Should Go to College

The governor's budget for higher education has been received with howls of indignation from Minnesota's college officials, as well as from civic boosters and others who protest the breach of what The Forum calls a "grand tradition of funding higher education," which is to say a tradition of perpetual, undiscriminating and fruitless increases. Thus, The Forum predicts that if the governor's budget stands, it will require the "elimination of programs" and "most importantly ... close the doors of Minnesota Colleges and Universities to many students."

I doubt, however, that a flat budget would be as catastrophic as *The Forum* suggests. In truth, the doors to college *should* be closed to many students, probably most of them, no matter how flush the state's budget may be; and many programs, particularly those designed for weak students, should be eliminated as well. Education is sacred, but it ought not to be a sacred cow. A great deal of nonsense parades under its banner and, as with any large enterprise, much money goes into wasteful practices.

Presently, more than half of our high school graduates enroll in college, even though a third of them are so poorly prepared that they require remedial coursework in basic subjects – things the elementary and secondary schools failed to teach them – once they get there. About half never graduate, even within six years. Even so, higher education still produces far more graduates than the economy can absorb. More than a quarter of the population over age 25 now has a baccalaureate degree or higher, but forty percent of recent grads hold jobs which, by their own account, do not require college. What interest is served by encouraging everyone to attend college?

Ever-expanding enrollments require, as an iron rule, ever-declining academic standards. With the exhaustion of the high school talent pool, traditional college programs come under pressure to indulge poor performance with grade inflation, and fluffy non-academic programs have to be invented to accommodate ever-descending levels of ability. Already the landscape is littered with courses in rap studies, hip-hop studies, celebrity studies and the like, all devoted to pampering dullards, nursing ethnic grievances, and flattering bad taste. The campuses have in part become extensions of the high school culture, so that the intellectual polish of university graduates is seldom distinguishable from that of 10th grade dropouts.

Large numbers corrupt the very meaning of higher education. It was classically understood that education meant acquainting young people with their culture's history and traditions, its arts and sciences, its great ideas; and it was also understood that education was to be pursued for its own sake, a "disinterested endeavor," as Mathew Arnold put it, "to learn and propagate the best that is known and thought in the world."

But those who can sympathize with that idea have always been few in number. Most students arrive on campus to bide their time socializing with their pals until they feel ready to enter the labor force. Similarly, our no-nonsense boosters (not a few of whom are within the ranks of college administrators themselves) have never grasped the ideal of knowledge-for-itself, and they have largely succeeded in hitching the universities to the goals of commerce. Many are puzzled as to why the universities are teaching art, history, or literature when it is not clear how such things promote economic growth.

In condemning spending cuts, *The Forum* does not express fear for the fate of the liberal arts. It merely issues a stern reminder that "colleges and universities are engines of long-term economic development," as if it were self-evident that higher education had no other purpose.

Money can make good things possible, and it can also perpetuate mischief. When money is used to stuff the campuses with people who cannot benefit from higher education and who even distort its true nature, it subsidizes mischief. It is not axiomatic that leaders who want to control wasteful spending are anti-education.

So, lighten up. A flat budget won't cause the heavens to fall unless the universities have lost all capacity for making distinctions between the essential and the ridiculous – a possibility that can't be ruled out.

Never let a crisis go unexploited. Throwing money at the schools merely allows them to drift along forever without reform efforts. Enlightened administrators (there are some) will embrace cuts as an opportunity to do some long-overdue trimming. Any damage to genuine educational interests is likely to rest with the universities and their grow-at-any-cost mentality than with the governor.

The Misuses of
the Nobel Prize

This year's Nobel Prize for Literature has gone to Harold Pinter, a playwright whose work is noted for its indecipherable characters, disjointed dialog, and general pointlessness. The Nobel committee, however, probably didn't honor him for his art so much as for his politics, which are stylishly anti-American. His view of the US ("arrogant, indifferent … the most dangerous power the world has ever known") was no doubt the most attractive item on his resume.

These days the committee seems more intent upon rewarding politically correct ideas, no matter how silly, than on recognizing authentic literary or scientific accomplishments. According to the *Atlantic Monthly*, good bets for next year's peace prize are rockers Bono and Bob Geldof, who propose to reform the world by giving debt relief to Third World tyrants who are not about to pay up anyway.

No wonder that the conservative journal *National Review* recently asked whether the Nobel Prize is any longer worth winning. To be sure, a clearly deserving figure like Mother Theresa or a V.S. Naipaul occasionally makes the cut, but increasingly, the prizes are being used to accentuate the Nobel Committee's political causes and grudges. Thus, the peace prize for 2001 was awarded (6 weeks after the attacks of 9/11) to the United Nations and its Secretary-General, Kofi Annan, as a rebuke, according to the committee, to President

George W. Bush for his impertinence in presuming to defend American security without getting permission from the UN.

A year later the peace prize went to former President Jimmie Carter (who runs his own foreign policy establishment in Plains, Ga. and who was the most prominent critic of George W. Bush's buildup in Iraq) as a "kick in the leg" (as the committee's chairman put it) to Mr. Bush and the US, and "to all that follow the same line as the United States." In 2005 it administered a second kick when it gave the peace prize to Mohammed ElBaradei, director of the International Atomic Energy Agency, for refusing to confirm Iraq's alleged weapons of mass destruction.

A third kick came in 2007 when it awarded the prize both to the Intergovernmental panel on Climate Change, and to Al Gore, whose campaign against global warming was a clear contrast to Bush's doubts.

And there was a fourth: As *Time's* Michael Grunwald put it, "it wasn't enough for the Nobel Committee to swerve off the road to run over Bush once, then back up and run him over twice more. Even though the official representative of ugly American culture and cowboy diplomacy has remained graciously silent in retirement, the committee decided to stick it to him one more time by choosing his newly minted successor who has been in office only nine months but has made some of the right noises about rejecting some of [Bush's] global policies."

(To his credit, Obama was said to have seen his award as "fawning" and as an attempt to influence his administration. "An American president wants to set his own agenda," an aide said. "Here he was forced into a role he hadn't sought.")

So, the committee's choices, however they might be rationalized, fit a close pattern: All four prizes went to (as Grunwald has put it) to a NPFNBGWB – a Nobel Prize for not being George W. Bush.

If the purpose of the Nobel Prize is to serve as an instrument of Leftist ideology, then the recipient's achievements are excess baggage. So last year the prize for literature went to an Austrian novelist named Elfriede Jelinek (who?) even though two committee members threatened to resign on the grounds that, except for their fashionable feminism, her books are "empty." Other recent winners for literature include Jose Saramago (who?) for writing "tradition in a way that … can be described as radical," and Dario Fo (who?) for his "strongly political plays" that "[scourge] authority and [uphold] the dignity of the downtrodden."

And then there is the case of Rigoberta Menchu. She got the peace prize in 1992 for an autobiography that portrayed her hardscrabble life as an illiterate peasant in Guatemala whose writings were said to have struck a powerful blow, as the Nobel Committee put it, for "social justice." She tells of a childhood spent toiling on coffee and cotton plantations; of her family's struggle against exploitive landlords (all of European descent, naturally); of the deaths of two brothers, one by starvation, and the other burned alive by government troops. Menchu's credibility on the Left was guaranteed by the fact that she is female, a person of color, and Third World – altogether the complete victim, the perfect realization of the Left's eternal fantasy of the suffering noble savage. Her book was put on required reading lists in American universities everywhere and she was showered with honorary degrees.

Six years later, however, a field anthropologist and a *New York Times* reporter exposed her book as a fabrication. Menchu had not spent her childhood toiling in cotton fields, but in prestigious private boarding schools. Her family's battle against avaricious landowners turned out to have been a feud between her father and his in-laws. Of her two dead brothers, one never existed, and the other was found living comfortably in a Guatemalan village.

How did the Nobel Committee respond to all this? Having been plainly swindled, did it then express outrage and indignantly rescind its award? No. It merely announced that the "details" of the case "are not particularly important." On the other hand, a good many universities *did* express outrage over the Menchu affair – not at her fabrications, but at the *investigators* who exposed them!

It's a pity that the Nobel Prize has fallen to such a low estate. It's important to have a pinnacle award to give recognition to literary, scientific, and moral achievements of the highest order. What will it take to restore Nobel's prestige?

Obviously, the Nobel Committee should quit using the awards to peddle its pet political causes. But another problem is simply that too many prizes are being given. (A similar problem afflicts the Olympic Games which shovels out medals for everything short of hopscotch.) First-order achievers do not show up annually and in numbers exactly equal to the awards available; yet since a large stock of prizes must be given, many will be given to third raters. If the awards were made, say, once every four or five years, genuine merit would form a larger pool and awards to politically correct hacks would be harder to justify.

In the meantime, the Nobel Committee might well profit from its own kick in the leg. Just imagine that one day a person of towering achievement is announced as having won the Nobel Prize – and then announces in turn: "Sorry, I can't use it. It puts me in the company of people like Rigoberta Menchu and Harold Pinter."

Academia's War
against the Military

At a forum held at Columbia University last September, PBS's Jim Lehrer asked the presidential candidates how college graduates might serve causes "larger than themselves," and Senator John McCain, a veteran of the Vietnam War, replied that while military service is one obvious means, Columbia, like most elite schools, does not permit either military recruiters or the Reserve Officers Training Corps (ROTC) program to defile its grounds. To the surprise of many, Barack Obama agreed: "The notion that [university students] … aren't offered the choice … of participating in military service, I think is a mistake."

But among academic and media elites, anti-military sentiment is always in fashion. A contemporary *Time* cover story, ***"21 Ways to Serve America"*** made not a single mention of the armed services, as if *that* kind of service were unthinkable.

In our politicized universities, such snobbery masquerades as lofty idealism, though it has more subterranean sources. Like moral exhibitionism and narcissism. ROTC was first purged from the campuses during the Vietnam era by anti-establishment students with riots and bombs, and today many of the rioters, now comfortably ensconced as senior professors, deans, and presidents, see its return as a slap at their legacy.

Class consciousness figures in too. Because the military is a traditional path of upward mobility for blue collar people, it is instinctively scorned by elite professors and well-born students who, like would-be aristocrats everywhere, are not amused by the rise of their inferiors.

Then there is academia's passion for causes. These usually have nothing to do with education, but that doesn't matter so long as they make academics feel good about themselves. When the Vietnam War ended, fashionable academicians had to invent a new reason to justify maintaining their anti-military posture. So, when the military's "don't ask, don't tell" rule was announced, the champions of gay rights pounced on it as yet another because that would serve to demonstrate their moral superiority.

Trouble is that the campus boycotts were in place long before the "don't ask" rule appeared in 1991. Worse, the military didn't make the rule, fellow Democrat Bill Clinton did. What to do? Well, the campuses could not, of course, blame those who formulated the rule, so they blamed its *executors* – the military – and left the boycotts intact.

However, misguided the "don't ask" rule may be, decades of moral posturing have accomplished nothing except to block students who didn't make the rule from exploring military careers. So, these students must either find ROTC programs elsewhere (which often involve long commutes to other campuses and military courses for which the home campus won't give credit) or else abandon their goal of becoming officers.

And that's a shame, because against the campuses' most cherished anti-military stereotypes, ROTC grads are as bright, idealistic, and forthcoming with their talents as any volunteers anywhere. As junior officers they are given opportunities and responsibilities that are seldom entrusted to people of their tender years, ones that draw out their best qualities and instill leadership skills that will serve them, and the country, in good stead for generations after.

For a couple of decades following WWII, almost all of the national leadership had first-hand experience of the military and its culture, surely a good thing a good thing in a country that values civilian control. Today only about one-sixth of Congressmen share this experience, and among graduates of the elite universities it's rarer still. In 1956 (a time of near-universal conscription) some 400 Princeton graduates entered the military as officers. In 2004 only 9 did. Each year a *quarter* of Yale's graduating seniors apply to Teach for America, a cadre that volunteers for service in the nation's toughest schools. But few Yalies will even consider the military. The difference is that the ideologues of academe have turned military service into something vulgar, unworthy of an Ivy League graduate.

Yet academic fashion may be changing. Just now, students on several campuses are petitioning to end the boycotts, and even in the Ivy Leagues some administrators are openly sympathetic. Harvard's ex-president, Larry Summers, made a point of speaking at commissioning ceremonies for his graduates (which, because of Harvard's general contempt for the military, have had to be held at nearby MIT) and his successor, Drew Faust, continues the tradition.

"You have awakened at dawn while your roommates slept in," Faust told a recent class. "You have jumped out of airplanes, challenged your bodies and your brains, and become mentally and physically prepared for service. You have our respect for your choices, our admiration for your commitment, and our deep gratitude for your willingness to confront dangers on the nation's behalf." She added that "every Harvard student should have the opportunity to serve in the military, as you do."

Refreshing words, those. They will be applauded by generations of ROTC grads who, like myself, were privileged to serve without being second-guessed by the legions of save-the-world academics who have too much leisure time.

An Educator
Who Needs Instruction

North Dakota Superintendant of Public Instruction Wayne Sanstead has replied to a commentary of mine by saying he found "very little" in the piece to which he could "relate." In particular, he could not relate to my view that the public schools are failing and that the most important reason for their failure is that their curricula fail to provide a coherent vision of what it is that students need to know.

His reply should leave little doubt that Dr. Sanstead, far from being devoted to the cause of education reform, is in fact an obstacle to it. Sadly, the state's chief educational officer has no perspective on the subject he is charged with supervising. What he does in his reply is to play some games that are marks of progressive educationists everywhere who wish to avoid genuine reform while appearing to be its champions.

One of these games is called denial. It's played in every state, and it goes like this: There is indeed a crisis in American education; thank God the crisis is confined to the other forty-nine states and does not include ours. Our state produces fewer illiterates, dropouts, unplanned pregnancies or whatever else the statisticians might scrounge up, than the national average. Therefore, our system is excellent; and a system that is already excellent doesn't need to be reformed, does it? What goes unmentioned in this orgy of self-flattery is that the national standard by which we measure ourselves is itself a disgrace. When tested against the rest of the industrialized world, our high school seniors invariably wind up at the bottom of the pack.

Then there's the obigatory cliché about money. "Our problem is not one of philosophy or consensus," Sanstead says; rather, "it is a problem of public-school finance." So: Do half of our high school seniors write at the sixth-grade level? Blame underfunding. Are they unable to identify Franklin Roosevelt, locate Mexico on a map, or perform long division? Then spend more money. And after spending has been doubled and then trebled and it turns out that our kids still can't write, still don't know who FDR was, why that just proves that we need to spend still more. The beauty of the alibi of underfunding is that it can never be disproved; even if a hundred spending increases have failed to improve education, that doesn't mean the next one won't succeed.

Throwing money at education fails because we no longer have a consensus on what education means. So, when we throw more money at something called "education," it invariably goes to into more administrators, more gyms, more coaches, more counselors, and more computers; but it never goes into beefing up the history program, or civics, or grammar or the arts and sciences or anything that might qualify as an academic subject. Because more money doesn't translate into higher student achievement, some of the most opulent "Taj Mahal" schools in America are among its worst failures.

American high school students are routinely outclassed by kids in other nations, including Third World countries, such as Vietnam, Estonia, Slovenia, Latvia, and Slovakia where per-student spending are a fraction of what it is here. The old one-room rural schoolhouse was almost certainly a better educator than is today's sprawling air-conditioned colossus with its sports programs, Olympic-sized swimming pool, its profligate technology, and its hundreds of electives, if only because its meager resources forced the rural school to concentrate on the things that matter.

Even when judged against our own past, standardized test scores are lower than they were in 1970 although real per-student spending has since trebled. Nor do students in states with high per-student expenditures reliably outperform their peers in low-spending states. A dozen states currently require all their students to take the ACT, but a comparison between state ACT scores and per-pupil expenditures reveals no positive correlation between student achievement and funding. Wyoming, for instance, spends $15,700 per student annually; yet students in Utah, Colorado, Montana, North Dakota, and Illinois, where per-pupil funding is thousands of dollars lower, all earn higher ACT scores.

Sanstead's third game is that old bureaucratic staple of referring the critic elsewhere. For this he recommends the recent work of a state task force which provides "an excellent education vision for our schools."

His first exhibit is the Fargo school system, which he says is "an excellent place to start." But purusing its curricular offerings, we instantly find that Fargo's schools are afflicted with the same randomized "smorgasbord" curriculum which, as the Nation at Risk report warned back in 1983 (and as many later national studies have confirmed) has been the ruination of education everywhere. The Fargo district's course catalog bulges with nonacademic electives - over 200 of them, some 90 percent of all the courses listed - like Restaurant Skills, Clothing Concepts, Highway Safety, Family Relationships, Community

Living, Social Skills, Auto Tune-up and and scores of other Mickey Mouse treats for kids whose "learning styles," as the course catalog puts it, may "limit their performance in other departments."

Not bad for an underfunded system, no?

Next, let's look at the reports of the three task forces whose "excellent vision" is highly recommended by Dr. Sanstead. These reports do indeed provide a vision, and it is a vision of admirable clarity. But it is not a vision of anything remotely related to education. These reports should be read by anyone who wishes to understand why our schools are failing to produce literate people.

The three reports are, "Education: North Dakota's Key to Recovery," by the Education Advancement Task Force; "Public Elementary and Secondary Education," by the Education Action Commission; and "Vision 2000," a series of reports by the North Dakota 2000 Committee.

The vision in all of these reports is that of a 21st Century industrial dystopia in which education is accorded virtually no value in itself and is important only insofar as it can be harnessed to the state's economic goals. Its common vision is the transformation of the schools into little more than suppliers of skilled labor through a curriculum completely cleansed of the liberal arts, sciences, and humanities. This cleansing is to be conducted, as the "Vision 2000" report puts it, by "private sector representatives in the design of human capital development efforts"; or, as the Education Action Commission puts it, by school-business-labor "partnerships." Clearly, the schools are to become subordinates of commerce.

One struggles desperately through these reports, with their pretentious jargon about "skills," "human resource infrastructures," "education enterprises," and "intellectual assets," hoping to find the smallest affirmation of the legitimacy of the independent life of the mind. And one struggles in vain.

To be sure, there are occasional references to the "quality of life," and the need to foster "critical thinking" and "further learning"; but from the context of these reports, it is clear that these things are intended to be construed only as business capital. In these reports no dimension outside of commerce exists.

"North Dakota's future," the Education Advancement Task Force observes in its opening statement, lies in its capacity to "combine agriculture with high tech and small business development." But because the schools "lack the content needed to secure the state's future," they must "restructure ... to provide for practical knowledge and skills for technical occupations."

And we are informed by the Vision 2000 Committee (in its "Flagship for a New North Dakota Discussion Report") that "the need is more than just education or training. It involves recognizing that knowledge (and the ability to use it through enhanced thinking and reasoning skills) is the single most important variable in determining the potential of a person and, therefore, the potential of a state's human capital." That last phrase says it all.

The work of the Education Action Committee, however, deserves special mention. Its "Vision and Consensus for Action" is a work of exquisite purity, a truly antiseptic picture of the final triumph of technique. It is 36 pages of totalitarian horror.

One reads in morbid fascination the story of Amber, a typical high school student on a typical day in the 21st century. Amber does not really have a school, as we think of schools today; hers is not so much a physical place as it is an amorphous series of clearinghouses, resource centers and telecommunications networks, among which she floats according to her interests at the moment.

The nerve center of all this appears to be contained in an "assessment center" located in an efficient, multipurpose "school/community complex" which resembles a shopping mall. Amber seems not seen to have teachers either; what she has is an assortment of consultants called "learning tutors" and "assessment proctors," because in the 21st Century students mostly teach themselves. Classes are more or less optional and Amber frequently chooses to stay home in order to do assignments on her computer, free from the bother of human contact.

It is all reminiscent of a painting in the style of socialist realism, a stirring picture of (as the Action Committee puts it) "the sun ... shining brightly over the rippling fields of the North Dakota prairie," with heroic peasants, workers, and students walking victoriously into the sunset. It is a sensory feast. And yet ….

And yet it is a feast which leaves one famished. Neither Amber nor anyone else in this picture seems to possess either an intellect or a soul. Amber inhabits a world of perfect efficiency, but it's an efficiency which has no discernible purpose, at least none apart from the interests of business and - The State. Hers is an anomic, bloodless, technology-worshipping world in which teachers have nothing to teach, in which there is no body of transcendent knowledge to be passed through the generations, no convictions that need to be shared, nothing to be savored for its own sake. Amber's world is devoid of art, poetry, literature, and everything else that is not immediately "useful." Her self-education is nothing more than a series of random projects reflecting her transient whims.

And so, it is throughout the remainder of this appalling document. We are given a Huxleyan paradise of international computer hookups, satellite instruction, resource centers, transportation networks, "teacher-business- employee exchanges," "flexibility in curriculum and school time," "entrepreneurial and economic experiences," and randomized "education plans" specifically tailored to each student's peculiar interests. And all - all of it - is in the service of a grim Calvinism which insists that above all else, education must provide the "motivation and entrepreneurial and career skills that can contribute to growth in their personal lives and in the state's economic growth and development."

Now mark this: Apart from references to Amber's dislike of English and math, her project in international relations and her "history" of a neighboring village (and the inexplicable fact that she has somehow taken up German) there is nowhere in this treatise on "education reform" a single reference to any aspect of a liberal education. There is not one mention of world history, geography, science, art, literature, civics, economics, or any academic discipline to be found in the entire document. There is nothing to suggest the need for an acquaintance with the culture one inhabits, nothing in praise of intellectual curiosity, nothing even about the value of reading a book for the pleasure of it. It is wholly devoted to the production of skilled laborers and child entrepreneurs.

And mark this too: It comes with the recommendation of the highest education officer in the state.

I hope no one will conclude that I take pleasure in criticizing North Dakota's school system, or anyone else's; I will be the first to insist that the state's confusion over education is no worse than that found in almost every other state, and that it only reflects what is truly a nation-wide crisis. I will also say that the North Dakota students in my university classes generally perform as well as those from neighboring states, and perhaps even better. But even so, they are the best of a very bad lot.

I once asked a freshman college class of 55 students who Adolph Hitler was. With the exception of a very bright Chinese student, not one of them knew. I asked another class of 75 who Winston Churchill was and was received with blank stares. I cite passages from the Declaration of Independence and the Gettysburg Address and find that my undergraduates have no idea of where they came from or what they mean. I sometimes ask them who their heroes are, and after an awkward silence they are likely to mumble something like, "my dad, I guess," or else cite the latest rock superstar.

I have graded hundreds of student-written book reviews and have been solemnly and repeatedly informed that reading Plato or Machiavelli or Reinhold Niebuhr is a waste of time because (as one student put it) "no one is ever going to agree on the matter, and it all lies in the fact that everyone has different morals and beliefs." And because: "The biggest problem is that there is no right or wrong answer. People's beliefs are based on their own judgments. Everybody has the right to their own opinion." And because: "The concept of justice is different with each passing individual and is just all in their minds."

Just so. Everything is all in our minds. If our high schoolers learn nothing else, they learn that outside of their own skins nothing is real. And they have drawn the appropriate conclusion too, which is that studying illusions is a waste of time. Here, in a nutshell, is the inescapable result of presuming to operate schools in the intellectual vacuum that is dogma in our teacher colleges and, from thence, our public schools. One wonders: Can students who reduce all values to subjective opinions find any value in what they read? Can they themselves live deeply?

I am shocked anew, every year, by the numbers of college freshmen who cannot construct a compound sentence, who do not know in what continent Vietnam is located, who cannot name a single book by a Nobel laureate; and by the militant anti-intellectualism that flourishes in the back rows among the smirking 25-year-olds with their baseball caps, bubble gum and tattered denims who now present a discipline problem in university classrooms because they have no real idea of what college is about or even of why they are there.

Dr. Sanstead says that he agrees with my "general thesis that education does not have the priority it deserves." But that is not my thesis. My thesis is that it is impossible to establish priorities for an enterprise when no one knows what purpose that enterprise is supposed to serve. The smorgasbord curriculum, which turns the responsibility of teaching students over to the impulses of students themselves – and tells them that literature and history, cake decorating and knitting are all of equal importance – is the education establishment's confession that it hasn't the faintest idea of what that purpose is.

The priority in education reform must be the development of a consensus as to what the schools should be teaching. And that is something for which those now in charge of education show a peculiar lack of concern.

Charity for the Landed Aristocracy

Nothing more sharply illustrates the immortal nature of government than the federal farm program, which began during the New Deal as "temporary" assistance for the rural poor and which now, in its 82nd year, flourishes as a permanent entitlement for well-to-do landowners. Last year Uncle Sam dished out another $22 billion in assorted subsidies of which 74 percent went to just 10 percent of America's farms, most of them owned by millionaires. Hardly anything went to the truly needy. That's because the needy farms – those legendary 3-generational, struggling, *wholesome* small family farms like the Joads' in *The Grapes of Wrath* – are today about as common as unicorns.

So, today's subsidy programs justify their existence by sending aid to farms that *don't* need it. Today it's Robin Hood in reverse: The median wealth of subsidized farmers is about five times the median wealth of the city dwellers who are forced to pay the bill.

Farm programs are a cornucopia of privileges, including direct payments for growing specific crops (and also for *not* growing them), export subsidies, import quotas, countercyclical payments, crop insurance, ethanol mandates, price floors, marketing loans, rules to keep out competitors, and so on, all justified by the assumption that agribusinesses, not matter how opulent they may be, should be uniquely immune to any possibility of risk. In this state it is blasphemy to say otherwise.

The result is that since 1995 North Dakota's farmers have snagged $15 billion of other people's money, with the richest 10 percent getting 62 percent of the loot. Johnson Farms near Walhalla, one of the largest farm operations in the state, have acquired some $5.3 million and the Kohler Partnership by Valley City has socked away $4.2 million.

Governor John Stewart ("Jack") Dalrymple III, a landed patrician who was born in Minneapolis, attended out-of-state private schools, graduated from Yale, and claims that his soul was formed on the humble "family farm," is the scion of a great-great grandfather whose bonanza farming operation dates back to 1875. The family's spread, once running 32,000 acres, was at the time the largest cultivated farm not just in North Dakota, but in the entire world. It remains today as one of the two or three most highly subsidized enterprises in the state, having accumulated $4.7 million between 1998 and 2012. Not bad for a plain, down-to-earth farm boy and an avowed budget hawk.

Uncle Sam's generosity is such that it has tempted even those otherworldly Hutterites, whose land holdings keep spreading across Canada and the US, to join the state's long list of mendicant millionaires. This might seem inconsistent with their values, but subsidies work wondrous effects upon the human psyche: All who receive them will swear on a stack of bibles and with tears in their eyes that subsidies are good not just for themselves, but are essential to the nation's well-being, necessary for humanity, and pleasing in the sight of God.

Nor are the representatives of the people's interests neglectful of their own. The wife of Frank Lucas (Chairman of the House Agricultural Committee) availed herself of $14,584 for her farm last year. Representative Doug LaMalfa (R-CA) took in $188,570, and Steve

Fincher (R-TN), who has famously denounced food stamps for the poor as "thievery," has received $3.48 million since 1999. Collin Peterson, the ranking minority member of the House Agricultural Committee, feathered his own nest with $65,431 in 2011. Over the past 14 years similar relief has been granted to Vicki Hartzler (R-MO). To Kristi Noem (R-SD) and John Tester (D-MT), each of whom has received over $440,000.

Currently, 23 members of Congress get direct payments, and still others receive heavily subsidized crop insurance. (Who gets how much of this is unknown since Congress prudently forbids disclosure.) Some 90,000 US investors and absentee landlords get payments, including Mark Rockefeller, who received $340,000 last year not for cultivating his land, but just for owning it. Some 2,700 absentee landowners who live in places like Hong Kong and Saudi Arabia also extract millions annually from the US Treasury.

It may get worse. Among other things, the current House farm bill would increase crop insurance payments by another $9 billion, raise price floors for some commodities, and make the new subsidies permanent.

If this socialism-for-the-rich were finally ended, would the heavens fall? No. Most farmers get along without federal handouts, thanks; and even when some do fail, the land, buildings, machinery, and expertise, contrary to popular belief, don't suddenly disappear into thin air – they merely change hands, as they always have, often by absorption into larger or more diversified operations that are better equipped to survive bad years.

Now please: Don't fall for that saccharine slop about how the rustic charm of the intimate "small family farm" must be preserved as an indispensable part of Americana, no matter how outrageous the cost. Except in the rhetoric of farm-state Congressmen who are haunted by the specter of electoral defeat, that era has long since passed. The romantic image of the intimate three-generational family farm is preserved as a cynical myth that serves only to camouflage scandalous subsidies for the well-to-do. The character of modern agriculture is more industrial than pastoral; today's mechanized farms are about as charming as steel mills.

This theft of your tax money serves no legitimate national purpose. It just keeps compounding the wealth of opulent people who can never have enough. It goes on and on because of the crony capitalism that props up agriculture as well as every other policy area regardless of its merit. Obsolete programs become immortal because of the asymmetry that exists between the heavy benefits received by a small clique of recipients and the far smaller burden to millions of individual taxpayers footing the bill.

Which is too bad. The citizenry ought to get mad as hell at this cronyism, and yet generation after generation goes by and it never has.

Higher Education's Horror File

It is a principle, widely accepted in American education, that while everyone needs to be educated, there is nothing in particular that an educated person needs to know. In this relativistic age any course of study is the equal of any other, and any fantasy is deemed educationally valid if someone in authority proclaims its relevance to … something.

That's why I keep an assortment of news clippings in a folder labeled with the name "Horror File." Its stories are about what happens to education in an intellectual vacuum, and they range from a recent account of blind kids in Chicago who are required to take courses in driver education, through the Massachusetts education professor who sees no reason why Ph.D.'s should have to know how to read.

Anyway, it's spring and I'm cleaning out the old files. Before they go, I'm submitting a few snippets for your amusement. They're all on higher education, and while they are not typical of the enterprise – yet – they may suggest that the ivory tower isn't as certain of its mission as it once was. Christopher Lasch, in his *Culture of Narcissism,* called higher education a "diffuse, shapeless, and permissive institution that has absorbed the major currents of cultural modernism and reduced them to a watery blend, a mind-emptying ideology of cultural revolution, personal fulfillment, and creative alienation." Maybe Lasch was thinking of recent accounts like these:

~ The Astrological Institute of Scottsdale, AZ wins accreditation from the Commission of Career Schools and Colleges of Technology, thereby making its students eligible for federal grants and loans. The Institute's courses have titles like "Master Class on the Asteroid Goddesses," and "How to Write an Astrological column." The Commission was satisfied that the Institute's teachers are qualified to read the stars and that its graduates will find jobs, chiefly writing horoscopes and giving advice about the future.

~ Oberlin College offers a for-credit course in "The Life and Times of Drew Barrymore." It is taught by the students themselves, who show Barrymore's movies on DVDs and then lead discussions. It's one of a series of courses at Oberlin that has also included the TV series "Days of Our Lives" as well as indigenous courses in "Art and Science of Home Brewing," and "Whiskey Appreciation."

~ At New York College in Potsdam, Prof. John Massaro teaches a political science course titled "Walk Tall: Beauty, Meaning, and Politics in the Lyrics of Bruce Springsteen." Each class features two hours of lecturing, one hour of listening to Springsteen's recordings, and one hour of discussion. Rejecting his colleagues' advice to teach Neil Young instead, Massaro says that although Springsteen is "not cool," he is "my thing" and that by the end of the term he usually has a few converts.

~ At Syracuse, English professor Greg Thomas teaches a course titled "Hip-Hop Eshu: Queen B@A$H101 – the Life and Times of Lil' Kim." Hearing of the class, the rapper said she was "honored" to have a course "on my sensationalist lyrics, unique style and fashion and leadership role within the hip-hop community."

~ Whole new disciplines are appearing on the campuses. One is "Buffy Studies." A Nashville conference on "Buffy the Vampire Slayer" drew 325 scholars from as far away as Singapore. The event was hosted by Prof. David Lavery, the acknowledged "father of Buffy studies." Some 190 papers were presented to the conference on such topics as "slayer slang," "Buffy and the new American Buddhism," and "Postmodern Reflections on the Culture of Consumption." Buffy studies are now taught around the globe. A dozen scholarly texts have appeared so far, most recently Jana Riess' *What Would Buffy Do? A Vampire Slayer as Spiritual Guide.*

~ And porn studies, according to *Time* magazine, are flourishing too. At Northwestern University, a course in obscenity "examines how publications like *Hustler* can define class stratification in the U.S.," while a class at SUNY-Buffalo "tracks pornography's pivotal role in the development of communications systems." At NYU, a film showing porn star Annie Sprinkle coupling with a transgendered man led one undergraduate to deconstruct her "biases about what is a man and what is a woman … it made me want to explore these stereotypes and get past them."

~ Jim Harrick, a basketball coach at the University of Georgia, gave a multiple-choice exam to his "Coaching Principles" class which included 20 questions like these: "How many goals are on a basketball court?" "How many halves are in a college basketball game?" "How many quarters are in a high school football team?" "How many points does a 3-point field goal account for in a college basketball game?"

~ According to the Mercury News, San Jose State University is turning away qualified students from its incoming freshman class because there isn't enough room for them. It seems the college has too many "professional students" who don't want to leave, ever. Two such students have been enrolled for 15 years each, earning enough credits to have graduated more than 3 times over. Since San Jose State is a public university subsidized by taxpayers, professional students can afford to hang around forever.

~ Washtenaw Community College in Michigan has a new plan to fire 700 of its part-time adjunct teachers and procure their replacements from a local day labor agency. The college expects to save $800,000 annually on faculty costs.

~ The American Association of University Professors cites a recent case in which a federal ethics review board has required a linguist studying a preliterate tribe to "have the subjects read and sign a consent form" before conducting his studies.

~ And finally, there is the Gallup-Zogby Poll which finds that, on a battery of questions assessing basic cultural knowledge, "contemporary college seniors scored on average little or no higher than the high school graduates of a half-century ago." Among Ivy League seniors, 98 percent were able to identify Beavis and Butthead, while 81 percent were *unable* to identify Valley Forge or sentences from the Gettysburg Address. Now what could account for that?

The Mystique
of Urban Growth

The metropolitan growth plan proposed by the Greater Fargo-Moorhead Economic Development Corporation has fortunately failed. It was publicized just 3 weeks before election day and was no doubt intended to be a stealth issue introduced too late for an opposition to form. The *Forum*, always on the side of boosterism, soldiered for the plan and reported favorable opinions among all those it interviewed, except for a lone "skeptic" who thought it didn't push growth far enough.

But here are some of the plan's underlying assumptions that would have been exposed as ludicrous had it been subjected to open debate:

First, it was packaged exclusively in terms of economic advantage, as if no other dimension of life mattered. Its champions might have argued that growth will bring distinctive new architecture, special shops, theme parks, a flourishing city center, and various other amenities that make cities more cultured, more interesting, more livable. But no; quality-of-life issues are of no interest to our down-to-earth, no-nonsense visionaries who believe urban well-being flows from two mutually reinforcing insights: (a) we must attract more people in order to fill jobs, and (b) we must create more jobs in order to attract more people. Progress – it's wonderful. The late economist J.K. Galbraith called this the "squirrel wheel" model of economics.

Second, the Plan does not examine the negative consequences of population growth, but merely assumes that bigger is always better.

Yet since the time of the ancient Greeks, philosophers have believed that cities have an optimal size beyond which key human values will be threatened. Thinkers from Plato through Rousseau have found most commonly that the optimal limit falls in a range of about 30,000-50,000 inhabitants – a fraction of the Fargo-Moorhead metropolitan area's current population. And with striking agreement, contemporary social scientists also say that unlimited growth has negative consequences. Kirkpatrick Sale (who summarizes much of this research in his book *Human Scale*) says that a host of social pathologies typically "begin to gather … somewhere around the 100,000 level."

Crime rates, for instance, show "a very sharp jump" after that figure is reached. Smaller cities, by contrast, are healthier and show "markedly lower incidences of bronchitis, ulcers, high blood pressure, alcoholism, and drug addiction." Recreational facilities in smaller cities are "usually better … and easier to get to." Educational advantages peak in "cities with a maximum of 70,000 to 90,000 people." Nor is gargantuan size necessary for cultural pursuits. Quality libraries, museums, and even symphony orchestras are easily supported by cities of 50,000, and they have higher per capita rates of participation besides.

Smallness has clear advantages for the exercise of citizenship. As the size and complexity of the polity increases, policymaking necessarily loses coherence, and the city becomes less easily governed. Apathy spreads as a diminishing proportion of the citizenry are confident, they can meet with their leaders, or believe that individuals can make a difference. Citizenship is reduced to casting a ballot every couple of years and self-government becomes a sham. "The larger the place," said Prof. Robert Dahl in his classic address to the American

Political Science Association in the 1960s, "the less likely is the citizen to be involved."

If every other argument fails, the fallback rationale among our boosters is that population growth will enhance the bottom line – raw economics. But economic advantage also observes the law of optimal size beyond which further growth no longer promotes higher employment rates or a wider range of jobs.

Municipal services like police and fire protection, sanitation, road repair and so on follow a familiar U-curve in which per capita costs start high in very small towns but then, with an expanding tax base and a relatively compact territory fall rapidly at first, then flatten out; then as population growth continues, costs once again begin to turn upward. In other words, growth at first brings economies of scale, but as it passes an optimal point, continued expansion eventually brings on *diseconomies* of scale because the per capita costs of providing additional infrastructure and services outrun additional tax revenues. Past a fairly modest population size (usually said to be about 60 to 80 thousand) further growth no longer pays for itself. Kirkpatrick Sale says that the optimal point for economies of scale is "in a range that I have calculated averages out to 63,000." The per-capita costs of running cities of 1,000,000 are nearly three times as high as per-capita costs in cities of 100,000.

Why do our boosters salivate like Pavlov's dogs each time they hear the word growth? The historian Daniel Boorstin, in *The Americans*, *traced this phenomenon to the idea of manifest destiny, the 19th Century view that motion* – pushing the frontier all the way to the Pacific – became synonymous with progress. When the Pacific stopped the movement over land, progress then had to take a new form, which became movement in place, that is, growth. Whether it applies to cities, populations, businesses or whatever, growth is still seen as an unmitigated good no matter what the consequences and even if we no longer know why. Like happiness, growth is just … *good*, a value in itself. Today it's in our genes.

I've lived in the F-M metro area on-and-off since 1970. As the metro area has grown, I have not noticed an improved quality of life, merely more sprawl and more congestion which by 4 p.m. makes traffic on the major avenues intolerable. Yet our boosters, for reasons they themselves cannot seem to articulate, want us to have still more of it. As for me, no thanks.

Does America
Need Immigration?

Does immigration, whether legal or not, serve any national interest of the United Stares?

Well, many businesses and agricultural interests do benefit from cheap immigrant labor, and lots of upper-class households are pleased to employ immigrants to get low-cost childcare, domestic servants, and groundskeepers. When a friend asked the billionaire mayor of New York City, Michael Bloomberg, about deporting Hispanics working here illegally, Bloomberg replied, "You and I are the beneficiaries of these jobs. You and I both play golf. Who takes care of the greens and fairways in your golf course?"

But cheap labor is less beneficial to low-skilled Americans whose wages are driven downward by the pressure of immigrant labor. Though proponents claim that immigration stimulates the economy, it defies all reason to believe that people who arrive uneducated and impoverished could contribute more to the country in taxes than they extract from it in medical care, education for their children and other resources of the welfare state that are diverted from America's own poor.

In 2011, 57 percent of all immigrants with children under 18 were on at least one form of welfare, compared with 39 percent of native households. The lowest welfare rates were among immigrants from UK (7 %), India (19 %), Canada (23 %) and Korea (25 %). The highest were among those from Dominican Republic (82 %), Mexico and Guatemala (75 % each), and Ecuador (70%).

Hispanics have high rates of welfare dependency because most arrive here with little wealth and no skills. They also tend to form a "culture of poverty," one which replicates itself over succeeding generations. Research by Harvard Prof. George Borjas in 2011 concludes that "the close link between the skills of parents and those of children suggests that current immigration policy has already determined the skill endowments of the workplace for the next two or three generations."

Hispanics account for the nation's highest school dropout rate, and those who are U.S.-born are twice as likely to be on welfare as native citizens. Though they are commonly praised for their strong family values, the fact is that fifty-three percent of their births are out of wedlock.

Immigration, as the *New Republic's* T.A. Frank writes, is an "immense blow to America's working class and poor" because it "undermines unions and labor standards, lowers wages, heightens social tensions, strains state budgets … [and] subverts the rule of law and exacerbates class divides."

What about immigrants with high-tech skills? We constantly hear that America is in peril because it isn't producing enough people in science, technology, engineering, and math. But the National Science Board reports that we are already producing *three times* as many STEM graduates as their jobs available for them. Last year the Census Bureau reported the country had 1.8 million engineers who were either unemployed or doing work that was unrelated to their training.

Importing foreigners with similar skills simply increases the present glut. Currently, 45 percent of all graduate students in engineering are foreigners, and their numbers, if they stay here, will depress salaries and make engineering careers still less attractive for their American peers.

The myth of STEM shortages has been cultivated for decades by university administrators who use misinformation about the job market to keep their enrollments at saturation levels. High tech businesses profit from exploiting the same fiction. The *Wall Street Journal* has noted that many U.S. firms want to "staff their operation with Indian expatriates who earn significantly less than their American counterparts."

If immigration's net economic effects are negative, then what about its cultural effects?

In the 19th Century, serious resources, in both the public and private sectors, were devoted to turning immigrants into Americans because strengthening national unity was thought to be important. Today it isn't. Immigrants arrive in such mass numbers that for many of them, if not most, assimilation has become unnecessary; millions settle directly into self-sufficient urban colonies which have their own schools, native-language newspapers, radio, and TV stations. They feel little need to join the core culture, to absorb Americana, or even to learn English because they find everything they need in their own urban colonies. They are *in* America but not *of* it.

It isn't entirely the immigrants' fault that they don't assimilate. For its part, America fails to insist upon assimilation because, rather than proclaim our best traditions, our schools, in league with American elites and many ethnic leaders, are busily deconstructing American history and glorifying Third World countries, often with flattering, if fake, histories of their cultures. Instead of encouraging unity, they stoke ethnic grievances and encourage separateness. Multiculturalism, as the historian A. M. Schlesinger, Jr. put it in *The Disuniting of America*, is a "cult" in opposition to "the original idea of America as 'one people, a common culture, a single nation." Underlying the rage for mass immigration there is, among many of our elites, an unmistakable element of anti-Americanism.

Most immigrants today are impoverished and unskilled people who, understandably, simply want a better life for themselves and their families. But does their desire for self-improvement mean that the citizens of the US, or Europe, have an obligation to sacrifice their own economic and cultural well-being?

Does America still retain a moral right to ask whether it really has an obligation to import poverty, deplete its own welfare system, and weaken its national identity on behalf of every Third World resident who comes here seeking a more comfortable life? Are we obliged to take in everyone who claims a right to sanctuary from persecution? If we are, then how do we distinguish between the millions who are really fleeing persecution from the millions who come here merely to share the wealth?

In 1960 only about 5 percent of Americans were foreign-born. Today it is 14 percent. If that number keeps rising, the social order will eventually become weakened by demands on its culture and its economic resources that America will be unable to serve as a sanctuary even for the truly needy. And if western identities are overrun by cultures that won't assimilate, how will any government muster the popular support needed to deal with a national crisis?

It might be good to reexamine the premises underlying our immigration policy before committing ourselves further to something which, in the long run, may prove irreversibly disastrous.

Are Republicans
The Stupid Party?

Since 2008 the Republican Party, with its embrace of Sarah Palin, Joe the Plumber, and the Tea Party, has assumed a populist character that is a curious turn for the party of Abraham Lincoln and Edmund Burke. But these days populism is where the votes are. Religious fundamentalists, for instance, now comprise about 25 percent of the party's base, and its presidential candidates are dumbing themselves down in order to court voters who are suspicious of too much intelligence or of ideas that contradict Scripture.

The suspicion of science, for instance, is such that among the eight current candidates for the GOP's nomination, only John Huntsman forthrightly acknowledges the reality of global warming and the theory of evolution. He's polling at the bottom of the pack. The other candidates fudge these issues or dismiss them as hoaxes and "just theories." Not for nothing is the GOP commonly referred to as the "anti-science" party.

But it's the church-state issue that gets scary. Minnesota's GOP representative Michelle Bachman has ties to "dominionism," a cult which claims that Christians are ordained to rule the world and that God demands the subordination of women and gays. Both Bachman and Rick Perry sympathize with WallBuilders, a sect which preaches that the founders of the Republic intended America to be officially Christian.

A clutch of similar outfits rejects the idea of church-state separation in favor of a sharia-style Christianity that applies God's presumed wishes to everything from school prayers through guns. Their influence resonates in the Tea Party, the GOP platform, and even in the social science curriculum of Texas schools. They form a network of churches, summer camps, colleges, counseling groups, broadcast networks, and publishing houses which the *New York Times* has recently described as a "parallel culture."

Most outrageously, they claim their ideas are sanctioned by the Founding Fathers themselves. David Barton, who leads WallBuilders, says that what Jefferson's "wall of separation" *really* means is that while the state is prohibited from interfering in religion, it also intends that "Christian principles stay in government."

Yet it should be, but isn't, common knowledge that the key men among the Founders – who were products of the Enlightenment – clearly regarded religion as both a private foolishness and a public menace. Personally, many accepted no religion stronger than Deism, a minimalist theology which held that even if the cosmos had been created by some supernatural Being, this Being subsequently departed the scene to amuse Himself with more interesting projects elsewhere, perhaps geometry, as Einstein suggested. This Being has no further interest in humanity and does not expect any interest from it.

Here are some representative views of the Founders, drawn mostly from their private correspondence:

Ben Franklin: "I cannot conceive otherwise than that He, the Intimate Father, expects or requires no worship or praise from us, but that He is even infinitely above it."

Thomas Jefferson: "In every country and every age, the priest has been hostile to liberty. He is always in alliance with the despot." Further: "I have been examining all the known superstitions of the world, and do not find in our particular superstition [Christianity] one redeeming feature."

John Adams: "This would be the best of all possible worlds if there were no religion in it." Further: "The Judeo-Christian religion is the most bloody religion that ever existed." Adams' treaty with Tripoli specifically noted that the American government "is not in any sense founded on the Christian religion."

James Madison: "Religious bondage shackles and debilitates the mind and unfits it for every noble enterprise." Further: "The purpose of separation of church and state is to keep forever from these shores the ceaseless strife that has soaked the soil of Europe in blood for centuries."

Thomas Paine: "Of all the systems of religion that were ever invented, nothing is more … repugnant to reason … than this thing called Christianity."

On **George Washington**: A near contemporary, the Reverend Dr. Bird Wilson, said that he had "perused every line that Washington ever gave to the public, and [did] not find one expression in which he pledges himself as a believer in Christianity …. He was a Deist and nothing more." Wilson judged all of the first six presidents to have been "infidels."

Given the historical record, why are so many people so easily seduced by cultists? Jefferson had a sound answer, which was related to the intelligence of the citizenry: Education in the public (or "common schools," so called because all social classes were to learn the same subjects) he said, should be "chiefly historical" because historical knowledge was thought to provide citizens with the best defense against the "designs of men," that is, demagoguery.

But our public schools have more or less given up the teaching of history – and other basic subjects – because the educational nihilism that dominates today's curriculum with its hundreds of electives, regards few if any as having any special importance. Knitting is held to be as important as history and lawn care is as good as classic literature. We have a chaotic political system in good part because we have a chaotic educational system in which knowledge is fragmented to the point where it has no public usefulness. Our citizens are disarmed of the knowledge needed for the understanding and defense of the republic they inhabit.

Too bad. We would have saner candidates for office if the electorate were better educated. As it is, our historical amnesia makes us sitting ducks for designing men.

Does Higher Funding Improve Education?

America's public schools are financed, for the most part, by a mix of local property taxes and direct state aid. But because property values differ (sometimes radically) between districts, some will be disadvantaged, both in terms of tax burdens and levels of funding, compared to their wealthier counterparts. The system's inherent inequities have inspired legal action in almost every state, and now North Dakota is being sued, again, by several districts which claim, among other things, that state funding does not allow them to meet educational goals that are mandated by the state itself.

On grounds of equity the claimants may have a strong case, but on educational grounds they do not. The link between money and student achievement is uncertain at best; it is often noted that real per-student spending in the US has more than tripled since 1970, although standardized test scores have stayed flat. Indeed, Prof. Eric Hanushek, who is a leading scholar of school finance, notes that "detailed studies at the school and classroom level" show "no systematic relationship between resources and outcomes once one considers families and other factors that determine achievement." In particular, he finds "no reason to believe that equalizing expenditure also tends to equalize student performance."

Why is education so impervious to money? In large part it's because we have no idea of what it is that we are trying to buy.

Suppose you wanted to buy a widget. You're not quite sure of what a widget is, though, so you ask around. At Wal-Mart all the clerks know of them: one thinks they are a kind of tool; another looks through crafts, a third scours sporting goods … yet after an exhaustive search, no one manages to turn up a widget. At Sears too, widgets are highly regarded although none are found either on the shelves or listed in the catalogs. At the hardware and home improvement stores widgets also enjoy great prestige, though it seems that no one can quite describe them. Finally, after many fruitless tries at the curio shops and flea markets, it dawns on you that not all the money in the world will get you a widget if no one knows what a widget is.

Although education once meant the arts, sciences, and humanities, it has become gospel in the teacher colleges that the word has no objective meaning. What is now packaged as "education," therefore, is a miscellany with something for everyone: sports, "life skills," job training, consumerism, careerism, quack therapy, hobbies … just take your pick. To be sure, the package still includes some traditional academics, but these have no special status; indeed, in our teacher training colleges it is a matter of strict principle that *nothing* has any particular importance. So, when we spend money on "education," we do so almost randomly and in the childlike faith that some portion of it will fall upon some aspect of schooling that might, some day, some how, prove to have some value although we have not a clue as to what it could be.

In progressivism's relativist fairyland, the fundamentals will always go begging. Hence one of the parties to the lawsuit claims that it can't afford a teacher of art – yet it *can* afford both a new gymnasium and a $300,000 upgrade for an auto repair shop. "Adequate educational opportunity and quality are a function of available dollars," the suit says. But if you think that hairdressing is as good as history, or that knitting is as important as classic literature, then doubling or quadrupling your expenditures is likely to do nothing to produce better learning.

When public education first began, its leading figures knew that both the values of mind and the workings of a free society required shared frames of reference. Thus Jefferson, normally a foe of centralization, proposed a common curriculum nation-wide (with an emphasis on history as a defense against demagogues) so that "the great mass of people" might be the "guardians of their own liberty," and learn, as well, the "first elements of morality."

Likewise, Horace Mann believed that democracy required a "common school" to make its citizens self-reliant, equal, and free. Even the progressive John Dewey finally came to believe that "men live in a community in virtue of the things which they have in common," and that these things – "beliefs, aspirations, and knowledge" – were advanced by "education, and education alone." Dewey's contemporary, William C. Bagley, insisted that democratic schools must strive for "as high a level of common culture as possible" to insure that "collective decisions … (are) made on the highest possible plane." Accordingly, he ridiculed the notion that every locality "must have a curriculum all its own" as being "not only silly, but tragic."

In this same spirit, North Dakota's constitution tasks the schools with advancing the "high degree of intelligence, patriotism, integrity, and morality" that is needed to maintain "government by the people" and to insure the people's "prosperity and happiness." To this end it calls for "a reasonable degree of uniformity in course of study."

While many assumed that local control would uphold these ideals, what has evolved instead is the "shopping mall" curriculum that panders to student self-absorption and accords transcendent importance to almost nothing. History, great literature, and the things that form the moral basis of Western civilization have given way to electives in dating and advanced racquetball. With that, we no longer have anything resembling a theory of public education.

Which is why, despite their misplaced egalitarianism, I hope the claimants win their case. If the state has to spend a lot more money on education, then maybe – just maybe – it will finally take a serious interest in what it should get in return. In place of the nihilism that spills from the teacher colleges we might get a rational debate on the meaning of education. Local governance is still essential. But an atomized and separate curriculum in every district – as if math were important in Jamestown but not in Valley City – is insane.

Shared knowledge is as important today as it was in Jefferson's time. That is why we ought to be devising statewide, if not, indeed, nationwide standards. With any luck, the constitutional mandate of a "reasonable degree of uniformity" may then come to mean something more than an equal opportunity to squander resources and miseducate kids.

Diversity and its Wrongs

Higher education's fixation with "diversity" goes on and on. Just now North Dakota State University is polling its students to see how they "feel" about it, and the neighboring campuses are gearing up to recruit more minorities. An anti-racism campaign is underway. A consultant says "diversity" includes race, gender, ethnicity, and disability, although of course that is *it* – on our politically monolithic campuses hardly anyone thinks that diversity should include anything so outlandish as, say, ideas.

In fact, the diversity-multicultural movement has little to do with education. Historian Oscar Handlin calls it an "assault on the core themes of American education" that is "part of a wider effort to alter the country's character." It is an ideology of social engineering that aims to remake society by first remaking education. That means emptying education of its cultural ballast, i.e., the heritage of Western civilization which is, according to the multicultural gospel, shot through with racism, sexism, classism, ableism, looksism and … well, you know the litany.

This kind of diversity really means surrounding ourselves with victims, which include "persons of color," the sexually ambiguous, the lower classes and others wounded by the culture's oppressiveness. On the campuses they are highly sought after. Victim-centered education generates the network of compensatory programs that has given the burgeoning multicultural population a great deal of leverage on the campuses in determining what shall be taught and by whom, as well as the language and decorum that will be permitted on the campuses.

This includes racial favoritism, watered-down academic standards, encouraging self-pity among minorities, and lowering the general quality of the student body. One of multiculturalism's worst evils is that it stigmatizes even the ablest among ethnic minorities as "affirmative action babies," as if racial preferences were needed by all members of a minority group in order to match the standards expected of the dominant culture.

Does poor schooling produce self-defined victims who can't do college work? Well, we might work at improving the elementary and secondary schools – but it's far less trouble to pass on the schools' failures by expecting the colleges to lower their standards to accommodate the victims after they are enrolled. Courses like Stanford's "Language of Hip-hop Culture" and "Black Hair as Culture and History" neatly solve the problem. In the surreal worlds of multiculturalism all topics are of equal value.

What about self-esteem – a huge industry on the campuses these days! Prof. Lionel Jeffries of the City College of New York assures his African American students that the treasures of classical Europe were in fact the creations of black Africans which were then stolen by the Greeks; those blacks ("sun people") are superior to whites ("ice people"); and that the slave trade was financed by rich Jews.

Just so, the highest achievements of Western civilization are displaced from the curriculum as politically incorrect. The works of Sophocles, Shakespeare, Dante, and Locke – dead, white, European males all – are routinely displaced by those of Maya Angelou or

Rigoberta Menchu (who received a Nobel Prize for a "memoir" that turned out to be bogus). Absurd, you say? Remember, fascist: Judgments of quality are meaningless – and likely racist!

Of course, the local campuses will say that none of this can happen here. But when students are recruited on the basis of their claims of victimhood, they must then be accommodated as such. And, according to Professor Clifford Orwin of Toronto University, "It is inevitable that champions of the different 'cultures' … will insist on increased representation in the curriculum" for their own agendas. Censorship and cartoon academic standards are already a blight in higher education; and as "diversity" expands, the curriculum will veer further from the arts, sciences and humanities toward feminism, witchcraft, date rape, the 1960s, or whatever.

Variety, as always, is the spice of life. But sympathy for the underdog can't justify debased schooling that benefits no one.

In *The Disuniting of America*, the eminent historian Arthur M. Schlesinger, Jr. argued that it is not an office of public education to magnify differences and nurse grievances, whether in the name of therapy or of social reform.

He adds that all it takes to end the multicultural plague is courage. It's time, he says, for the "great silent majority of professors (to) cry 'enough' and challenge what they know to be voguish nonsense."

A Plain Joe Looks
at Higher Education

At the colleges around North Dakota, they're giving the governor a hard time and I guess I can't blame them. They're mad because he wants to cut their budgets and they say that if that happens, then a lot of bad things will follow. Like, maybe not so many kids will sign up next fall, and if *that* happens, then the colleges will lose still more money and some teachers will get laid off. Some students may get so disgusted they'll move out of the state, and others who might've moved into the state will change their minds.

Also, manufacturing could be depressed, and even foreign trade could go down. So, cuts are a bad deal all around because they mean that the state's economy won't grow as fast as it should, and the population won't grow either. Hey, come to think of it, education could suffer too.

And the colleges say that the worst of it is that budget cuts aren't needed anyway because all the fat that used to be there got trimmed out two or three cuts back. So, all that's left is lean and mean, right?

Well, I'm not so sure. Looking through their catalogs I see a lot of programs that are still kind of plump to me. Take my old alma mater, the University of North Dakota: If it's really down to bare bones, how come it brags about having courses in 160 different fields? Yeah, 160! They give out degrees in everything from raising horses to how to fly an airplane. It seems like education these days is anything you might dream up.

It's the same at North Dakota State University. They've got a lot of courses with great names, but you have to wonder if all this stuff has to be learned in college. I mean, things like "Creative Family Management," "Creative Awareness," "Consumer Issues," "Issues in Sexuality," "Women and Communication," "Athletic Training Terminology," "Language Bias," "Bowling," and so on. Gee, you can even get *degrees* in stuff like "Corporate and Community Fitness," "Apparel and Textiles," and "Leisure Studies."

And Minot State offers courses in things like "Microwave Cooking" and "Creative Stichery," while Dickinson State has a program in truck dri – oops – "Highway Transportation Specialists." Or it did. They had to do some cutting and the guy with the knife had a lucid moment.

And how come the catalog at Valley City State, which says it's a liberal arts college, needs only two and a half pages each to list its courses in English and history but needs *six* for jockstrap courses like "Philosophy of Volleyball" and "Philosophy of Wrestling" – hey, all this philosophy is too deep for me! – and ten pages for the courses in business?

But this'll knock your eyes out: When I counted the courses in education departments around the state, you know how many I found? About a thousand! Yeah! It's hard to be exact because a lot of these ed courses are hybrids from overlapping departments. But I keep reading about all these reformers who have been trying for ninety years to close down the ed schools because they don't provide future teachers with what they need to know, and here we've got a *thousand* of their courses right under our nose!

And maybe those reformers have got something because a lot of this stuff doesn't look like rocket science to me either. I mean stuff like this:

Phys ed 225, *Camp Management,* NDSU; "Theories of Camp Management and Counseling. Camp Skills and Techniques."

Education 97, *Community Concepts of Residence Hall Living,* UND. "Assists Resident Assistants in gaining a more complete understanding of components of a successful residence hall environment, with implications for job satisfaction and individual development."

Phys Ed 427, *Leisure and Society*, NDSU: "Survey of the leisure problems of today. Emphasis on the critical analysis of completed writings and research in parks and recreation."

Phys ed 250, *Recreational Leadership*, Dickinson State. "The introduction, to, history of, and related concepts of recreational program delivery in the private, community, or school setting."

Phys ed 102, *Jogging and Conditioning*, Minot State. "Instruction, practice and participation in the basic skills, body mechanics and terminology associated with jogging and power walking."

Yeah, walking. I guess nothing in life is so simple that some colleges won't offer formal courses in it for credit, right? Maybe even a master's degree. The thing is, these course titles sound really sophisticated, and yet the subject itself doesn't seem, well, all that – *important.* I mean, I learned stuff like this in the Boy Scouts and didn't even get a merit badge. The only difference was that the Scout leaders could write better.

The experts say they just can't cut any more of this stuff from the curriculum without damaging academic quality. Well, I'm no expert, but I've gotta tell you – a lot of what they say is indispensable looks like plain old featherbedding to me. I mean, next they'll have Ph.D. programs in "Philosophy of Cheer Leading," if they don't already. The governor wants to cut spending by five percent? Hell, I'll raise him five.

There's one last thing I don't understand. Every time the subject of education comes up, all I ever hear about is – growth. I hear it from the campus honchos, and from businesses, politicians, and guys who write newspaper editorials. It's just growth, growth, *growth,* all the time. I mean, the people in higher education don't seem to know whether they're running colleges or chambers of commerce.

I never hear anyone ask whether college kids are learning history, or literature, or science, or whether our college grads will be able to help pass on the culture to their kids and grandkids. All anyone talks about is whether enrollments are going up. And when you ask why growth is supposed to be such hot stuff, all you get is a blank stare – like they think you're crazy! I guess when nobody knows what they're doing, they still need a goal of some kind, right?

Well, I'm not as smart as those theology guys, but it just seems to me that growth can't be the highest thing there is. I mean, studying

Plato and Shakespeare should still be important all by themselves even if it doesn't create jobs and make the economy grow. You know what I mean?

A couple of thousand years ago there was a dude named Aristotle who was really smart. He said that there are "branches of learning and education which we must study merely with a view to leisure spent in intellectual activity, and these are to be valued for their own sake." He invented a whole bunch of tough subjects like physics and biology and logic, and he said that education was so important that we had to protect it from vulgarity, that is, from stuff that's trivial. Our college presidents used to talk like that too.

I wonder what Aristotle would think about higher education today and what we've done with it.

Hey – we've come a long way, baby!

Right?

The Pedagogy
of Good Old Boys

Len Martin lived in Valley City, where he was for a time a schoolteacher. He was also an anti-tax protester and anti-foreclosure agitator who blamed many of society's problems on Masons and Jews. He was also a member of a vigilante group called Posse Comitatus, a network of good old boys who seemed to believe that their patriotism absolved them of the responsibility for observing laws they didn't like. One of his associates was Gordon Kahl, a North Dakota tax protester who in 1983 killed two US marshals and was himself killed in a shootout in Arkansas. Martin later ran for the post of Superintendent of Public Instruction and shocked everyone by getting a fifth of the vote. A devoutly religious man, Martin and some friends held a prayer meeting and asked for a miracle. When the letter below promptly appeared, Martin, mistaking sarcasm for praise, believed his prayers had been answered.

The primary election for the post of North Dakota Superintendent of Public Instruction was hardly an indication of widespread support for the pedagogical theories of Len Martin, whose 22 percent of the vote nevertheless came as a shock to the education establishment. Neither was it a vindication of Martin's backwoods Posse Comitatus, whose desire to save the world proceeds less urgently from its expertise in educational matters than it does from the prospect of impending foreclosure on its members' farmlands.

Nor is it proof that 22 percent of the electorate has lapsed into insanity. Most likely, what the vote represents is a more or less inevitable reaction to the chronic failure of public education and the refusal of the respectable people in charge to do anything about it.

"Len Martin offers North Dakota a chance to return to godly values, to godly families, to return prayer to our schools and truth that will set us free again," reads a Martin campaign ad.

There, in a nutshell, is Martin's philosophy of education. Or the most intelligible part of it anyway, there being some additional detail concerning the evils of sex education, secular humanism, Masons, Jews, and persons deemed insufficiently Aryan.

It's pretty crude, but a fifth of the voters found it more intelligible than the educational program they have now. And the cultivated people in the educational establishment will, as a matter of principle, *never* have any program at all. Why not? Well, it's partly because of that hyper-pluralism for which we Americans are so justly famous. Educational policy is not made by philosopher-kings whose wisdom is devoted to a transcendent public good but is mostly the product of the tradition of romantic progressivism in which, as Richard Hofstadter says in *Anti-intellectualism in American Life*, "American educators entered upon a crusade to exalt the academically uninterested or ungifted child into a kind of culture-hero. They were not content to say that the realities of American social life had made it necessary to compromise with the ideal of education as the development of formal learning and intellectual capacity. Instead, they proclaimed that such education was archaic and futile and that the noblest aim of a truly democratic education was to meet the child's immediate interests by offering him a series of immediate utilities."

So, we have what 1983's *A Nation at Risk* report called a "smorgasbord curriculum," a curriculum which denies the possibility of an adult consensus on the meaning of education and instead charges the kids themselves with the responsibility for deciding what they need to know. The kids do this by browsing through an endless desert of hundreds of electives reflecting hobbies, vocations and personal interests that might have seized them at any given moment. Such courses, intended to cater to the transient appetites and whims of children, are "homogenized, diluted and diffused," as the report puts it, "to the point that they no longer have a central purpose."

Where once the curriculum invited students to explore their cultural heritage and to grapple with the great questions – is there a moral order in this universe; how have history's great men and women confronted the problems of good and evil; how do we give our lives meaning and dignity? – we now invite them to load up with courses in cake decorating, film appreciation, interior design, grieving, bachelor living, sheet metal working and approximately two hundred other instances of random froth.

The intellectual vacuum that is modern education is more than matched by its moral emptiness. Where once the schools transmitted the religious and moral traditions of the Western world, we now have bloodless courses like "values clarification" which affirms that no principle, no cause, no culture, no person can be shown to be better than any other. Instruction takes place in the surreal atmosphere of an extreme relativism which bills itself as value-free, but which is in fact a nihilism so extreme that it cannot, without contradicting itself, demand civility in classrooms, condemn cheating, or affirm the superiority of knowledge over ignorance.

In fixing something, the beginning of wisdom is in having some knowledge of the thing to be fixed. You can't repair a malfunctioning machine if you don't first know what the machine is supposed to do; and you can't make the schools work if you have no idea of what purpose they are supposed to serve. We have no such idea. We have no consensus upon which to act, nothing to serve as a basis for reform. Len Martin at least has a firm, if also ridiculous, idea of what he believes to be a proper education. The sophisticates who run the state's educational establishment proudly confess – no, they boast – that they haven't one. Politics abhors a vacuum; therefore, we have the phenomenon of Len Martin.

Is it possible for us to unite, over and against our sectarian interests, on behalf of a firm public consensus as to what the schools should be teaching?

Can our elected leaders, the State Superintendent of Public Instruction, the governor, members of the state legislature, and others professionally involved in education define and defend a vision of education that the public will respect?

Without the armament of a coherent philosophy, education will remain mired where it has been for the past hundred years, concerned only with incremental putterings in the prevailing absurdity. Without a guiding theory, "reform" will continue to mean nothing more than feel-good slogans, improvements in physical plant, organizational tinkering, more administrators, more technology and of course the obligatory demands for higher funding. And the academic performance of our kids will continue, year after year, in their free fall.

Education is the most expensive commitment of state and local government. Perhaps the first order of business for the education establishment should be to figure out what that commitment is all about.

Old Wine
in New Bottles

Every so often the education establishment launches another attack upon the young, and the latest is led by an outfit called "Partnership for 21st Century Skills." It's composed of business interests (mainly those with computers to sell), teacher guilds, and state authorities who have discovered that the emerging historical era is different from all others because, well, *this* one, you see, involves *change*.

As usual, the change they're most concerned about involves commerce and global economic competition. So, P-21 wants to make education "relevant to the demands of the 21st Century" by "integrating" the academic curriculum, or what's left of it, into such commercially useful skills as problem-solving, teamwork, communication, and "global awareness," the better to prepare children for their proper cells in the new global hive.

But while it bills itself as cutting edge, the P-21 boomlet is merely the latest in an endless procession of fads that have been at war with liberal education since the Progressivist movement began in the late 19th Century. Progressivism teaches that nothing is permanent except change itself, and that the curriculum must be constantly adjusted in order to keep students abreast of the random winds of social and economic flux. So, as education historian Dianne Ravitch has written, "educators forgot how to say 'no' even to the loopier notions of what schools were for." When the consensus on what an educated person needed to know dissolved, then "every perceived need, interest, concern, problem or issue found a place in the curriculum … and hawkers of new wares could sell their stock to the school …because all needs were presumed equal in importance."

More than a century after the appearance of Progressivism, its boosters are still tying to cleanse the schools of obsolete and "useless" academic subjects such as history, literature, art, civics, and other subjects that used to be part of the repertoire of an educated person. It is contemptuous of such notions as knowledge for its own sake, and of the joys of discovering the "best that has been thought and said"; after all, hard-headed practical men have always known that the purpose of education is not to liberate the individual, but to fit him into the existing social order.

Edward Ross, an early skills evangelist, proclaimed in 1901`that the schools' mission was to take "little plastic lumps of human dough … and shape them on the social kneading-board." Subsequent fashions, such as the "social efficiency" and" life adjustment" movements of the early and mid-20th century, likewise condemned the traditional curriculum for its inexplicable concern with the cultivation of mind and spirit, and demanded its replacement with strictly utilitarian, down-to-earth job training.

Yet the totalitarian sweep of P-21 is jaw-dropping. "Every aspect of our educational system," its manifesto warns, "– pre-K12, post-secondary and adult education, after-school and youth development, work force development and training, and teacher preparation programs – must be aligned to prepare citizens with the 21st century skills they need to compete."

Yes, *every aspect*. Where in Orwell's darkest vision is there a match for that?

A century of utilitarian fads has compromised liberal education until it's now widely assumed that all schooling should be project-based, experiential, and "practical." By 1949 the reformer Mortimer Smith had described the typical American curriculum as a "vast bubbling confusion … in which hairdressing and embalming are just as important, if not a little more so, than history and philosophy." And so, it remains to this day. Perhaps a few remnants of traditional learning, such as poetry and art, might survive for a while – provided only that they lend themselves to advertising jingles and commercial illustrations. Otherwise, almost no value is accorded to the linking of students' lives to the collective experience of the human race.

How do we answer the modern vandals who are ransacking the schools?

First, we might observe that P-21's desired traits are mostly intuitive, and that successful people have always had them; innovation, critical thinking, and the like do not require formal instruction. Further, they are inseparable from the content knowledge that our faddists invariably despise. You cannot, for instance, think critically if you have nothing substantive to think critically *about*. Nor are the P-21 skills as fecund as advertised; Steven Spielberg's savvy in directing films won't enable him to conduct the Cleveland Symphony or manage the Red Sox. Mastery of specific subject matter is still required.

The classic case for liberal education lies, with no irony intended, precisely in its – yes, *practicality*. "The most obvious fact about society," wrote R.M. Hutchins in 1967, "is that the more technological it is the more rapidly it will change." Hence the paradox: "The most impractical education is the one that looks most practical, and the one that is most practical is the one that is commonly regarded as remote from reality, one dedicated to the comprehension of theory and principles." In short, liberally educated people are better equipped to make sense of the world and to see beyond their immediate circumstances than are those who have been narrowly slotted into transient economic arrangements.

Finally, we might even risk the heresy that there is more to life than commerce. The cultural heritage includes intellectual, moral, and esthetic dimensions which, when explored, make life richer in almost magical ways. What liberal education teaches us is the enjoyment of life. This is impractical? Purging these things from the curriculum for the sake of turning kids into efficient workers isn't just impractical, it's sadistic.

But of course, our one-dimensional philistines see none of this. They are slaves of unexamined assumptions. Until these assumptions are rudely and publicly disturbed, the schools will remain the "vast bubbling confusion" they have been for generations. By mustering the imagination to consider the first principles we may yet restore education to the realm of permanent things.

Education's Slavery
to a False Idea

Is there an educationist left who hasn't announced that education, as traditionally understood, has to be scrapped because the "emerging global economy" demands it?

Mayville State's Vice President Ray Brown wants to "redesign" education in a way that designs it right out of existence. To Brown, though, that's no loss because education doesn't really exist anyway, at least in any objective or public sense. He espouses a relativism that is vintage Progressivism, which for a hundred years has been the unassailable ideology in the dungeons of every teacher college in the land. In this view, education has no meaning because there is no particular body of knowledge that educated people are supposed to possess. The word means whatever you choose it to mean, and Brown informs us that there are many "alternative models" available for whatever purpose you may have in mind. Just – pick one out.

Brown wants to pick one for the (strange) purpose of "recreating rural communities." He believes, with shocking historical ignorance, that "during the early 20th Century a consensus was reached that public schools should be the same across the country," and that they still operate … largely for a national agenda" with standard texts and curricula.

But with its hang-ups about "artificial situations" (educationese for what – literature, history, math?) the standard model is too outmoded to address "real community problems" and has to be discarded.

In this state, Brown says, such problems are mainly those of declining local economies. So, his chosen model of education would involve job creation, "exciting" school-to-work projects, and a list of good deeds that includes everything except – there being no need to go to extremes – the intellectual development of students. In towns like Hatton or Hillsdale, N.D., the highest purpose of education will be to dissuade the remaining inhabitants from leaving.

The real horror of it is that in our schools of education – the teachers of our teachers – this sort of nonsense masquerades as vision. "I can not imagine," says Brown, whose imagination may require a federal subsidy, "a greater challenge facing North Dakota's citizens as we prepare for the next century."

So let me help him.

Education is basically the process of transmitting the culture from one generation to the next. Being educated means being at home with the best traditions of the civilization we inhabit – its arts and sciences, its philosophic, religious, and moral traditions, the lives and deeds of its great men and women. Education has a definite meaning because there are definite things that individuals and societies must know as a condition of their own, and their culture's, well-being. And these things are not innate. They must be taught.

What are its purposes? To provide cultivation of mind and character, to expand our capacity for the understanding and enjoyment of the world around us; to inform us of our rights and obligations as citizens and as moral beings; and even, by indirection, to prepare us for self-sufficiency with knowledge that is common to all work.

And its content? At its foundation is literacy; and yet the reading ability of half the American population over age 16 ranges from the fifth-grade level to complete illiteracy. Even with its small population, North Dakota has more than 50,000 functionally illiterate adults. Perhaps if the schools focused less upon job training and eccentric personal interests, that number wouldn't be so high,

Then there is what E.D. Hirsch calls "cultural literacy" – knowledge that serves as a vocabulary "throughout the land" because a well-functioning culture requires that it be widely shared. But most of our high school graduates do not know within a half-century when the Civil War was fought, can't identify the Magna Carta, can't explain the basic ideas of the Declaration of Independence, or Lincoln's Second Inaugural Address. In multiple choice tests, their ability to identify the most important writers of the past two centuries often falls below randomness.

And it's not much better in math and the physical sciences, where half of all doctorates awarded by American universities go to foreign students because our own high school graduates are unprepared in demanding subjects.

Why are Americans so ignorant of basic things? The only reasonable explanation is that our educational establishments don't regard them as particularly important. Why don't they? In large measure it's because our controlling assumptions about education are those of Jacobinism – a romantic 18th Century doctrine that sees society as artificial and an enemy of the child's natural tendency toward self-development. In this view culture is not a heritage but a threat. "The apparent ease with which children learn, Rousseau wrote, "is their ruin."

If so, then the less they are taught, the better. And in our schools of education, where the ghosts of Rousseau and his heirs, notably John Dewey, still haunt the premises, transmitting the culture may be seen less as an obligation to students than a as violation of their autonomy. So how will they develop? The Jacobin solution, which dominates American public schools everywhere, is the "cafeteria curriculum," a chaos of hundreds of mostly shallow, non-academic electives which invite students to decide for themselves what is worth knowing.

Speaking of the teacher colleges, Richard Hofstadter observed, in his classic *Anti-Intellectualism in American Life*, that "America has the only educational system in the world vital segments of which have fallen into the hands of people who joyfully and militantly proclaim their hostility to intellect."

So, the problem is not that education needs minor readjustments of the status quo. Tinkering won't do. What education needs is a radical rethinking of its underlying assumptions. At bottom, the problem is the manner in which our educationists think about education.

Why We have
Too Many Lawyers

Sunlight is said to be the best disinfectant and right now it looks like a healthy dose of it is finally about to fall upon one of the darkest corners of higher education. When it does, it may prove to be a curative for one of academia's most repellant practices, which is the manner in which many colleges and universities go about recruiting their students.

In an ideal world, students in every academic field would receive honest counseling about the career prospects they are likely to face upon graduation. But in our fallen world, campus advisors commonly shrink from divulging news that is too pessimistic, lest enrollments might suffer. Dissimulation about the job market, however, can be financially ruinous to students who are led to believe that their career prospects are promising when their advisors either do nothing to dissuade them, or even entice them with information they know to be false.

Take law, for instance. For years, bloggers and watchdog groups have complained about misleading come-ons practiced by law schools, though little has been done about them. Presently, however, the schools are being seriously challenged by some of their own graduates, who are joining class action lawsuits against them. So far, 17 schools have been named and that number is certain to rise because the sort of come-ons practiced by them is widespread. One of the lawyers leading this litigation expects that "nearly every law school in the country will be sued before long."

The law graduates are suing because they believe they've been deliberately conned. They committed much time and money (usually in the range of $100,000 to $250,000, depending on how selective the school is) to the belief that once they had a law degree in hand, a high-paying career was virtually assured. Yet upon graduation many find themselves heavily in debt (about $140 thousand on average, according to the *NY Times*) and either jobless or underemployed in non-legal fields.

They blame their calamitous career decisions on data, published by the law schools, which entices enrollments by inflating their previous graduates' history of success in finding jobs. Many of them breezily assure prospective students that they will get excellent jobs as lawyers within a few months of graduation. Indeed, almost all the law schools accredited by the American Bar Association, even those in the lower tiers, have reported placement rates of 90 percent or more, with some claiming rates as high as 99.8 percent. While such claims may seem incredible, they have usually gone unchallenged, perhaps because the culture has long associated a law degree as a guarantee of upward mobility, but also because prospective students naturally assume that their institutions are trustworthy.

But much of the success claimed by law schools is due to creative accounting. Research by University of Colorado professor Paul Campos finds that more than half the jobs making up those 90 percent-plus rates are nothing more than temporary or part-time spots as paralegals, clerks, interns, and other kinds of low-level, poorly paid legal drones. Others wind up in white-collar or even blue-collar trades that make no use whatever of a law background. Even those graduates who have become too discouraged to look for work of any kind are counted by their law schools as employed because, as a technical matter, the Bureau of Labor Statistics counts dropouts from the labor force as not being *un*employed.

But when the smoke and mirrors are cleared away, Professor Campos finds that the success rate among graduates of even elite schools (the 50 most selective) in securing real law careers within nine months of graduation is a dismal 45 percent.

Since the late 1960s, higher education in general has been a bubble whose price keeps rising even as its value keeps declining. Its relentless expansion does not reflect any sort of national need for college graduates, nor even a genuine – even if misguided – student demand; what it reflects is a cynical, see-no-evil scheme by universities to maintain institutional success by keeping their enrollments as high as possible without regard for market conditions or the injuries that may befall to naïve students.

How do the law schools get away with this? For one thing, there is no connection between the schools' post-graduation placement rates and their students' eligibility for federal loans; two-thirds of a school's graduates may never have found work in the legal profession, yet their new enrollees will still be eligible for money from Uncle Sam. The schools have a strong incentive to keep luring new enrollees because, on average, they get 69 percent of their funds from student tuition. Once that money is in hand, the schools will care little about what happens to their former students.

Further, the schools have no legal responsibility for the failure of their graduates to find careers. As a *New York Times* essay has put it, the schools have no "skin in the game," because even when their graduates receive a useless degree, they have no entitlement to get their money back. And because of the Direct Plus Loan program (passed by Congress in 2006) which cushions student loans, the taxpayers are stuck with paying for many student defaults.

As the truth has got around, law school enrollments have dropped from 52,000 in 2010 to 38,000 in 2014. But even that lower number is far higher than the number of jobs available. So, the characteristic response of the schools has been to maintain enrollments by lowering their admission standards. This means that the problem of unemployment will worsen as more weak graduates will be unable to pass the bar exam.

So let the buyer beware. Even if the pending lawsuits should eliminate outright lying, college will remain a high-stakes gamble for the foreseeable future. Those considering a career in law – or in any field – should realize that the interests of the campuses are not identical to their own. Students should carefully investigate the job market for themselves before committing their time and fortune to an endeavor that, alas, no longer guarantees success.

Just What We Need:
More Ph.D.s

In higher education, no ideal is higher than the ideal of getting bigger. Constant growth is commonly taken as a mark of administrative competence, and it confers institutional status as well. It's just about the only widely accepted means of measuring the success of campuses in comparison with each other. In North Dakota, though, the goal of permanent growth may be threatened by a shortage of students, particularly among potential graduate students who are spearheading the expansion.

Although enrollments are rising steadily, their rate of growth may be too low to keep fueling the state's Ph.D. programs which, especially at North Dakota State University, are multiplying like rats. They are already so numerous that NDSU's programs are duplicating those at the University of North Dakota, and if more students aren't dredged up, the two campuses will be locked into a ferocious competition for the same warm bodies. Indeed, they may even have to contemplate the horror – *the horror!* – that at some point there may be implacable limits to further growth.

In fact, holders of Ph.D. degrees have been in oversupply since the late 1960s, though America's universities keep churning out some forty-five thousand more every year. Concealing the fact that such a glut exists is a major industry in higher education, and so is the effort to maintain high recruitment levels by developing flaky new "disciplines" too recent and too circumscribed to have histories of unemployment; NDSU's proposed doctorate in "food safety" comes to mind, as does UND's degree in "social communication." The universities are forced to keep inventing ever-more exotic Ph.D. programs in a desperate race to stay ahead of a market that keeps collapsing just behind.

President Joseph Chapman of NDSU defends his multitudes of doctoral programs by affirming that there is a "proven demand" for them. But a demand of what sort? Dr. Chapman, who cites surveys affirming strong student interest, appears to understand this demand not as a reflection of a public need (say, for engineers or professors) but of the private wants of students themselves. So if Bubba, who lives in Fargo, thinks it might be cool to claim the title of "Doctor" with, say, a Ph.D. in bowling, and thinks it bothersome to have to go 70 miles north to UND to get it, then NDSU – responding to a *demonstrated demand!* – will create a Ph.D. in bowling.

And if it matters, a public rationale can be tacked on too, which is that such programs, if numerous and ethereal enough, will help to grow the population, which in these parts is a mystical aim that surpasses all understanding. "We need to attract people to this state," says a vice president at NDSU in defending the proliferation of Ph.D. programs. What is the plan? It seems to be that people who agree to settle here will get a specially tailored Ph.D. of their choice. And by the thousands, apparently.

But it is as futile for universities to serve as handmaids of boosterism as it is unbecoming. This same sleazy, zero-sum game of Ph.D.s-for-everyone-and-in-everything is being played everywhere. Anyone shopping for a designer degree can find one to suit his taste in virtually any state including, no doubt, ping-pong, and floral arrangement.

What is to be done? Well, if the unfettered growth of Ph.D. programs is a function of demand, then the thing to do is to reduce demand. Long ago, Robert M. Hutchins, the legendary president of the University of Chicago, foresaw the ravages that are now being inflicted upon education by the vanity of degree-seeking. So, he famously proposed a scheme for reducing the value of degrees by a process similar to inflating the currency. This was to be done by awarding a Ph.D. diploma to everyone. Every child born in the U.S. would have one stapled to his or her birth certificate as a right of citizenship. Since *everyone* would be called "Doctor," a Ph.D. degree (and all lesser degrees) would lose all of its snob value, and those who were not serious about learning would stay away.

Clearly, this is an idea whose time has come. And we needn't wait for federal action to stop our state's race to the bottom. On its own, North Dakota could print up a batch of very impressive diplomas in any field desired and award them in mass mailings to every resident. It could also offer them to out-of-staters who would promise to move into the state and stay for a specified time. Those who bring along businesses, or show unusual fertility, might receive multiple degrees.

But, you say, this is all nuts? Well, okay, maybe so. But it's no nuttier than the mindless, grow-at-any-cost delirium that is driving our campuses to ruin right now.

"Professor X" and
His Troubles with Mediocrity

Two or three times each year the nation's colleges and universities announce, in fits of ecstasy, that enrollments have once again broken all records. In academia nothing is so highly prized as unrelenting growth – in admissions, revenues, plant, sports, corporate ties, or whatever; after all, in the absence of any sort of coherent educational purpose, *something* has to serve as a measure of progress, doesn't it?

Growth isn't just pure mysticism, because it does have utilitarian value as a hedge against campus unemployment. Higher education was disastrously overbuilt in the 1960s and if enrollments were to slip now, layoffs among faculty (though of course not among administrators, who grow like weeds) would surely follow. Hence higher education has had to become a perpetual growth machine locked in an endless bidding war for warm bodies.

The trouble is, when higher education takes in everybody, it gets hordes of students who, for want of talent or of dedication or both, don't belong there. So nationally, 28% of freshmen quit within a year, and even after 6 years only 61% have graduated. (At North Dakota's public 4-year colleges – where few if any are turned away – the completion rate is even lower, currently averaging just over 43 percent) Add up all the tuition, time, and public resources that come to nothing, and then ask: Is this really progress?

In a recent issue of *Atlantic Monthly*, "Professor X," a professor of English, laments the absurdity of making college a universal right and then expecting most students to meet high academic standards. X's students commonly can't write a coherent sentence and their general knowledge base is often so small that it won't serve to process new information. Lacking cultural reference points, they can't even form a proper class. And because the idea of knowledge-for-itself is alien to them, they can't see the relevance of subjects like history or literature that aren't tied to immediate career goals. So, X says his classes teem with "frustration and bad feeling" as students, unaware of their own deficiencies, blame their failures on out-of-it teachers or on seemingly nonsensical subject matter.

Enticing the unprepared is not just wasteful, it's unethical. Prof. X cites the case of "Ms. L.," a middle-aged blue-collar student who, by getting into college, believed herself to have triumphed over adversity. Yet it soon becomes obvious that she can't do college work. Unable to absorb class material, she is shocked when her chaotic research project gets an *F*. Thereafter her pride in having written a "college paper" gives way to a "wall of defeat and hopelessness and humiliation." In her own mind, "Ms. L. had done everything that American culture asked of her. She had gone back to school to better herself, and she expected to be rewarded for it, not slapped down."

Though weak students may find that college is a cruel deception, the colleges often see *them* as cash cows because their high failure rates often force them to pay for the same classes two or three times over. X surmises that if academia could somehow schedule a graveyard shift to cram in still more weak students, it would probably do so. "No one," X says, "is thinking about the larger implications, let alone the morality, of admitting so many students to classes they cannot possibly pass."

Every professor knows them: the part-timers who need credits for job advancement but are sadly out of their element; the serious kids who try hard but simply lack the necessary talent; the utilitarians who are miffed that too much class time is "wasted" in discussing ideas; the slugs who glare defiantly from the back row and refuse all engagement; and the innocents who just don't *get* the idea of college. A further class of victims includes, of course, the genuine talents who are deprived of stimulation in classes that are dominated by mediocrities.

Although open enrollments lower academic standards, the campuses have no incentive to end them. So, some reformers propose a partial, non-intrusive remedy, which is for governments to devise their own admission standards and tie them to financial aid. Students enrolling on the public's dime would have to demonstrate not just need, but also some genuine aptitude. Because most full-time undergraduates receive federal aid, this simple requirement might have sweeping effects in keeping out the unpromising and in elevating the student culture. At present, Pell grants go to students who need only to show "satisfactory academic progress," which usually translates into a C and which, in the current context of grade inflation, means almost nothing.

It's worth a try. College isn't for everyone. Nothing is deadlier to higher education than the pretense that it is.

Why Are
Professors Liberal?

A fish is said to be unaware of the water it swims in and just so, Professor M., a liberal professor at Moorhead State University avows that he is unaware of any liberal predominance in higher education. Surveys purporting to show it are, he says, based on that old bugaboo, "flawed methodology"; and even if faculties really are lopsidedly leftist there is no reason to believe that this translates into a bias affecting either classroom teaching or campus policy.

In fact, surveys have been conducted for many years by professional pollsters and social scientists on both the right and the left, and they show close agreement that the campuses are heavily liberal. But why quibble? Does Professor M. need a formal study to tell him that the sky is blue? In his first week as a college freshman, he must surely have noticed that his campus, wherever it was, had a point of view that was strongly leftist in every field, even in math and the physical sciences; and today the most meticulous examination of the social science and humanities faculty at Moorhead State would probably fail to turn up, among its roughly 300 faculty members, even a half dozen who would confess to being right of center.

In the general population, 38% of Americans identify themselves as conservatives and 24% as liberal. But a 2005 survey of 1,643 professors across 183 four-year campuses by Stanley Rothman showed that in academia liberals outnumbered conservatives 72% to

15%. Rothman polled members of 22 departments where liberals predominated in every field without exception. Not counting those who described themselves as centrists, the breakdown was:

Field of Study	Liberal	Conservative
All faculty	72%	15%
Social Sciences	75	9
Humanities	81	9
Other	67	20

In the social sciences and humanities where ideology most matters, ratios of liberal to conservative were highest in English departments (88 to 3) and lowest in economics departments (55 to 39). In the physical sciences, the liberal presence ranged from chemistry (64 to 29) to biology (75 to 17), to physics, (66 to 11). In no field was there anything close to parity between liberals and conservatives.

Other studies find that in the humanities and social sciences about 12% of professors identify themselves as "far left," while only .4 percent identify as being on the "far right."

A recent survey of US campuses by the University of Toronto found that in the humanities, 81% of professors identified themselves as left of center, while in the social sciences 75% did, with the rest identifying as moderates and conservatives. In departments of law, business, science and engineering, the left also far outnumbers the right, though by lower ratios.

Of course, ratios differ between campuses as well as departments and regions. Some fields are notorious for their lack of conservatives. Christopher Cardwell and Daniel Klein, in a survey of 11 campuses in the California system found a left-right ratio of 44 to 1 in sociology and 30 to 1 in anthropology. The left is strongest in the elite universities. Harvard's faculty, for instance, is reported to vote Democratic 96 percent of the time.

The absence of campus conservatives and libertarians can get scandalous. University of Virginia researcher Jonathan Haidt once polled a live conference of roughly a thousand social psychologists, asking how many of those present considered themselves liberals. About 80 percent raised their hands. When he asked how many were conservatives, the number of hands raised was – *three*! Prof. Haidt said that this was statistically impossible. He surmised that majorities of such intensity tend to form "tribal-moral communities" that can be vengeful to those outside the tribe. No doubt others in the crowd stayed silent for fear of their careers if not their lives.

How did the left achieve majorities of such proportions? A common explanation is "self selection," meaning that different occupations attract different kinds of people. For example, nursing is 94 percent female, so that it's normal to think of it as a woman's profession. Most males, therefore, may not even consider a nursing career.

Just so (as liberals explain it), people who are intelligent, love ideas, and are willing to work for modest salaries become liberals and then go into academic life. On the other hand, those who want high incomes – and who maybe aren't so bright – will, as my liberal correspondent Professor M. put it, "seek jobs in the private sector."

The problem with this explanation is that it's the ideology of the already selected. So, conservatives have a different interpretation of the self-selection theory, which is that they opt out of academic careers because they discover that the academy is an inhospitable place to work. Having experienced the academic culture as undergraduates, they know that the campuses practice racial favoritism, censorship, and the conformity known as political correctness that is contrary to their own values and to the purposes of education.

When everyone else is on the left, campus conservatives become oddities who must constantly watch themselves. Rather than voicing their convictions and engaging in spirited debates they will likely hold their tongues and stay in the closet. Before committing to a career that will likely leave them marginalized and frustrated, many, probably most, will ask, "Do I want this?"

More important, as higher education expands its repertoire of world-saving causes, it is also redesigning its infrastructure. Prof. Mark Bauerlein has written that a progressive "orientation has been embedded into the disciplines" so that "some fields' very constitutions rest on progressive politics." This means that part of the qualification for teaching these fields is a *sympathy* for them. Examples include the many courses whose titles end in "studies":

ethnic studies, feminist studies, gay and lesbian studies, and other programs that patronize victim groups claiming oppression by Western culture. (Just now Victoria University in Canada has announced that it will have the world's first endowed chair in transgender studies.) If you fail to accept the leftist interpretation that these identity groups are victims of Western culture, you won't get the job.

Nor will Marxist-based "culture studies" accept those who are unconvincing in their disdain for capitalism. Nor will social services programs likely hire faculties who do not accept the mandate, as the American Council on Social Work has put it, "to integrate social and economic justice grounded in an understanding of distributive justice, human and civil rights, and the global interconnections of oppression." Many other disciplines are designed in such a way that leftist sympathies are required to teach them.

Even job advertisements turn away conservatives with pious affirmations that the hiring campus is an "equal opportunity employer" – doublespeak for racial preferences – and that it "especially welcomes" applications from minorities and "persons of color," which is a polite way of saying that white male conservatives need not apply.

Conscious prejudice also works against conservatives. Dutch social psychologists Yoel Inbar and Joris Lammers once asked 800 psychologists what they would do if choosing between two equally qualified candidates for one job opening. Thirty-seven percent said unapologetically they would choose the liberal candidate over the conservative. Others said they would also apply a bias against conservatives in evaluating their papers, in approving grants, and in extending invitations to symposiums.

In replenishing their own ranks, professors naturally want their students to have teachers who are intelligent and level-headed, that is, people like themselves. To do otherwise would be irresponsible. Subjecting their students to someone whose outlook may be, well ... kooky ... is something they could not in good conscience do; they will instead feel honor-bound to limit applicants to those who are safely within the liberal fold.

But okay. Why does all this matter?

The answer is that the left presides, unchallenged, over practices that are simply ruinous to education. It has turned the campuses into places of censorship (the last place on earth where it should exist), developed compulsory reeducation programs that are nothing short of indoctrination, withdrawn the protections of due process, cultivated hostility to the Western cultural tradition, dismantled the core curriculum and, in general, exchanged the best traditions of higher education for political fashions that have turned our universities into bastions of intellectual conformity. Debate no longer exists on our campuses; at best we have an occasional family quarrel among liberals. All of this destruction is due to the left's monopolized campuses that permit no opposition. There is no one else to blame.

"Any political position that dominates an institution without dissent," writes Mark Bauerlein, "deteriorates into smugness, complacency, and blindness." He adds that "without genuine dissent in the classroom and the committee room, academic life is simply boring." It is hard to imagine that anything like this state of affairs could exist in higher education if it even a quarter of the faculty and administration were conservatives.

But it's also hard to foresee any event that could end the liberal dominance and add dissenting voices to the campuses. My guess is that the left will go on pushing its anti-education agenda for decades more to come, undisturbed by any form of opposition whether internal or external.

Which is too bad, because two heads are always better than one. In his classic work *On Liberty*, John Stuart Mill said that those who censor debate lose as much, if not more, than those who are censored. A party may be in possession of true ideas, but if it is never challenged by criticism, its understanding of *why* its ideas are true will go to rust and it will be unable to defend them. "He who knows only his own side of the case," Mill wrote, "knows little of that."

In the absence of dissenting parties, our campuses have armored themselves against dissent and we are all losing more than we can know.

Hollywood's Love Affair with Tyrants

"The sin of nearly all left-wingers from 1933 onward," wrote George Orwell, "is that they have wanted to be anti-fascist without being anti-totalitarian." From the nineteen-thirties through much of the Cold War, many of the left's artists and intellectuals have refused to notice that the apparatus of repression used by the communist regimes they admired was no different from those of the fascist regimes they despised. If Stalin's or Mao's admirers were asked about their heroes' gulags, terror, and deliberate starvations, they commonly dismissed them as either trivial or as "historically necessary."

Though once plentiful, the far Left's men on horseback are now piteously reduced to a senile egomaniac in Cuba and the memory of Venezuela's Hugo Chavez, a pale copy now deceased. With the passing of the international class of artists and theoreticians who flourished during the Cold War, the worship of tyrants is now more or less confined to: Hollywood.

For the past five decades Hollywood's celebrities have trooped to Havana where Fidel has flattered them with his interminable monologues ("the most important 8 hours of my life," recalls director Stephen Spielberg of one of the Maximum Leader's shorter speeches) and the illusion of importance. Celebrities like Redford, Belafonte, Sarandon, DiCaprio, Spacey, and scores of others have sat at Fidel's feet for a weekend and then returned home with breathless and widely publicized accounts of Fidel's brilliance and charm ("one of the Earth's wisest people," says Oliver Stone) and of his statecraft: "Cuba," exclaims Jack Nicholson, "is simply a paradise!"

How do they deal with that pulchritudinous pachyderm that sits squarely in the living room, Cuba's, um … totalitarianism? Well, Hollywood's celebrities don't deny the absence of liberty; they simply dismiss it as an eccentric concern, of interest only to nit-pickers abroad and of little importance to the Cubans themselves. Rights, you see, are unimportant because most Cubans have higher concerns. "Cuban human rights violations," explains producer Saul Landau, "take the form of procedural violations. They involve legal and political rights rather than economic and social rights."

Got it? Human rights are mere technicalities. A right to speak, to associate, to own property, to enjoy the protection of due process – even to *leave the country* – is lost on these noble primitives. So, what if Cubans can't own satellite dishes or use the Internet without minders hovering over their shoulders; or that secret police and neighborhood watch committees keep the population atomized and docile; or that in a half-century there have been no elections and dissidents languish for decades in prisons? So long as they get free education and health care, why should Cubans need liberty?

Ed Asner, defending the 2003 arrest of 75 Cuban dissidents, mostly artists, writers and economists who received sentences of up to 28 years, said "I understand that the trial was very fair … By Cuban standards the trial was fair and judicious." Were the standards themselves fair? To Asner the question seems irrelevant. Otherwise, Hollywood celebrities who complain that the US doesn't appreciate its own artists seem to have no complaint about Castro's treatment of its artist-dissidents.

After a half-century of Fidel's wise and benevolent rule, food is still rationed (in the pre-Castro years Cuba was a net food exporter), wages (according to Fidel's brother Raul) average $22 a month, and the economy has been continuously dependent on foreign tyrants and remissions from expatriate families. But Hollywood's let-them-eat cake crowd ignores the chronic poverty and instead rhapsodizes about the country's spirituality and its absence of consumerism. The *Washington Post's* Michelle Singletary found Havana's empty shelves "kind of refreshing."

And what about Cuba's highly vaunted egalitarianism? Well, where the naïve visitor might see an apartheid system of hospitals, hotels, restaurants, shops, and beaches reserved for Communist Party and military officials as well as tourists but off-limits to ordinary Cubans, Hollywood reports a classless society. In widespread prostitution practiced by even highly educated but impoverished women and state-sponsored sex tourism, it marvels at an "erotic" culture. In a country where even aspirin is seldom available and surgical patients are expected bring their own soap, sheets and light bulbs, it finds a model of free health care. And in people so long deprived of self-determination that many have come to fear it, Hollywood finds proof of Castro's wise and kindly rule.

Why do prestigious people romanticize tyrants?

One oft-cited explanation is that tyrants are a fantasy about ourselves. The milquetoast who identifies with Fidel becomes Robin Hood, a man on horseback, the begetter of a new society, the intellectual in power, an existential hero … choose your scenario. Perhaps there is an element of revenge too. If America doesn't acknowledge your true worth, Fidel thumbs his nose at it for you; the enemy of your enemy is your friend. And if you don't much like the human race, he torments a fair portion of *that* for you too, and at no personal risk to yourself. As the Argentine socialist Jacobo Timerman (who was himself jailed for 3 years as a political prisoner) has put it, "Foreign Castroists have all the motivations and none of the hardships."

Some social theorists say that artists and intellectuals tend to see themselves as members of an aristocracy and resent liberal society because it does not include them in its ruling class. Snubbed by the open society, they exact a vicarious revenge by lavishing praise upon its enemies. Bertoldt Brecht was once asked how he could justify his loyalty to communism when his plays were banned in the USSR. His reply was: "Well, at least there they take me seriously." The egotist welcomes suppression as a tribute to his importance; on the other hand, liberal society's indifference is an insult. It is better to be persecuted than to be ignored.

And for their part, tyrants embrace sycophantic celebrities ("useful idiots," in Lenin's term) because they help to prop up regimes that would otherwise have little legitimacy. Prison memoirs often recount the demoralization of dissidents wrought by troupes of artists and intellectuals who heap praises upon their jailers and trivialize the dissidents' sacrifices and misery. Dissidents take mortal risks on behalf of liberty only to have their heroism dismissed by giddy celebrities. Tyrants can operate gulags with confidence when they know that prestigious visitors will justify them.

As Cuba's personality cult declines into a feeble gerontocracy (and then, inevitably, into the banality of military rule) Hollywood's celebrities are having to look elsewhere for their next tyrant-hero. For a while, their new pilgrimages took them to Venezuela, Where Fidel's understudy Hugo Chavez – "a great man," according to Sean Penn –

won their admiration by jailing rivals and erecting a cult of personality in the grand revolutionary tradition.

Unfortunately, Chaves was felled by cancer before the consequences of his live-for-today plundering became fully manifest. His uncharismatic successor will reap the whirlwind. Thus, for the moment, Hollywood is bereft of tyrant-heroes.

Just before Chavez' demise, however, Director Oliver Stone produced a pseudo-documentary film ("South of the Border") which portrayed him as – guess what – a wise and benevolent leader who was victimized, in Stone's words, by "years and years of blighted journalism." When a *New York Times* reviewer observed that, as with some of his earlier film biographies, this "glowing portrait" of Chavez showed a disregard for historical facts, Stone accused the reviewer of "nitpicking" and "splitting hairs."

"What about human rights?" the reviewer asked.

"Human rights," Stone replied, "is a buzz phrase."

A Popular Revolt
Against Racial Preferences

Among the losers in the last general election was the scheme of state-sponsored racial discrimination known as affirmative action. In Michigan the voters passed, by a 58 percent majority, an initiative banning race and gender preferences in public agencies, and they did so against the preachments of the entire state educational establishment which outspent supporters of the ban by three to one. They also uprooted "landmark" decisions by the US Supreme Court which just three years before had allowed Michigan's colleges and universities to turn away applicants with oppressive characteristics like maleness, whiteness, Asian-ness and Jewishness, provided that they do so, in a "limited and nuanced manner," as Justice Sandra O'Connor put it, and that they put a final end to it … oh, some time within the next 25 years or so.

In 2005, before the voters spoke, the "limited and nuanced" rule meant that applicants applying to the University of Michigan with SAT scores of 1240 and GPAs of 3.2 had a 90 percent percent chance of being accepted, *if* they were black or Hispanic – and just a 10 percent chance if they were white or Asian.

That same rule also produced a student body of black and Hispanic enrollees whose mean SATs were 230 points below those of whites and Asians and who were five times as likely to be on academic probation. In the law school, admissions for blacks, Hispanics, and Native Americans fell to 5.5% from 39.6% when the preference rule ended. It was against such "nuances" that Michigan' s voters seem to have rebelled.

When the returns were in, Mary Coleman, president of the University of Michigan, expressed outrage at the voters' "unconstitutional behavior" and threatened to sue. In a campus speech she thrice avowed that "we are Michigan, and we are diversity," and warned that ending racial preferences could lead to discrimination – by *other* people. Perhaps wondering why so many racists, sexists, and assorted yahoos cling to outmoded ideas like merit and the chance to advance oneself by hard work, Coleman proposed a vigorous public relations campaign to help voters understand that subordinating merit to skin color both enhances fairness and makes for a smarter student body.

But for the moment Michigan joins California, Florida, and Washington, where voters have also failed to understand that throwing one person under the bus in order to advance the fortunes of someone else is a noble act. Since a quarter of the population now lives in those states, foes of discrimination are calling the latest vote a "death blow" for preferences. Indeed, one day the universities may have to stop reforming the world and resume tasks for which they are better suited. Tasks like, well, educating students.

"Diversity" may be passe outside the campus walls, but inside them it remains the Holy Grail. Its disciples accord it near-mystical powers in transforming race relations and stimulating learning, although there is little evidence that it does either. In a careful survey of student and faculty attitudes in 2002, a research team headed by Professor Stanley Rothman noted that on ethnically diverse campuses "the predicted positive associations of educational benefits and inter-racial understanding failed to appear." Other researchers find that low admission standards for minorities in prestigious universities are often set-ups for academic failure later on. But on the campuses, news of this nature is either ignored or denounced as racist blasphemy, and the fact that researchers on both the Left and the Right arrive at similar findings makes no difference. When facts disturb cherished campus illusions, so much the worse for facts.

Who benefits from official discrimination? Mostly, the ideologues of diversity and the permanent apparatus. The diversity industry provides careers for both campus administrators ("diversity offices" have sprung up everywhere) and for professors who teach ethnic studies because the more respectable academic fields are overstaffed.

As more oppressed groups are discovered, exotic new programs in ethnic studies, feminist studies, whiteness studies, queer studies, subaltern studies, fat studies and many others must be constantly invented to drive home the vicimhood of their clientele and elevate their self-esteem. These "studies" are all crap, but they do provide job security and they proclaim the superior idealism of their sponsors.

When large numbers of faculty and administrative careers are irreversibly locked into these fields, the question of whether they are of any benefit to students becomes moot. Those who benefit from the new status quo will fight to preserve it. The diversity industry symbolizes the growing divergence between the interests of educators and the interests of education.

Affirmative action puts public authority on the side of racial discrimination and involves it in such sordid practices as deciding who qualifies for the spoils distributed along racial and ethnic lines and who doesn't. It even requires peering into ancestral histories (the "one-drop rule" again?) in order to decide doubtful cases.

Because preferences encourage minority students to think of themselves as weak, they lower incentives for individuals to succeed by their own efforts. In relaxing standards for minorities (the soft racism of low expectations," as President George W. Bush put it), standards are also compromised for the whole student body. A cruel side effect is that preferences stigmatize as "affirmative action babies" minorities who are perfectly capable of excelling on their own merits. And preferences gloss over the most basic reason the colleges offer preferences to minorities in the first place, which is the second-rate elementary and secondary education minorities get in low-income neighborhoods.

When we allow government to judge people according to their immutable characteristics – those beyond anyone's power to determine – rather than according to their merit, we are tolerating injustice. When Martin Luther King's admirers want the schools to judge people by the color of their skin rather than by the "content of their character," what do they do – turn King's portrait to the wall? Affirmative action's synthetic idealism is rife with hypocrisy and masks practices that are plainly wrong.

Such things don't bother the courts, but they do the voters. Initiatives similar to Michigan's are forthcoming in other states, and because the polls indicate that majorities are generally hostile to preferences it may well be that the final end to official prejudice is not far off.

Fair-minded people should hope so.

Why School Board Elections
Change Nothing

Why are the public schools so resistant to reform?

The US Department of Education recently reported that 20 percent of American eighth graders are functional illiterates (relax, North Dakotans, here it's just 15 percent). It also says that 57 percent know almost nothing about history, and by the way their scores in math are awful too, have been for decades, and never seem to improve. In part, DOE blames out-of-field teaching, but it also blames a curriculum so infested with non-academic electives that there isn't enough time to teach the basics.

So, at a forum for school board candidates who wanted to show their stuff, I asked about this. The high schools' "Program of Studies" (I said) lists well over 200 courses, though only 22 credits are needed for graduation and of these, only 8 are academic subjects that are specifically required. Otherwise, the curriculum is packed with electives like "Personal and Business Law," "Relationships," "Fashion Trends," "Advanced Racquet Sports," and "Sewing for Fun."

Q: "Do you see any semblance of purpose here?"

A: "*Yes!* said all five of those presents. Learning, all agreed, should be fun, which is why hobbies and sports are important. Also, the basket-weaving stuff keeps dropout rates low. Most importantly, the schools must prepare students for "real life," which is why we need all those courses in job training, daily living, and the like. One candidate, warning against "cookie cutter education," even thought 200 electives were too few.

Q: "Is there a particular body of knowledge that an educated person needs to possess?"

A: All five hopefuls took up the question (which was, really, "Do the liberal arts matter?") And while two of them paid tribute to the 3 Rs, the consensus was: No.

The evening was an eye-opener for me. Though the candidates were all intelligent people, their responses struck me as stale bromides rather than insights they had arrived at themselves. They seemed to have no differences among themselves concerning such basic questions as the nature and purposes of education, of what is essential and what is peripheral. Instead, they limited themselves to questions of school funding, teacher salaries, new equipment and so forth. It was as if the philosophical questions were long since settled and agreed upon by all sophisticated people, so that nothing more was needed except tidying up the details.

Their ideas and even their language mimicked the assumptions that have ruled the teacher colleges for a hundred years. These assumptions have seeped from the teacher colleges into the public schools and from there into our livings rooms where its pretentious jargon has become part of our common discourse. Today everyone speaks of the idiom of progressivism even if no one understands its true meaning.

What is this ideology, known as progressivism, that dominates our thinking about education?

Rooted in 18th Century French Jacobinism, progressivism is based on a utopian view of human nature. "The fundamental principle of all morality," said J.J. Rousseau of his pedagogical theories, "is that man is a being naturally good, loving justice and order, that there is not any original perversity in the human heart, and that the first movements of nature are always right." John Dewey, an American disciple of Rousseau's, and a founder of American progressivism, agreed: "The child's own instincts and powers," he avowed, are the "starting point for all education."

With its faith in childish impulses, progressivism is thus a revolt against all human experience, most especially the Judeo-Christian tradition which sees the natural man not as innately good but as a fallen creature whose instincts and impulses need to be tamed. For that reason, traditional education has always stressed the cultural heritage with its religious and moral demands for self-control.

But if childish impulses are a creative force, then instruction from the adult environment must be a form of contamination. Dewey saw this clearly enough and warned against instilling the "values of adults rather than those of children and youth." Another early progressive, Friedrich Froebel, wrote that "education should from the first be passive, observant, and protective rather than prescribing, determining, interfering. ... All training that ... interferes with Nature must tend to limit and injure." In short, learning should come spontaneously from children themselves.

Though this ideology violates common sense, it forms what education reformer E.D. Hirsch, Jr. calls a "thoughtworld," a belief system so monolithic that in educationist circles there is no thinkable alternative. The embodiment of this thoughtword is what the 1983 *Nation at Risk* report called the "smorgasbord" curriculum which caters to the tastes of children. "There is no such thing as degrees or order of value," wrote John Dewey, "therefore we cannot establish a hierarchy of values among studies." If everything is relative, then setting educational priorities is neither possible nor desirable. All we need to do is offer a broad miscellany of subjects and then stand aside and let students themselves decide what is worth learning.

So modern education promotes, as Richard Hofstadter acidly put it in his *Anti-Intellectualism in American Life*, "Not chemistry, but the testing of detergents; not physics, but how to drive and service a car; not history but the operation of the local gas works; not biology but the way to the zoo; not Shakespeare or Dickens, but how write a business letter."

School boards are made up of intelligent, civic-minded people who volunteer their time, with few thanks, to make the schools better. But while they want to cultivate critical thinking in students, they do not see that they are in need of it themselves. The theories which now govern the schools are not, as they seem to believe, eternal principles proven by experience or by science, but are part of an exceedingly radical ideology that is hostile to the very idea of education.

Just so, the smorgasbord offered by Fargo's high schools includes 13 courses in athletics but only 4 in history; 14 in stenography and 1 in philosophy; 17 in housekeeping and 2 in government; and so on. In math not a single course is required. For students who can't read, remedial courses are available – but only as electives.

So, I listened gloomily as the five candidates zestfully demonstrated their mastery of progressivism's fashionable jargon by flippantly noting that content knowledge conflicts with "higher order skills," that it is better to be "life-long learners" than to learn things in school; that instruction in the arts, sciences, and humanities must give way to "real life situations," i.e. job training and hobbies. Ridiculed by virtually all reformers outside the thoughtworld, nonsense like this survives only because of the public's naïve faith that the "experts" who run the teacher colleges and the public schools *must somehow*, against all appearances, know what they are doing.

When the ideology of progressivism is uncritically accepted by candidates and voters alike, elections will do nothing to improve the schools. They will only serve to further legitimize the status quo. Debate will be limited to the minutiae of schooling – to budgets, buildings, personnel, equipment and so on – and will never deal with its governing ideas. The public will remain largely unaware that the schools are operating far below their potential. In short, elections yield personal victories for candidates but never mandates for change.

At the conclusion of his important book, *Cultural Literacy*, E.D. Hirsch, Jr. says that our great challenge is "to bring the hidden curriculum into the open where it belongs and to make its contents the subject of democratic discussion." Doing that was, indeed, the implicit point of my questions to the school board candidates.

Do we really want better schools? Until we free ourselves from assumptions that are too hallowed to be questioned, we'll never get them. Those who lack the imagination to challenge the prevailing orthodoxy can never be educational leaders; they will forever remain the slaves of the conventional wisdom and the status quo.

Which is why, next time we have a school board election, the first item on the agenda for debate ought to be the ideology of progressivism.

The Schools Have Forgotten Their Mission

Forum columnist John Sundvor is of course correct then he writes that the problems of public education are too complex and too massive to be cured by a simple resort to school vouchers. Nevertheless, he is quite wrong in dismissing them as merely a quick fix. No one pretends that vouchers by themselves are sufficient for the reconstruction of education, but it is also unlikely that reform will ever take place without some form of parental choice.

The public schools, Sundvor says, "will not be made better by putting a few good students into private schools and leaving the troubled students behind." That is true, but it misstates the issue. The real fear among those who oppose school choice is not that a few students would leave the public schools, but that they would leave in droves – in such numbers as to raise the specter of empty classrooms, mass teacher layoffs and a residue of aging hoodlums who are more or less uneducable.

Suppose a mass exodus did ensue: Would that be a bad thing? What does it say about the public schools when their champions admit that they could not survive in a system where parents are free to choose where they send their kids? And what moral precept justifies the holding of good students' hostage – that is what it is – to a system which even Sundvor insists has failed, as a kind of human sacrifice to students who are not good?

The main argument for vouchers is that schools, like most enterprises, are made better by the challenges of competition. Why do good students leave the public schools? Because the private schools are usually better. How did they get that way? By having to compete for good students. And why are the public schools failing? Because as monopolies they don't have to earn their students. For them, failure has no consequences. No matter how badly they perform, they will be guaranteed a reliable supply of captive students.

An institution's profoundest corruption is the forgetting of its purpose. And the purpose of public education has been all but lost in a sort of collective amnesia. Even the governor, who supports vouchers, does so for the wrong reason, believing that the public schools have failed to train students for high-tech jobs – as if it were self-evident that their mission is not to produce intelligent minds but to provide a skilled labor force. And Sundvor, his critic, leaves that view unchallenged.

Nevertheless, there are still parents who know the difference between education and training. Faced with schools that are increasingly dominated by a utilitarian-industrial ethos, they ought to have the right to opt out in favor a traditional liberal arts education.

The public schools' confusion is faithfully reflected in their curriculum, or what now passes for one. The smorgasbord curriculum – a mishmash of mostly nonacademic electives – flourishes in the surreal atmosphere of an extreme relativism which affirms that calculus and cake decorating, biology and basket-weaving are all of equal worth. It is a confession by professional educators that they have no idea of what education is or what it is that an educated person is supposed to know. In the absence of any settled conviction as to what constitutes an education, the schools are left with no alternative but to abandon the responsibility of educating students to the students themselves.

Indeed, the kids find lots of fluffy treats to choose from, scores and scores of them: aerobics, interior design, consumer education, small engines, personal law, aviation, clothing dynamics, foreign foods, living on your own, families and relationships, welding, and loads of narcissistic courses devoted to the exploration of feelings. There are two things to be said for this program of studies. One is that it precludes all threats to self-esteem that might otherwise accrue to academic failure. The other is that it defies all possibility of parody.

This insanity cannot be lost on the students themselves. They are asked to believe that while it is very important that they spend long years in school, what they learn, or don't learn, while they are there is a matter of little consequence.

If we have forgotten the *what* of education, so also have we forgotten the *how* of it. Lacking any firm pedagogical principles, the teacher colleges have placed their faith in fads. Thus, the schools lurch along from year to year, adapting themselves to TYNT – This Year's New Thing – with no sense of continuity or any hope that something permanent might develop from them. This inconstancy is taken as proof of open-mindedness and a willingness to experiment. In educationist circles, no virtue is more highly regarded than a demonstrated inability to distinguish between the permanent and the episodic.

But witness the flotsam of old TYNYs: look-say reading, the "new math," values clarification, life adjustment, the self-esteem movement, and countless others that are nothing more than old wine in new bottles, stale progressivist ideas recycled with new names that leave our libraries bulging with titles like "Why Johnny Can't read," "Why Johnnie Can't write," Why Johnnie Can't Add," and so on. When the "academic curriculum lost its importance as the central focus of the public school system," writes Dianne Ravitch in her history of education, *Left Back*, "the schools lost their anchor, their sense of mission, their intense moral commitment to the intellectual development of each child." The result is that in a world of endless distractions, children are left in a world of images shaped by the popular culture, "everything becomes trivia, famous for a minute or two, then gone."

Without an external challenge, we should not expect the public schools to recover their sense of mission and undertake their own reform. The problem here is less one of vested interests than of how our educationists understand the world. The word "reform," after all, implies that one state of affairs is better than some others.

But what if you refuse to believe that one thing *can* be better than another? The catch is that in the educationist profession, whose ideas almost exclusively determine school policy, is itself heavily influenced by a positivist philosophy which denies the very possibility of making the value distinctions that any idea of reform must presuppose. There are not may among its ranks who can deal with a concept like "better than" without experiencing severe disorientation.

If there is still hope for the public schools, it surely resides in the same competitive forces that have made many of the private schools, even with their weaknesses, seem comparatively attractive. There is no reason why the stimulus of competition should strengthen private schools but not the public ones. More likely, the specter of free choice will prove to be the tonic that the public schools need to get hold of themselves and decide what they are all about.

But whatever their ultimate effect, vouchers are probably inevitable if only because public education is truly bankrupt. A high school diploma, with few exceptions, is hardly worth the paper on which it is printed. The public schools are in desperate need of fresh thinking, and the prospect of impending extinction is said to concentrate the mind wonderfully.

Who Should
Enroll in College?

A couple of weeks ago the Commission on National Investment in Higher Education reported that, in the absence of a sharp increase in taxpayer support, "millions of Americans will be denied the opportunity to go to college because of the combined effect of enrollment growth, a sixfold increase in costs, flat funding, sky-rocketing tuition and shrinking resources."

At last - some good news about education!

The fact is that we are already cycling far too many people through college. Consider:

In 1967 about 12 percent of all college graduates were either unemployed or else employed in jobs which traditionally do not require a college degree. By 1990 the figure was 25 percent. By 2013 the New York Federal Reserve Bank reported that 44 percent of young college graduates had jobs for which a degree is unnecesary.

All of this flies in the face of the orthodox view, beloved of officialdom and the educational establishment, that what the country needs is more people with college degrees. It is true that talented people with genuine intellectual interests and clear goals should always be welcomed in higher education, even shanghaied if necessary. But the aim of our education boosters is seldom that of inspiring in students a love for art, science, or learning for its own sake.

President Clinton, who once announced the discovery of a new human right - college for everyone - also proclaimed that one of his top goals was to "help the nation's schools prepare students for work," and urged, accordingly, American educators to de-emphasize academic courses in favor of applied skills. And that view of education's purpose is widely accepted among our college students, many of whom cling to the belief that the main, if not sole, purpose of college is to enhance their economic status.

But a college degree, formerly a sure-fire ticket to economic success, no longer is. While demand remains strong in a few fields, notably in medicine and in careers that use quantitative skills, most degrees are in chronic surplus and have been for decades. There simply isn't room at the top for everyone. The supply of degreed people in the labor force (presently more than 30 million) is already more than the social order can absorb.

So why do high school students keep signing up in droves for college?

Again, consider: High school graduates aged 25-32 and working full time have median earnings of about $28,000 while those with baccalaureates earn $45,500, a premium of 60 percent. Over a lifetime, median earnings for college graduates are expected to make $1.19 million, almost twice what high school graduates will make, and $335,000 more than those with associate degrees. Such gaps are cited with great enthusiasm by universities seeking ever-higher enrollments.

But wait - is there not a paradox here? If large numbers of college graduates are in oversupply, then their earnings should be going *down* when in fact they are going *up*.

But the paradox is not hard to explain. A good many economists stress that the rising value of a college degree is mostly a matter of relativity. Adjusted for inflation, the median earnings of college graduates between 1979 and today have remained essentially flat (rising by an unimpressive 4 percent), while the earnings of high school graduates *dropped* by a disastrous 14 percent.

The earnings gap yawns downward and it is far less a reflection of the scarcity of college skills than it is of the collapse of the high school diploma's credibility as an employment credential. Thus, high schoolers who have little interest in college may nevertheless feel compelled to enroll, less in the expectation of gain than in the hope of avoiding ruin.

They are put in that predicament by high schools that have become synonymous with low standards, grade inflation, and a curriculum devoted overwhelmingly to non-academic froth. Thus, the National Employer Survey has revealed that more than three-fourths of the nation's employers (who are well aware of the horror stories about straight A students who can't write a compound sentence) ignore any talents their high school applicants might really have and increasingly require a college degree even for unskilled jobs. And why not? They are so numerous that they can be had cheaply, and there is even a fair chance that a college grad can read and write.

Only about 60 percent of college freshmen ever graduate. Of those who do, a good many get useless degrees in lawn care and the like. No one wins by this sort of nonsense except the academic empire builders who regard their campuses less as places of scholarly achievement than as growth industries.

Instead of treating the colleges and universities as places of remediation for the failure of the high scools, we would do better to restore serious college entrance standards. Doing so would force the public schools to take academics seriously and restore credibility to the high school diploma. Let's get realistic about college: most who enroll have neither the intellectual ability nor the clarity of purpose to benefit from a college education worthy of the name. Demagogic pretenses to the contrary will inevitably lead to a baccalaureate as devoid of meaning as the high school diploma is now.

What matters is not how many people we have in college but what they learn and how well they learn it. If the worst fears of the Commission of National Investment are fulfilled and millions of indifferent and redundant graduates fail to appear on schedule, it will be something less than tragic.

Introducing Honesty
into School Ratings

Once every year, the trade journal *Education Week* publishes an edition – "Quality Counts" – that is an indispensable tool for sizing up the state of the nation's public schools. This year's edition looks at the impact of No Child Left Behind, a muddled law that requires the 50 states to report progress in such things as reading and math – and then invites each state to define "progress" for itself. This loophole yields more flim-flam than reliable data, so the success of NCLB can be hard to assess. Therefore, "Quality Counts" tries to put some realism into the picture by using data from a respected testing agency, the National Assessment of Educational Progress, whose own standards are ballast against educationists eager to create the illusion of progress while avoiding, at all costs, actual reform.

So, while Tennessee counts 87 percent of its 4th graders "proficient" in math, we learn that by NAEP's reckoning only 28 percent belong in that category. Alabama claims a 38 percent gain in 8th grade reading proficiency, while NAEP records an actual decline. In Arizona, the number of students passing exams in reading, writing, and math jumped 30 percent in a single year – a brilliant achievement that occurred after the state exams were "revised."

North Dakota too is a generous judge in its own cause. In both math and reading it counts almost twice as many of its students to be proficient as does NAEP. Among eighth graders, proficiency in math would seem to be growing impressively – the state reports a gain of 22 percent over last year – except that NAEP reports a slight decline. Amid all this rampant dissimulation, only Massachusetts, which since its founding has consistently produced America's best schools, assessed itself honestly.

Clearly, this patchwork of optional state standards, each hostage to political expediency, is worse than useless. With no common idea of what students at any grade should know, and of how well they should know it, accountability is impossible, goals lose their meaning, and the pressure to show quick results creates an incentive to keep lowering academic standards.

In this environment, even successful reforms in one area may do harm to others. Dianne Ravitch, who is one of our best writers on education, says that because only math and reading "count" for NCLB purposes, "important subjects like history, science, foreign languages, and the arts have been ignored."

Indeed, in some school districts, Ravitch says, "children are prepared like trained seals, ready to check off the right box on a standardized test, but completely unprepared to read a complex text, understand the historical roots of contemporary problems, or appreciate the arts as a part of their lives."

What to do? If honest standards appear to spur improvement (as they seem to do in math, at least), then perhaps extending NCLB to include history, science, languages, and the arts would make those subjects "count" as well. Ravitch is one of a growing number of reformers who insist that accountability shouldn't be limited to reading and math, and that until long-degraded, yet essential academic subjects – those that go to the heart of what it means to be an educated person – are similarly revived, our kids will be schooled but not educated. By merely extending the NAEP template to other key subjects, the totality would add up to something like a national curriculum.

If this seems radical, let us remember that three consecutive US presidents – Clinton and the 2 Bushes – have proposed nationwide content standards. They've done so because the horror stories about American education simply won't quit, and because there are few local constituencies for real reform. Just the other day, the American Institutes for Research announced that most of our college seniors can't handle ordinary tasks like comparing credit card offers, summarizing the results of a survey, or understanding the argument of a newspaper editorial. Yet the response of education establishments, everywhere, is an unctuous vow to "continue the excellence."

Public education is failing because most of its subject matter is irrelevant. Over time, the curriculum has been purged of substance until it is now mostly a flea market of electives in dating, dancing, woodworking, and tennis – who any longer teaches history? Though we prize local control, we cannot expect self-correction from school systems that refuse to admit that anything is wrong.

Right now, nothing is more important than restoring purpose to education and cleaning out the soporific fluff which, for far too many years, the schools have waged their war against the mind.

Why We Have
Too Many Ph.D.s

In the growth industry known as higher education, success is gauged by enrollments, revenues, new programs and by how rapidly they expand. Currently, graduate programs are the rage everywhere, with doctorates being offered in trendy fields such as "sports management," "food safety" and other indispensable areas of knowledge. Our state has also joined the race in earnest, notably with North Dakota State University's plan to add a jaw-dropping 16 new doctoral fields to its existing 26, and thence to award 50 Ph.D.s annually.

"We must graduate more doctoral candidates than we are," NDSU's President Joseph Chapman says. "To me, it's the most critical issue we face."

But why is this a "critical issue"? The fact is that the state is already awash in doctorates. So is the whole country. Their chronic overproduction has been a scandal in higher education since the late 1960s.

Writing in the *Washington Monthly*, Paul de Moulin reports that in science and engineering alone, some 40,000 holders of doctorates are currently stuck in dead-end, fringe jobs in academia. A Stanford study shows that most engineering doctorates never find work in their fields, anywhere. Among Ph.D.s in all fields, unemployment is as high as it is in the general labor force, while *under*employment – Ph.D.s working as clerks and cab drivers – has become so common that it no longer shocks.

Why do the campuses want to produce still more Ph.D.s? Why, instead, aren't they cutting programs, limiting enrollments, warning students of their poor prospects? Very simply, it is contrary to their interests to do so.

Think about it: Rewards to universities are determined not by the fortunes of their graduates (who are seen as water under the bridge), but by the traffic lining up at the registrar's office. Big enrollments mean big money from tuition, as well as more from government and private grants. Growth means more faculty, more administrators, and staff – promotions loom. And as the institution grows, so does the prestige of those who run it.

And since 70 percent of the institution's costs are in labor, high intakes of graduate students are essential in keeping costs low. Graduate assistants are exploited at great profit as classroom teachers who are paid subsistence wages, and they do pedestrian research tasks which, while of dubious educational value, might help land the university a patent. Through research contracts, their labor can even be sold at a profit to private industry with no nonsense about meeting minimum wage laws or fringe benefits.

Likewise, the campuses are utterly dependent upon holders of advanced degrees for their teaching staff. An astonishing 70 percent of undergraduate classes are taught by "adjunct" professors who work part time and/or seasonally for a fraction of the cost of regular faculty. So, the campuses profit from growth while the cost of producing underutilized Ph.D.s is borne by unwitting taxpayers.

But what about the graduate students who submit to this exploitation? Why do they keep marching, lemming-like into the flood, commonly spending ten years working toward a career for which there is no demand?

One answer is the flood itself, which makes grad school a safe place to sit out bad job markets. But another, as de Moulin notes, is the impact of reports (often generated by the schools themselves) that foresee shortages of professors just around the corner. Edward T. Lewis, once a president of St. Mary's College in Maryland, forecast severe shortages of professors that would appear in the 1990s, which "will be across the board [i.e., in all subject areas] in two or three years, and before 2000 almost half of the current professors will retire."

One of these reports was generated by William G. Bowen, a former president of Princeton, and it has become legendary. Published in 1989, after a glut had been accumulating for more than 25 years, it predicted "severe" shortages of Ph.D.s beginning in the early 1990s, especially in the social sciences and humanities. Bowen claimed that only 7 qualified professors would be available for every 10 positions unless the country began immediately to begin producing a two-thirds increase in the production of Ph.D.s. Of course, the glut only worsened, no doubt in part because the report inspired false hopes among college graduates who might have done something more useful with their lives.

Based on doubtful assumptions (such as high retirement rates) these projections are invariably wrong. Yet they succeed in kindling students' hopes and in keeping the government, which doesn't want an educational crisis, spooked. So, graduate students and cash keep rolling in.

How will UND and NDSU entice so many new doctoral students? In part, by further flooding long-saturated fields in English, history, education, etc., where a single job opening typically draws hundreds of applicants. They'll do this by claiming that these fields, against history and common sense, will soon develop shortages of professors.

But others will percolate upward into degree inflation. "Food safety," until recently an undergraduate minor at NDSU, has been garnished with several leftovers and rehabilitated as a doctoral field. So it will also be with "transportation," "communication," "human development" and other proposed ball-of-wax degrees whose advantage over well-focused baccalaureate degrees is unclear.

This race to the bottom, with doctorates offered in everything and for everyone, isn't just a local absurdity, it's the inevitable result of making the body count the measure of institutional success. It's so senseless that some reformers are calling for federal action to stop it.

Who will stop it here? Not the State Board of Higher Education, which adores the idea of growth. Its president, with startling originality, praises the new doctorates as a means of bringing "new jobs and new wealth to our state."

But there is surely some discontent within the academy itself. Professors in the liberal arts and humanities especially, are the natural defenders of educational integrity. Yet most have so far remained silent while their profession dissolves into incoherence and their campuses become kept institutions. They must be sick to death of hearing, over and over again, that universities are handmaids of business and boosterism and that their chief purpose is to advance the goal of economic growth.

The legislature may also offer some hope. It has a fair number of skeptics who are able to distinguish between universities and chambers of commerce. Let's hope that, with public prodding, they wake up and do something. If no one does, we'll soon have doctorates in walking, sitting, and breathing.

Higher Education's
Fashionable Idea of Justice

Vice-President Joe Biden says that 20 percent of college coeds have been victims of sexual assault, an assertion that on the campuses is eagerly seized upon as proof of a burgeoning "rape epidemic." The FBI, however, says that because sexual encounters commonly involve drunkenness, faulty memories and other ambiguities, the real incidence is probably below 2 percent.

Whatever the case, the Obama Administration wants to show that it's tough on rape and it's doing so by removing prosecutions away from law enforcement agencies and into campus proceedings where convictions are much easier to obtain. Under Title IX of the Educational Amendments Act of 1972, the US Department of Education has issued rules to the campuses that withdraw the protections of due process from those accused of rape, including the right of the accused to cross-examine their accusers. It has also virtually eliminated the presumption of innocence by swapping the "beyond a reasonable doubt" rule for a "preponderance of evidence" rule that allows conviction with only a 50.01 percent likelihood of guilt. Though this is basically a coin toss, campuses that don't comply will risk losing their federal funding.

But gutting students' due process rights further empowers a campus culture that even now has little sympathy for the dispassionate rule of law. In our politically correct campuses, students will likely be judged less by the facts of the case than by their membership in whatever identity group the institution sorts them into. Depending on their ethnicity, social class, gender, and other factors, some students are more equal than others; and in questions of rape, campus "justice" invariably means a presumption of guilt against men.

Two episodes illustrate the destructive potential of campus justice.

In an infamous case at Duke in 2006, three athletes were accused of assaulting a stripper who performed at a party for the lacrosse team. Although the accuser's story was inconsistent (and contradicted by her co-performer) left-wing campus zealots instantly proclaimed the athletes guilty. Student mobs marched and banged pots and pans, carried banners that read "castrate," and distributed "wanted" posters with photos and email addresses of the accused.

Faculty members also joined the fun. A faction of radical professors calling itself the "Group of 88" weighed in with a full-page ad in the student newspaper thanking the pot-bangers for their service to the cause of social justice. The ad also included quotes solicited from students who dutifully affirmed that the campus was indeed saturated with racism, sexism, classism, and the whole bag of politically incorrect horrors which the athletes supposedly epitomized.

The accuser was black and female, therefore doubly a victim. The defendants were athletes, white (except for one), affluent, male and, God forbid, probably even heterosexual – all characteristics so inherently damning that concrete evidence of rape hardly mattered. Professor Waheema Holloway, who drafted the ad, gleefully noted that the accused were "almost perfect offenders."

The atmosphere on the campus became so belligerent that Duke closed the lacrosse season and fired the team coach. In the city of

Durham, opinion was so prejudiced against the players that their legal counsel requested a change of venue.

But despite the flamboyant stereotyping, no real evidence against the players ever turned up. DNA tests cleared the accused, while Mike Nifong, the prosecutor, was removed from the case and eventually disbarred for withholding evidence. After 13 months the case imploded so spectacularly that it left many academic and legal reputations in ruins.

Today the affair remains as a monument to higher education's surrender to fashion and ideological zealotry. The accuser, who had a history of mental instability, is at this writing in jail for the murder of her boyfriend. At the end, Duke paid an estimated $100 million in settlements and legal fees.

Were Duke's radical professors repentant or remorseful? Of course not. The Group of 88, who were never held personally accountable, defiantly continued their morality play with undiminished zeal long after the charges were dropped. Prof. Holloway vowed to press ahead "regardless of the 'truth' established" about the allegations in the case. If the jocks didn't really do it, so what? The point is that they *could* have done it; and among Duke's postmodern culture the "could haves" are much more powerful than mere facts. Only one member, a math professor, ever publicly apologized for the group's behavior.

Unable to nail the three athletes except by character assassination, the Group of 88 then pinned the crime – even though there was no crime – on the oppressive atmosphere of Duke's campus. Duke's president responded in the classic bureaucratic fashion by appointing a study group which in due course reported that, indeed, the campus' "social space" was dominated by – brace yourself – *white heterosexual males*! A reeducation campaign was clearly in order.

So, the report recommended abridging students' freedom to choose their own dorm roommates and other associates when in public places. Inevitably, it also recommended adding more female and minority members to the faculty, more courses in race and gender, and compulsory reeducation classes in multicultural sensitivity. Presently there appeared a new anthropology course elegantly titled, "The Hook-up Culture at Duke: What does the Lacrosse Episode Tell us about Power, Race, Class, Gender, and Sexed Normativity in the US?"

At Duke and elsewhere, this sort of harassment is practiced for both fun and profit. It transpired that the study group which recommended this regime of thought control was heavily staffed by the Group of 88 – the same people who, as a Duke math professor put it, exploited "the false allegation of rape to … cash in with new courses for themselves, new faculty hires, and new avenues of institutional support for their political agenda."

* * *

We've had a similar experience closer to home. In a nationally publicized case at the University of North Dakota in 2010, the Student Rules Committee used the "preponderance" rule to convict a student, Caleb Warner, of rape after an encounter with a coed he met at a frat party. His accuser filed charges, weeks after the alleged event, with both UND and the Grand Forks Police Department. The police investigation found no evidence of assault – but it did turn up an email from the accuser inviting Warner to a second encounter. She was charged with lying to the police and when a warrant was issued for her arrest she promptly disappeared.

But long after the police dropped the case against Warner, UND continued to twist the knife. Having found Warner guilty by its own rules, it banned him from the campus for 3 years; he was left with a derailed education, depression, and perhaps the lifetime stigma of a sexual predator. His appeals to reopen the case were denied and it took another 18 months (plus legal assistance from the Foundation for Individual Rights in Education) to squeeze from UND even the most anemic admission of error: "A continued finding of a violation [of the student code] is not substantiated."

Higher education's general indifference to the constitutional rights of both students and non-conforming faculty has become so commonplace that it no longer shocks. But here and there, principled academicians have begun protesting the absence of legal rights for the accused. At Harvard and the University of Pennsylvania, law schools have petitioned their campus administrations about the preponderance rule, as well as campus denials of due process that allow judicial panels to convict with a bare majority rather than requiring unanimity.

Because of a letter ("Dear Colleague") sent to campus administrators from the Office of Civil Rights (of all places) in 2011, men accused of rape are no longer guaranteed the right to cross-examine their accusers, or to have their own witnesses present, or even to be represented by a lawyer. The letter also attempts to abolish the prohibition against double jeopardy by allowing accusers to appeal judgments of not guilty. In some instances, when defendants are allowed to raise questions, they may do so only in writing in advance of the trial and not during the actual proceedings.

Apart from the withdrawal of Constitutional protections, judicial competence is also an issue. Those assigned to judicial panels are usually campus employees, including clerks, who commonly bring little or no investigative or legal expertise to their task. This exposes defendants to the risk of amateurish bungling even if the adjudicating panel's intentions are otherwise well-intentioned.

Colleges must of course have their own procedures for monitoring unruly dorms, punishing plagiarism and the like, for which elaborate formal protections may not be needed. But when accusations of serious crimes have the potential to destroy careers and even lives, police work should be left to the police, and justice to legitimate courts. Title IX, which requires campus interference in rape cases, needs revision.

In any event, some chickens are coming home to roost. As government and academia conspire to boost convictions at whatever the cost to fairness, a growing clientele of embittered men is queuing up to sue their campuses for defamation of character, breach of contract, distress, gender discrimination, and deprivation of due process.

The hubris that now characterizes the academy's ambition to perfect the world has grotesquely distorted the ideals of higher education. The corruption of the academy, which once stood for the disinterested pursuit of truth, has yielded to the radical Left's vengefulness against all those who fail to join its authoritarian fashions. In place of yesteryear's campus officials who defended civility, we now have presidents who act not as leaders, but mainly as fund-raisers whose principles are fashionably flexible. What is necessary now is to install campus leaders and supporting superstructures – alumni associations, political leaders, and regents – who are not afraid to criticize practices that are clearly contrary to the mission of higher education.

The College Dropout Rate
is Too Low

Higher education has lately discovered that too many students are dropping out before graduation. Nationally, only 61 percent of freshmen who enroll in 4-year institutions get degrees, even after 6 years, and locally the rate is even lower. At the University of North Dakota just 54 percent ever graduate; at North Dakota State University it's only 47 percent. Just across the river, Moorhead State University reports an anemic 40 percent. Half of our students spend two years or more on campus only to leave short of a degree and often with a a burdensome debt. So, there is a fever to keep them enrolled, somehow, until they get a diploma.

But in fact, high dropout rates are an excellent thing. Indeed, it would be good if they were even higher. When I query professors about their job-related gripes, I usually hear something like, "too many students who aren't college material," or "students who just aren't engaged." A large body of research agrees. Most students are on campus, as sociologists Burton Clark and Martin Trow have put it, to "join a world of football, fraternities and sororities, dates, drinking, and campus fun" before venturing into the adult world of labor. In other words, they are not really college students. On the campuses this is hardly a secret, but it is deemed irresponsible for academicians to speak of it publicly. Doing so might suggest a need for higher entrance standards, and nothing so horrifies administrators as the specter of declining enrollments.

Still other students enroll because they are pressured into it. The entire culture warns them that without a degree they will be condemned to menial jobs and blighted lives.

This has become so firmly a part of American lore that ten angels swearing to the contrary could no longer disturb it.

A couple of generations ago, a baccalaureate degree in almost any major would have employers pounding at your door. Possession of a college diploma identified you as being above the general run of the population. But today the official rate of unemployment among college graduates between ages 22 and 27 is 8.5 percent, not much lower than what it is among the general citizenry. The real shocker, though, is that among recent graduates who do have jobs, a sobering 46 percent complain that they are *under*employed – that is, they hold jobs that don't require a college degree, or else jobs that are only part-time. Fifteen percent of cab drivers and firefighters have baccalaureate degrees they don't need and will probably never use.

The unemployment rate for high school grads is much higher than it is for college graduates, but it's not because the demand for high school-level skills has fallen; it's because the unskilled jobs formerly reserved for them are now being claimed, out of desperation, by college graduates. When choosing among a pool of applicants, employers will likely choose those with college degrees just because they can get them for the same wages as those who never went past high school.

This dismal job picture isn't just a quirk of the recent recession. Despite occasional spikes in demand for particular majors, college underemployment has stayed at a steady rate since the early 1990s. Indeed, college graduates have been a glut in the labor market since the late 1960s when the higher education bubble first began. Half of recent college graduates are "boomerangers," young adults who are unable to find self-supporting work and who have had to move back into their parents' homes.

If most students enroll for the wrong reasons, the campuses have unseemly motives for accepting them. They may seek certain characteristics, such as jocks for their athletic programs, and minorities for their ethnic-identity programs, neither of which requires intellectual talent. Also, higher status – very important now that higher education operates according to the corporate model of governance –accrues to institutions that can boast of a huge and ever-expanding student body. And as state funding keeps declining, the campuses must rely more on growing hordes of tuition-bearing bodies to compensate. Weak students are even in demand as cash cows because they tend to repeat courses and require additional instruction for their academic weaknesses.

In this mix, student quality has low priority. Among the nearly 3,000 four-year colleges and universities in the US, only a few dozen is "selective," meaning that they reject as many applicants as they accept. Otherwise, more than 80 percent of campuses admit virtually anyone who applies, including those whose low ACT or SAT scores should be red flags. It has long been scandalous that a full third of freshmen require corrective instruction in the basics they were supposed to have mastered in elementary and secondary school.

Many who do manage to graduate do so only because lower academic standards and grade inflation disguise prevent certain failure. Basic courses like English have been tossed from required courses, and history has been dropped from course requirements in most campuses, even those in the Ivy Leagues. These days, students can satisfy their course requirements the same way high schools do, by loading up with cotton candy subjects like yoga and hip-hop studies.

As such, the "education" represented by most diplomas is pretty shallow. In 2005 a Pew survey of 14,000 college seniors found that most couldn't do simple calculations like comparing credit card offers, and most lacked the ability to understand a newspaper editorial. If some vital public interest is served by recruiting kids who are barely literate, and patronizing them through graduation with Mickey Mouse subjects, I can't imagine what it is.

Academia proposes to reduce dropout rates while at the same time continuing to enroll everyone who applies. But this is not Lake Wobegon. Half our kids are below average, and despite the fake idealism of politicians and campus administrators, average kids simply can't make good use of college. By their self-serving admissions practices the campuses are creating the very problem they so piously deplore.

And they have no incentive to change. If reform is to come, it must come by the pressure of legislatures, alumni associations, donors, and other external agencies that care about quality. In the meantime, let's hope that the dropout rate remains high.

Education's New
Gender Gap

Not so long ago the "gender gap" in higher education meant a shortage of female students so embarrassing as to warrant heroic, if frequently unprincipled, efforts to increase their numbers. Today this shortage has been filled to overflowing.

In the early 1970s women were just 43 percent of undergraduate enrollments, while today that ratio is almost exactly reversed, with female enrollments outnumbering those of males by 58 to 42 percent. Today women earn about 60 percent of all baccalaureate and master's degrees and their share of MDs and law degrees has increased, respectively, five- and ten-fold since 1970 and are about to surpass men's. Don't expect any affirmative action programs for males, though. The feminist passion for gender equality has mysteriously cooled; and admissions offices, formerly friendly to quotas for women, have inexplicably become converts to strict meritocracy.

So, what gives? It seems unlikely that males have suddenly become politically incorrect. Nevertheless, there appears to be no consensus about what is happening except that males have fallen into some sort of mysterious malaise that is found in all social classes, all ethnic groups (most grievously blacks, whose high school dropout rate reaches 50 percent), and most of the countries of the developed West. "It is almost as if many are surrendering while still in their teens," says political scientist Andrew Hacker.

Some analysts speak of a "war against boys" in elementary and secondary schools that sours them against further education. Others say that boys have characteristic behavioral problems that the schools have failed to take into account; still others say they've been seduced by a rap culture whose heroes and "artists" are mostly semi-literate goons; and so on. Some even say that males are not declining at all but are merely being suddenly outpaced by females making up for lost time.

What is clear is that many schools have adopted a more feminine character that may be a turn-off for boys. Impulse control, focus, and collaborative habits of study (more often associated with girls than with boys) are encouraged, while acting out, goofing off, and competitiveness (more often male traits) get less indulgence.

There is also an effeminate New Age pedagogy in place that stresses "feeling" over thinking; and the Digital Age rewards early maturation along with verbal and social skills thought to be strong suits in girls.

Whatever the explanation may be, boys, more often than girls, say they do not enjoy school and that education is not important to them. They show this with grades that are lower than girls', and also with higher dropout rates. Some educators propose segregating classrooms, and even entire schools, by gender to see if males will then become more serious. Even now, a few schools are experimenting with the idea (and are being sued by civil rights organizations), though there is as yet no consensus on whether these experiments show any significant change.

But the new gender gap, still largely ignored by researchers and the media, will inevitably produce consequences that transcend the schools. As educational credentials (and therewith, social influence) shift from men to women, the social order in the near future will be profoundly changed, perhaps with disorienting effects. What to look for?

Changed personal relations, for one thing. Historically, women have tried to advance themselves by marrying above their social station or, failing that, settling for a life of (ahem) "spinsterhood." But now, facing a shortage of educated men, the shoe will be on the other foot. Large numbers of women will have to settle either for a life without a mate, or else a dimwit with whom intelligent discourse may prove impossible. We may therefore expect a continued fall in the marriage rate and, presumably, in the birth rate as well, which even now is at a bare replacement level.

But since many women will still want children, out-of-wedlock births (which have held stable for several years) are likely to resume rising. Despite its Hollywood chic, illegitimacy often means inept child-rearing; and because it is strongly related to such pathologies as crime, addiction, and intergenerational poverty, it already ranks among America's worst domestic problems. Educated women will surely prove to be devoted mothers, yet many of the stresses of single parenthood will still hinder them. Since the majority of college-educated workers will be female, we will see greater pressure for paid maternity leaves, subsidized day care, and perhaps an inversion of Ozzie and Harriet-style marriages, with women playing the role of breadwinners while men become stay-at-home dads.

Our politics will also shift leftward. Though married women usually vote Democrat and Republican in equal shares, single women are far more liberal than men (though this fades somewhat with rising income), voting a whopping 70 percent Democratic in recent presidential elections. Left to themselves, women would have elected both Al Gore and John Kerry by wide margins.

Women are also reliably leftward of men on such defining issues as gun control, welfare, military intervention, and the death penalty. And since voting rates and other forms of political activity rise with educational levels, women's issues will become more prominent while both men's issues and their electoral clout will recede.

The expanding numbers of women in idea-generating and-disseminating institutions such as the universities, think tanks, and the media may shift the national climate of opinion leftward as well.

But women's educational gains still do not extend evenly to every field. Spin it as you will, college women still cluster in subjects like literature and psychology rather than math, engineering, and science. So, as men sink further into slackerdom, key fields may go begging; we may either have to accept critical shortages in male-dominated fields, or become ever more dependent upon immigrants, who even now earn nearly half of all science Ph.D.'s awarded in the US.

Some sectors, though, may resist the *zeitgeist* and remain tight male islands. Though women earn nearly half of all MBA's, almost all Fortune 500 CEOs are members of an exclusive good old boys club. (At this writing there are just 24 of them.) Interesting battles may lie ahead. Similar challenges may await the military's officer corps. Which aspects of national defense, if any, lend themselves to male domination and which do not?

What else? Will this pink revolution proceed smoothly, or will there be backlashes and consequences not now foreseeable? Will men accept life as the "second sex" – as ultimately women could not – and careers that won't match their fathers'? And even if society should awaken to whatever the male problem is, will large numbers of men remain permanently behind as a lost generation? Or will they yet recover themselves?

Time will tell. Meanwhile, keep your powder dry.

Technology's
False Promise

In America the surest sign of an educational visionary is the fervent cry, "Bring technology into the classroom!" So, for 30-some years our visionaries have proclaimed with messianic zeal that if we wire every classroom, issue every kid a laptop – no, make it two, even three – and keep every teacher current, we'll have an educational Golden Age – "the greatest leap forward in achievement," as the US Department of Education has recently declared, "in the history of education." Thus, we are asked to believe that a blizzard of random data from the information superhighway will trigger quantum leaps in student achievement, release an explosion of creativity, and make life-long scholars out of kids who don't even read newspapers. The vision is so grand that we've spent scores of billions pursuing it. And now President Obama says he wants to spend billions more.

Few things are more embedded in the American soul than the faith that technology will save us from whatever predicament the human race might have gotten itself into. In *The Flickering Mind*, Todd Oppenheimer recounts that in the 1920s the development of motion picture technology promised a "learning efficiency" 50 times greater than that of textbooks. In the 1940s, radio was set to take over instruction and even eliminate blackboards. In the 1950s, behavioral teaching machines were to double student achievement, and in the 1960s, television was to be a cost-efficient substitute for live teachers. When each gadget in its turn failed to deliver, the visionaries blamed under-funding, teacher resistance, or red tape but never the limitations of the gadget itself.

By now we've immersed a whole generation of kids in computer-saturated schools. Has the Golden Age finally arrived? Are the Digital Natives the smartest generation ever?

No. A growing body of research says that not only are computers not turning our kids into geniuses, but that they do not improve student achievement at all. Standardized test scores like the SATs and ACTs are lower now than 45 years ago, despite all the new gimmicks and a three-fold real per-capita increase in school funding.

Reading is crashing too. Mark Bauerlein, whose book *The Dumbest Generation* tracks research on the Digital Generation, finds that between 1982 and 2002, the 18–24-year-olds who reported voluntarily reading a play, poem, short story, or novel within the previous year fell 28 percent. Increasingly, the Digitals are "bibliophobes" – smug anti-intellectuals who see book-reading as "an old-fashioned custom" which they have gone beyond.

Content knowledge is also declining. As with-it technology increases in prestige, basic subjects like civics, history, literature, and science are cleansed from the curriculum. Infantilism fills the void. Hence (as Bauerlein notes) 59 percent of teens can name the Three Stooges, but just 41 percent the 3 branches of government; 64 percent of 15–26-year-olds can name the latest American Idol, but just 10 percent the Speaker of the US House of Representatives; 98 percent of college seniors can identify Snoop Dog, but only 22 percent a line from the Gettysburg Address. In 1966, 60 percent of college freshmen thought it "very important" to keep up with political affairs, and in 2005 only 36 percent did.

Computer technology has achieved such towering prestige that it displaces the subject matter it is supposed to serve. Means and ends are reversed: Technology is no longer an instrument for teaching particular subjects but has itself become the primary subject of learning. A poll by Public Agenda shows teachers and the general public to be in agreement – both by a 3-to-1 ratio – that it is more important to teach "computer skills and media technology" than such culture-defining works as Plato and Shakespeare, Hemmingway, and Steinbeck. As technique becomes more important than substantive knowledge, schools are dropping subjects like music and art in order to make more room for computer labs.

And choosing the subjects to be taught may depend on whether they lend themselves to computerized instruction. If topics like literature, art, philosophy, music, and the like don't fit the expensive technology, then our educational Procrusteans may simply eliminate them, or else alter them to fit the new technology's strengths and weaknesses.

Most sobering of all, as many researchers now believe, lengthy immersion in cyberspace may impede brain development, especially in younger kids. Todd Oppenheimer writes that attention spans ("one of the most important intellectual capacities anyone can possess") appear to be withering along with imagination, reasoning ability, and social skills. Books require perseverance and reflection, while cut-and-paste "data" do not. Dialog with teachers sharpens critical thinking and empathy, while mute screens can't.

Immersion in cyberspace also appears to dull causality, the sense that one can affect changes in the physical world. Teachers complain about passive students who can't empathize with assigned material, can't deal with open-ended questions, and can't see relationships between ideas.

Nor is this a golden age for teachers. Traditionally admired as molders of intellect and character and as people who changed lives, the prestige of computers is such that teachers are now being reduced to "facilitators," subordinates to machines, who render technical advice and clear up glitches on student-driven projects and are otherwise more or less irrelevant. In the current catchphrase, teachers have been demoted from being the "sage on the stage" to the "guide on the side."

How did all this come to pass? Well, it's because, apart from fads and gimmickry, education has for a hundred years had little else to hang onto. Not having a clear mission, our schools have an identity crisis; they are public institutions, but they do not have a public mandate. They are supposed to "educate," yet the community offers hardly a clue as to what that means. After generations of tinkering with each year's New Thing we no longer know what a proper education should look like and, left adrift, the schools can only lurch from one fashionable delusion to another.

Wouldn't it be grand if impersonal technology could somehow impose a coherent mission upon the schools and thereby relieve us of all those messy debates about the nature and purpose of education? Isn't it pleasant to pretend that the next mechanical device might have the power to perfect an enterprise that we can't even define? Wouldn't it be nice if some automatic process could authoritatively decide just what things an educated person is supposed to know?

Our faith in gimmicks allows us to ignore the real causes of school failure and to avoid responsibility for reform. If today's college seniors know less about core subjects than 12th graders did 50 years ago, don't worry – the latest ed school revelation, the latest mechanical marvel, will *this time*, for sure, turn things around. All past fads may have failed, but the next one will definitely succeed.

But we won't get better schools until we put away our alibis and accept adult responsibility for real-world reform. That means recovering a consensus on what the schools are about and restoring the proven traditions of learning. We might start by bringing technology *out* of the classroom.

America's Vanishing Professors

For over 30 years, one of academia's dirty little secrets has been its ongoing liquidation of the professional teaching staff and its replacement by fill-ins who resemble day laborers more than career scholars. Now a report from the American Association of University Professors reveals the damage to date: Only 24 percent of teachers in higher education are still tenured and – shades of things to come – only 11 percent are on tenure track. The other 65 percent are "contingents" or "adjuncts" – part-timers, temporaries, and graduate students who are hired just because they are cheap. North Dakota follows the national trend: At UND and NDSU faculties are 63 percent and 72 percent, respectively, contingent.

It's due to what might be called a "paradigm shift," or a change in what seems normal. Once it was normal to think of universities as faintly otherworldly institutions devoted to the discovery of truth and the enlightenment of students. They were proud of their aloofness from mundane concerns, most especially those of commerce. But today they have adopted corporate habits and values; they have themselves come to behave like corporations in their pursuit of ever-higher enrollments, revenues, and status as ends in themselves. They boast of "partnerships" with industry and government, and they proclaim themselves "engines of economic growth." Practices which under the service paradigm were scandalous, like enticing semi-literate applicants who are treated more like "customers" than students, are now hailed as visionary.

And true to their new paradigm, our corporatized universities seek to control costs with compliant, cut-rate labor.

They find it in the armies of wannabe professors who, in resolute denial of a 40-year glut of Ph.D.s, keep streaming through the graduate schools only to wind up in adjunct hell bearing signs that read "Will Teach for Food." They typically teach courses that the tenured faculty won't touch, and they do it for a fraction of a tenured prof's salary with no job security, no fringe benefits, no real hope for a decent future and precious little respect. Their many aliases ("migrant laborers," "piece workers," "untouchables," "scab labor," etc.) suggest their status among liberal academicians who wear their idealism on their sleeves and who swear passionate, to-the-death struggle against the exploitation of labor – at Wal-Mart. Under its "air of gentility," says Sandra Bowen of City University of New York, higher education "is one of the most shocking labor abusers in the country."

But while contingents may deserve our sympathy, the larger point is that an educational system dominated by them doesn't work very well. There are too many things they are powerless to do, and their very powerlessness is itself a threat to academic freedom and the quality of instruction.

They can't, for instance, make up a real faculty. Part-timers and transients can't form departments, design curricula, or undertake long-term projects, like campus governance, that make professors collectively important to the institution. And for its part, the institution has no reason to invest resources in teachers who are not integral to it. Forget sabbaticals and grants, travel funds and audio-visual training; contingents seldom even get office space. "The nature of contingent employment," as the AAUP report puts it, "is stark: an exchange of constrained teaching for minimal pay."

Academic freedom, like other kinds, rests on a balance of power. But despite their majority status, contingents are too transient to form a community and wield steady influence; so, the tenured faculty's depleted ranks means that power must shift by default to administrators so that the old model of shared governance gives way to the corporate model of top-down control. That leaves no internal force to defend the ideals of liberal education against academic bureaucrats and the political and commercial interests eager to fit the universities into their latest plans. Worst of all, there is no one to resist threats to the most essential freedoms like speech and due process. The sacred traditions of free inquiry, of questioning authority and defending unpopular ideas have been entrusted to scholars who are disposable.

Though contingents are sometimes the best teachers on the faculty, their uncertain status is a handicap for everyone. Since their hiring often comes as a last-minute surprise, they are often not adequately prepared when their classes start, and they may be gone before ever getting to know their students. If so, they can't properly advise them or track their progress; personalized things, like the writing of recommendations, get lost in the shuffle. Without office space (a common complaint), they must meet with students at the local Burger King or else remain inaccessible to students needing timely help.

Meanwhile, the professors who once were campus anchors, the accomplished and sometimes charismatic teachers who provided continuity for the long haul and who inspired students and changed lives, are vanishing.

And until the universities stop pretending, they are Fortune 500 companies, they'll keep vanishing. The soul of a university is its faculty. If a degraded teaching force is not now troubling to higher education, and "if fully 65 percent of the academic workforce is employed in this way," then, as the AAUP report warns, "the other 35 percent cannot be far behind."

Higher Education's Hoodlums

A recent essay in the *Chronicle of Higher education* has leaked one of academia's unseemly little embarrassments, which is that it now has, of all things, a problem with classroom discipline. These days college students are known to shuffle in and out of class according to their whim, address teachers profanely, work on assignments for other classes, receive calls on cell phones, sleep, and pointedly ignore classroom proceedings. The *Chronicle* notes that students are "less attentive and more combative," while life is "nightmarish" for some professors who are forming support groups, taking workshops in classroom management, even calling the cops.

What's going on here? Some say that the new barbarism (actually, it has been in place for over 20 years, though seldom publicized) merely reflects a pop culture whose heroes are commonly hoodlums and cretinous goons. But its appearance also coincides with the decline of higher education as an elite enterprise.

So long as the campuses took in the best and the brightest high school graduates, classroom misconduct simply did not happen. The campus culture extolled (sometimes to the point of absurdity) maturity and intellectual seriousness; and having once joined that culture, students reliably put away childish things. College freshmen differed in age from high school seniors only by a single year, but in terms of classroom demeanor they might have been from different planets. Seriousness and civility went hand in hand.

Alas, the campuses now value large enrollments more than student seriousness, with the result that decent admission standards have been scrapped as a hindrance to growth. (In this state, essay exams on admissions forms have been discontinued on the memorable grounds that they might discourage applicants of doubtful literacy.) Just so, as the campuses take in ever-lower orders of talent, they also take in ever-lower orders of morals and manners. For decades the campuses have been growing splendidly – and they have also ingested a burgeoning lumpenproletariat that can't identify with academic achievement and can't see why it has to take courses in English and history when all it wants is a degree of some kind, any kind at all. So, it makes its boredom and resentment amply known in class.

My own response to incivility was to lay out the rules and then follow up, as necessary, with private admonitions, public rebukes, even seating reassignments to break up the social clubs in the back rows. Nevertheless, there was usually a miscreant or two who just would not behave. In such cases I brandished pink slips (withdrawal forms) and warned that with the next offense the registrar would get one with the offender's name on it: "You're fired!" The calming effect of this was amazing.

The trouble was, I had no authority to kick the bums out, and it worked only because the bums didn't know it. Student codes still reflect an era when misconduct meant loud frat parties, drunkenness, and plagiarism, not anomie and classroom disruption. Thus, professors must go on fumbling with a problem that officially does not exist. A professor who wants to deliver his class from an insolent and unceasing chatterbox must usually, therefore, appeal to a catch-all bureaucratic process that requires a formal complaint, committee referral, hearings, and so on.

But while students have a right to due process, machinery that grinds toward an uncertain resolution three or four weeks hence may not impress the brat who is out of control *now*, especially if the brat has no very strong desire to be in college in the first place. Professors, therefore, need some interim power. At the very least they should have the right to hustle troublemakers directly out the door, pending the outcome of due process later.

Teachers can't give their best to degraded classrooms, and neither can even the most diligent of students benefit from them. So, it's time for the campuses to face up to a problem that isn't supposed to exist – but does – and deal with it realistically. It won't just go away. A couple of people I spoke to at a local student affairs office thought it was worsening.

Perhaps the universities will yet survive the growth-at-any-cost pathology that is now ruining them. In the meantime, teachers and serious students shouldn't be left defenseless against its ravages.

Should We Really
Celebrate Diversity?

In higher education and elsewhere the "diversity" movement is no longer just another passing academic fashion but has become a kind of fundamentalist religion that remains totally impervious to facts. Everyone, everywhere, is now sternly commanded to *celebrate* diversity – or else. On the campuses and in the public square the movement has achieved such irresistible moral force that to question it is blasphemous. All intelligent, humane people *must* praise the wisdom of diversity, period. Doubters are certain to be shunned and denounced as racists, sexists, fascists, or bigots of some kind.

The stated purpose of the diversity movement is to help certain minority groups (which include blacks, Hispanics, Native Americans, gays, lesbians, transgenders, and others) who claim histories of oppression to feel more comfortable within the broader culture. It is also supposed to increase social harmony through the sharing of life experiences, and to make the social order intrinsically more interesting. The list of oppressed groups grows by the week. Just recently some Princeton students have proposed recruiting convicted felons onto the campuses because, as their petition put it, "individuals with past involvement with the justice system ... can open the door to increased diversity of experience and perspective."

A key task of the campus diversity movement is to create a therapeutic environment in which minority groups keep expanding their numbers until a "comfort level" is reached for each. Courses are designed for them which confirm their oppression, raise their self-esteem (commonly with faux ethnic histories featuring a purloined golden age), and ensure that no one flunks. They may also get separate facilities like separate theme dorms and student centers reserved for this or that minority, all provided in the name of inclusion.

The most important thing is that their environment must be free from all possibilities of offense. Those who are still smarting from histories of oppression might be traumatized in an atmosphere with too much liberty. Thus, it is necessary to curtail certain practices which were formerly regarded as essential to the educational enterprise – like free speech, academic integrity, due process, respect for unpopular ideas, and the transmission of Western culture. Imposing racial preferences along with the web of authoritarian practices known as political correctness is deemed necessary to create an atmosphere of comfort for diversity's clientele.

If all this is faithfully pursued – *behold!* – the social fabric will become richer, more tolerant, and smarter than ever before.

But there is a fly in the ointment. It seems that diversity's beautiful theory has been ravished by a gang of brutal facts.

The latest debunking of this fantasy comes from Harvard researcher (and author of the best-selling *Bowling Alone*) Robert Putnam – who, in the largest study of "civic engagement" ever conducted, reports (*Scandinavian Political Studies*, June 2007) that diversity does *not* promote social harmony but in fact *damages* our ability to trust each other and to function as a community. Putnam's

5-year project included 30,000 respondents in 41 sites over the US and it controlled for factors of age, gender, socioeconomic status, educational level, geographic region, and neighborhood as well as for ethnicity. It is to date the most exhaustive survey ever conducted on the subject of ethnic diversity.

But despite his own hopes to the contrary, Putnam's research unambiguously led to a conclusion that he himself did not want: "The more ethnically diverse the people we live around," he writes, "the less we trust them." This is indeed a bombshell. Yet it comes from a solid academic liberal who sat on his findings for five years because he was loath to upset his fellow liberals with news he thought would be "explosive."

While some previous research has found that diversity fosters out-group distrust and in-group solidarity, Putnam finds that it leads *both* ins and outs to "hunker down" – to "distrust their neighbors, regardless of the color of their skin, to withdraw even from close friends, to expect the worst from their community and its leaders, to volunteer less … and to huddle unhappily in front of the television." As diversity increases, whites trust each other less, blacks trust each other less, and so on for every ethnic group. As settings become more diverse, Putnam says, "Americans distrust not merely people who do not look them, but even people who do,"

As diversity increases, social bonds keep getting weaker. So, in rural counties of the Dakotas, 70 to 80 percent of respondents say they trust their neighbors "a lot," while in highly diverse Los Angeles and San Francisco just 30 percent say the same. The inverse relation holds true regardless of respondents' race, gender, wealth, ideology, or whatever. "Ethnic diversity itself," Putnam says, "seems to encourage hunkering."

Further, the relation between diversity and trust is "linear," meaning that instead of leveling off, mistrust keeps increasing so long as diversity does. And in the short run, at least, there is little to be done about it. "We have tried," Putnam concludes, "every conceivable artifactual explanation for our core finding, yet the pattern persists. Many Americans today are uncomfortable with diversity."

Rising diversity also inhibits altruism (the willingness to volunteer and to do good works) along with community collaboration. It reduces personal involvement in community affairs and lowers confidence in local institutions. In general, it seems to create a sense of alienation that makes most forms of social interaction more difficult.

(If you thought that a generation immersed in multicultural sensitivity would have a different outlook from that of their parents, you'd be right. Those growing up with racial quotas, compulsory reeducation, taboos, language police, kangaroo courts and self-censorship are *less* trusting than their elders. Gosh – how *does* one explain it?)

Putnam's findings are not unique. An earlier research project conducted by Stanley Rothman, Seymour Martin Lipset, and Neil Nevitte arrived at similar conclusions. "The predicted positive association of educational benefits and inter-racial understanding failed to appear," they modestly say. "A pattern of statistically significant association appeared, but it was in the opposite direction from that predicted by the diversity model."

If so, then as nations become more diverse, the "social capital" they need for maintaining mutual trust and unity will diminish. Which raises an important question: Will the steady influx of immigrants into their populations mean increasing balkanization and even threats of secession?

If the diversity movement is counterproductive, then why the passion for it? As one who has spent many years in the academic culture, I venture the following reasons:

First, it creates jobs. As the grievance industry turns up ever more oppressed identity groups, new courses ("whiteness studies," "subaltern studies," "fat studies," etc.) must be invented to accommodate them. These "studies" are intellectually empty, but they do provide steady work for legions of teachers who never got a start in academia or else were bumped from more respectable departments suffering declining enrollments.

Likewise, it's a bonanza for bureaucrats, whose big budget "diversity offices" are flourishing on campuses everywhere. Washington State's "Chief Diversity Officer," for example, has a full-time staff of 55 and a $3 million annual budget. (Hmm … how many minority scholarships might have been created with $3 million? Well, never mind – just a thought.) Bureaucratic expansion is an inexorable fact of life, and with it comes the familiar ratchet effect: Once in place, an academic fashion will instantly recruit staffs in such numbers that guarantee its permanence no matter how useless its presence may prove to be.

But it's surely the psychic payoffs of a *cause* that most fires up these save-the-word causes for which academia is famous. These endless fashions, though they have nothing to do with the advancement of knowledge, nevertheless appeal powerfully to self-regard. Their promoters' good works place them on the side of the angels and allow them to feel good about themselves. They are conspicuous champions of the oppressed and become social engineers. They bask in self-esteem.

The diversity craze also rewards minority students according to status to their alleged victimhood. Being designated a victim has lately become quite prestigious among many, especially those who need an alibi for poor academic performance and who might want to claim special consideration. Psychologist Ofur Zur has written that "the victim stance is a powerful one. The victim is always morally right, neither responsible nor morally accountable, and forever entitled to our sympathy."

But when we dutifully "celebrate diversity" we consent to the tyranny of political correctness and all its associated baggage, everything thing that is contrary to the objective needs of real education on campuses everywhere, including low academic standards and censorship. Higher education once took pride in giving a fair hearing to unpopular ideas. But no longer; fear of offending members of identity groups makes cowards of us all.

Both justice and practicality require that merit should be welcomed in all of its colors, even if that causes some hunkering. But diversity should be a legitimate byproduct of individual merit and not of group quotas and myths. The cult of victimhood justifies practices that would be wrong even if they somehow advanced the stated goal – which they don't.

To make an omelet, V. I. Lenin observed, you must break eggs. To this, George Orwell replied, fine – but where is the omelet? The wrongs of "diversity" are plain enough. But where are the benefits?

A Surprising Argument against Federal Subsidies

Much as we North Dakotans may romanticize our frontier history and its image of rugged self-reliance; we are also accustomed to being foremost among the 50 states when it comes to receiving federal handouts. Clustered just behind, other Republican-leaning "red" states, mostly in the plain's region and the south, are also given to gluttonous freeloading while moralizing endlessly about the liberal "blue" states' addiction to deficit spending and big government.

In putting Republicans in federal offices, red states vote contrary to their economic self-interests, which would be better served by liberal Democrats who make no pretenses about cherishing small, frugal government. They do so because red state voters are typically more concerned with cultural issues like immigration, religion, education, or abortion than with economic issues. Nevertheless, these states receive far more from the Federal Treasury than they pay into it, all without any perceptible sense of hypocrisy.

Who pays for the deficit spending on the extra goodies that go to the red states? Mainly, the blue states whose big-government values the reds so much disdain. So, while red North Dakota receives two dollars for every dollar it sends to the federal treasury, liberal New Jersey gets back just fifty-seven cents.

John Wayne would not approve. Nevertheless, the struggle for other people's money is earnestly joined in every state and Congressional district; and since seniority is crucial in determining who gets what share of the loot, voters everywhere are inclined to keep reelecting incumbents who claim that their seniority makes them indispensable when it comes to raiding the federal treasury on behalf of the home folks. At the top of the seniority ladder is, of course, a Congressional committee chairmanship.

This Hobbesian war of all against all is, naturally, a national washout, a negative sum game in which almost everyone loses almost all the time. And yet common sense would seem to suggest that the struggle must yield net benefits to those states which, like ours, beat the system by extracting more from it than they put back in. In such cases, injections of federal money should produce measurable increases in local prosperity.

But do they?

Pssst! – here's what your representatives don't want you to know!

Recently a team of Harvard Business School researchers headed by Professor Lauren Cohen found – to its own surprise – that even high levels of federal pork don't boost local economies. Their report ("Do Powerful Politicians Cause Corporate Downsizing?") concludes that earmarks and other federal aid tend to be counterproductive for everyone, even for localities that appear to come out ahead in the tax-and-subsidy ratio.

The team's strategy was to correlate shifts in Congressional committee chairmanships with economic changes in the newly installed chairs' home states. Since chairmen have far more power in dispensing pork than their more junior colleagues, it should be expected that earmarks to a given member's constituency would jump each time the member assumes control of a committee chair.

And indeed, that is exactly what happens. Each new accession results, as the report puts it, in "a positive shock to his or her state's share of federal funds that is virtually independent of the state's economic conditions."

During the course of 232 such shocks over 42 years, the team found that Senate earmarks going to the new chair's home state typically rose 40-50 per cent within the first year of the member's tenure, while in the House the new chair's tenure caused earmarks to rise by 20 percent.

What happens when the new funds reach home? Here's the surprise: It turns out that "the average firm in the chairman's state did not benefit at all from the increase in spending." On the contrary, the firms' usual response was to "significantly cut physical and R & D spending [typically by about 15 percent], reduce employment, and experience lower sales." These slumps persist until the committee chair shifts to another state.

What accounts for this counter-intuitive effect? The Harvard team's explanation is that when government competes for local factors of production it tends to drive up costs for private firms which then respond by retrenching their activities. Local economies simply choke on all that pork, and the sporadic nature of government involvement also undermines business confidence by creating uncertainty.

These effects are intensified in smaller states where such shocks will have magnified effects. Currently, North Dakota has very low unemployment and it ranks fifth in per-capita earmarks; in this environment private activity will be especially vulnerable to being crowded out by federal projects with a net loss to the state's potential.

A political case can be made for earmarks, which are cases of mandated spending commonly buried in omnibus bills, intended to sneak subsidies into the member's home district without any pretense of a national benefit. Though earmarks have a reputation as the most cynical kind of demagoguery (Alaska's late Senator Ted Stevens' "bridge to nowhere," which would have cost $398 million to serve an island population of 50 residents, is the classic example), they have nevertheless been important as bargaining chips for presidents seeking the support of stubborn Congressmen in voting for bills of broader importance. But the case for local economic benefits seems to be weak. On economic grounds they make no sense.

So instead of heaping praise upon the demagogues who promise free lunches, perhaps we should be careful of what we wish for. And instead of mindlessly reelecting incumbents who boast of their clout, perhaps we should have a strong presumption against them. Policy is personnel, and it's better when it's made by new people with new ideas.

Beware of indispensable men bearing gifts.

The Rise of America's Permanent Political Class

With elections for Congress still weeks away, I boldly make the following prediction: Of members seeking reelection (all but a few are) at least 90 percent will be re-elected, most by landslides. Party control of either house may change, but in terms of personnel the new Congress will look very much like the old one.

Don't be too impressed if I'm right, though, because for most of our history incumbents have won by lopsided ratios. Since 1980, 88 percent of all senators who have wanted to stay, stayed. In the House 95 percent have been safely returned. Occasionally (as in 1998 and 2000) reelection to House seats reaches 98 percent, a level which members of the old Soviet Politburo could only envy.

In the first Congresses, turnover was far more rapid because service was more demanding. Travel to the capital was arduous, even dangerous, and since members could take few comforts with them, most had to stay in cramped boarding houses. Washington was an unhealthy, foul-smelling swamp and most legislators saw their service as an unrewarding duty, paying just $6 per diem. Up to the 1870s the mean length of a House career was barely two years and in the Senate midterm resignations were common.

Today Washington offers the Georgetown brick house, the cocktail circuit, lunch with Hollywood celebrities. Members work amid marble and mahogany, and they draw six-figure salaries, get free or subsidized *everything*, and appoint themselves to "fact-finding" tours in exotic places where they stay in five-star hotels.

So, against the Founders' ideal of citizen legislators who served out of patriotism and then went back to their farms or businesses, we now have a professional political class, one so addicted to office that it uses the leverage of government to preserve itself in lifetime careers. Incumbents hold all the cards: Free postage, free travel, free audio-visual services, free research, free personal staffs and, simply by virtue of holding the office, free "propaganda of the deed," meaning that they get free publicity just by doing their jobs. They sell "access" to lobbyists and amass war chests so huge that would-be rivals who are not delusional don't challenge them. They bribe the voters with pork, and many House members even benefit from gerrymandering, a means of rigging the home district's demographics in their own favor. Their rivals can do none of this. (For more on this topic, see Matthew 13:12).

But careerism doesn't just degrade the democratic ideal, it also injures the careerists' ability to govern. Permanent incumbency requires permanent electioneering. Thus, a senator who spends a modest $12 million per election must raise, with alcoholic compulsion, over $38,000 for every week of his term. Fence-mending back home keeps senators away from Washington 80 days out of the year, representatives 120. Both spend endless hours on the minutiae of solving petty problems for constituents and other forms of self-promotion. Less than half their day goes into actual legislative work.

Senators frequently oppose executive appointees they know are highly qualified, simply to please key voter blocs in their home states. They shy away from supporting unpopular policies, no matter how necessary they may be to genuine national interests. Incumbents boast not of the expertise they bring to a national legislative body, but of the "clout" which, like ambassadors from hostile nations, they bring to an orgy of collective looting. Careerism, as Minnesota's former Rep. Vin Weber says, "explains why so few take political risks or propose bold programs."

If careerism is destructive to self-government, then democracy's response will have to take the form of constitutionally mandated term limits. That's a sobering step, but without them elections will remain a sham and responsible legislation will be the exception rather than the rule.

Term limits (most proposals are for 12 years in each chamber) won't quite level the electoral playing field, but incumbents who leave early will provide room for more new leaders with fresh ideas to enliven the national conversation. With no hope of establishing lifetime careers, more candidates will seek office for the right reasons and be better motivated to give the nation's business their undivided attention. Average citizens too may find a higher form of citizenship than that of lobbying senior Congressmen for federal pork.

Cynics say that the age of citizen legislators is over, that only professionals with long experience can govern effectively in this complicated age. What they mean is that democracy is obsolete. If so, term limits are a means of finding out. But even now, when modern legislation produces bills in thousands of pages, few members of Congress even pretend to read the bills they vote on anyway. That's why have have large professional staff.

This republic has survived wars and economic depressions, and despite self-serving defenses of the status quo, my guess is that it can survive citizen self-government too.

The Tyranny
of Multiculturalism

For decades, we have been told by governmental and educational elites that the ideology known as multiculturalism would serve to uplift disadvantaged ethnic groups, enrich the cultural tapestry, and make us all smarter and more tolerant. The universities in particular demand, to the point of nausea, that we "celebrate diversity" even though a host of evils, including racial discrimination in admissions policies, degraded academic standards, censorship and the general regime of authoritarianism known as political correctness comes bundled with it.

But the European Union's current experience with diversity ought to give us pause. Multiculturalism began there in the 1960s when Third World laborers were imported to offset declining national birth rates. It was naïvely assumed that these "guest workers" would eventually return home. But instead, their numbers have swollen, and today Europe is stuck with large alien populations that it can't always digest.

Usually, those hardest to assimilate are Muslims. Many live in ghettoes on the edges of large cities and their sense of alienation sometimes extends to sympathizing with terrorists. In March 2010 in Toulouse, a French-born jihadist murdered four soldiers, three children and a rabbi. When police killed him in a shootout, riots broke out in Islamic neighborhoods. Since then, attacks on police and Jewish centers have become so commonplace as to be barely newsworthy. There are even "no go zones" where French citizens, and even the police, are advised not to enter.

And Britain's domestic intelligence service, MI5, has reported that "over 100,000 of our [Islamic] citizens consider that the July 2005 bus-train attacks in London (which killed 55 people) were justified." The police were unable to extract information on the attacks from Islamic communities, although they were certain it was there.

Alienation works in both directions. Among Germans and Frenchmen, a plurality of 40 percent sees the Islamic presence not as cultural enrichment but as a threat to their national identities. Even now, many Europeans report that they feel like strangers in their own countries; expatriate Brit John Cleese of Monty Python has complained that "London is no longer an English city." In this environment, it should not be surprising that Muslims feel unwelcome and find it hard to feel affection for their host country.

But Europe finally may be waking up to its immigrant problem. Former French President Nicolas Sarkozy recently warned that "if you come to France, you accept to melt into a single community, and if you do not want to accept that, you cannot be welcome in France …. We have been too concerned about the identity of the person who was arriving and not enough about the identity of the country that was receiving him."

Germany's Chancellor Angela Merkel has bluntly called multiculturalism "dead," saying that the attempt "to live side by side and to enjoy each other … has failed, utterly failed."

And Britain's Prime Minister David Cameron now laments that "under the doctrine of state multiculturalism," Britain had "tolerated segregated communities behaving in ways that run counter to our values … We've been too cautious, frankly fearful to stand up to them."

Multiculturalism guarantees its own failure. It is an anti-Western ideology that wallows in white guilt and moral relativism; it says that Western civilization is no better than any jungle clan, that it has no real claim to anyone's loyalty, that it has been the begetter of racism, imperialism, inequality, and every form of evil … you name it.

So, when the West no longer believes in itself, immigrants will naturally ask: Why should *we*? If the West proclaims itself to be decadent, then why should immigrants wish to join it? So, on the advice of the West itself, they are keeping their own values and resisting assimilation. In this moral vacuum, it should be no surprise that Sharia law, so far without a peep of protest from the government, is taking hold as a rival legal system in Britain's Muslim communities. So are other alien practices like female genital mutilation and forced marriages.

The U.S. may now be approaching Europe's impasse. Its birth rate is at its lowest point ever, and its foreign-born population is now 14 percent and rising. Fear of a shrinking work force with a consequent decline in workers' financial support for retirees and the welfare state will likely mean pressure for more immigration, as it has in Europe. America's Anglo-European character may soon be a thing of the past; ethnic minorities will soon form a plurality of the American population.

Historically, the chief American instrument for melding immigrants into the national culture has been the public schools. They accomplished this by upholding ideals that everyone could admire. But under the spell of multiculturalism, America has given up on the idea of turning immigrants into new Americans; today the schools stress ethnic grievances and chauvinism while dwelling on the dark side of Western history and minimizing its more positive aspects. Our politicized universities eagerly do the same thing in their humanities and social science courses, and also their various ethnic studies programs. Multiculturalism has made it embarrassing on the campuses to exhibit love of country.

America takes in immigrants not because it needs a larger workforce but because the multicultural ideology, by emphasizing the sins of white privilege, has implanted a sense of duty to take in the Third World's poor and uneducated. No longer invited to assimilate, many immigrants seem to regard the US as a crash pad where immigrants may continue their cultures as they please. Hispanics are clustering in urban ghettoes where their large numbers make them self-sufficient and relieve them of any necessity for learning English or adopting American norms. Many observers say that Miami, while an interesting city, is no longer an American city. California is feeling the effects of ethnic change as well: Over half its population is now Hispanic and Asian, and one important political consequence is that the state no longer has a two-party system.

So far, the West has refused to consider the long-term consequences of immigration and has simply assumed that the current stream of arrivals will assimilate, just as earlier streams of northern Europeans did when their numbers were much smaller.

But immigration may soon reach a point where its cultural damage will be irreversible. The growth of ethnic voting blocs may increase their leverage over public policy to the point that their demands will become irresistible, including demands for control over immigration policy.

Until the Western world reclaims its belief in itself and is able to assess the West's experience with immigration honestly and without guilt, it ought to be wary of its current pace. Until there is a convergence of expectations between the host countries and the newly arrived, each will make assimilation more difficult. America needs the kind of broad public debate that Europe should have had 50 years ago.

Camouflaging Farm Subsidies

My tolerance for both Mitt Romney and Newt Gingrich increased considerably after I read the attacks leveled upon them for opposing farm subsidies. Maybe there is some principle left in this world after all, even in politicians.

"It appears that the world's most successful system of agriculture is not good enough," the *Forum's* editorial says, adding that Romney in particular "seems to have a poor grasp of US production in a global marketplace." That shouldn't have surprised *The Forum* though, since it admits that this marketplace doesn't exist anyway: "There is nothing free about global agricultural markets because most countries heavily subsidize their farmers."

Indeed, global subsidies have turned agricultural markets into something resembling arms race whose logic is that once you're in it there is no getting out. Leaving it would be a case of unilateral disarmament which leaves you at the mercy of hostile states that are not about to disarm. And it's a logic that is perfect for the agribusiness lobbies because it promises to keep the taxpayers in their grip forever.

But what would really happen if we were to free ourselves from a race that threatens to go on forever and allows no winners?

According to *The Forum*, the skies would fall. Preserving subsidies, it solemnly warns, is "a matter of food security and a matter of national security." Without the guarantee of permanent subsidies American agriculture will collapse, and then domestic food supplies will dwindle, and we'll be dependent upon imports from unstable and hostile places like ... well, like Europe, Canada, Australia, Mexico, Brazil, and scores of other fanatically anti-American countries who might choke off their exports at any moment and leave us to starve.

But I say that we may miss an opportunity here. Why wouldn't it be smart to stop spending scores of billions subsidizing our own farmers and instead rely upon subsidized foodstuffs from abroad? If other countries are foolish enough to help pay for our food, then I say - exploit the hell out of them! Why, we might store up cheap imported produce in warehouses for decades to come before foreign taxpayers wake up.

Public spending on agriculture in 2011, says *The Forum*, was $911 billion, which it claims is not all that horrific because most of it went into food stamps and school lunches for the poor. Well, fine - but so what? That datum is irrelevant to the question of whether farm subsidies are in themselves justifiable. No one misses the obvious fact that providing aid for low-income people in farm bills is simply protective coloration intended to camouflage the scandalous waste of billions going to agricultural interests that are far from poor.

A mere 7 percent of that near-trillion-dollar sum (*The Forum* adds) went into commodity support programs. That comes to "only" $50 billion annually, which *The Forum* regards as a great bargain, since it stabilizes business cycles and - get this - is "actually saving money for the US Treasury!"

But other countries have opted out of the arms race without calamitous consequences. New Zealand, for instance, has ended subsidies altogether, and yet its farmers somehow manage to get by. And so, in fact, do most American farmers, two thirds of whom do not get any subsidies at all. Of those who do get them, most get very little, since the lion's share of the loot (about three-fourths) goes to just 10 percent of the wealthiest landowners.

This whole picture is insane. Urban dwelling "farmers" like the Rockefellers have been on the dole for decades. So has North Dakota's governor Dalrymple, a self-described fiscal conservative who over the past few years has graciously consented to accept several millions of the taxpayers' dollars. There is no economic logic to subsidies but only the political logic of crony capitalism in which farm lobbies and their Congressional allies conspire to secure their mutual interests at the public's expense. Thus, Uncle Sam spends hundreds of millions to encourage the production of tobacco (with $1.4 billion spent over the past 15 years) while at the same time devoting more billions to discouraging its use. Our politicos justify such insanities by claiming that they are anomalies, just kinks that somehow survived the last farm bill and which will be duly ironed out - "next time." But these are not anomalies. And "next time" never comes.

America has homeless people in numbers that are about equal to its farmers. But Congress sees no reason to lavish billions on families who survive winters by sleeping in their cars. Why should it? After all, the homeless don't have lobbies that give millions to pliable legislators, nor do they form voting blocs.

The farm subsidy scam is a cynical, dirty business that should have been ended generations ago. Shame on *The Forum* for trying to sanitize it.

Killing the Messenger

Dr. Hamid Shirvani, North Dakota's chancellor of higher education, was fired while attempting to implement a reform agenda that, according to his critics, was linked to an imperious leadership style and a disregard for rules requiring open meetings.

How much of this was camouflage is hard to say. Reformers, by definition, are threats to those who are comfortable with the status quo. If it's impolitic to condemn reform, then condemning the reformer may get the same result. Hence an informal lunch-and-cocktail gathering can easily be portrayed as a sinister evasion of open meeting laws.

And of course, it also depends on what you mean by reform. Former North Dakota State University president Joseph Chapman was also accused of bullying his subordinates – *after* he was safely gone. Outside the campus, though, no one much cared because Chapman's idea of reform was maniacally focused upon the single issue of campus growth – growth intended to do nothing more than burnish his institution's prestige – and no one dissented because in these parts' growth is all but universally believed to be the highest aim of the human race, even though no one seems to know why. When someone in authority simply mentions the word "grow," millions of eyes suddenly glaze over, and millions of mouths begin drooling.

So, if a prestigious institution is what you seek, growth is the fastest and surest way to get it; and Chapman succeeded in making NDSU grow in terms of budgets, enrollments, construction, athletics, and whatnot. For that reason, all the local boosters, including the news media, proclaimed him the greatest man since St. Paul. If bullying secures ends that you approve of, then bullying is okay.

But if your idea of reform means that you want to create a smarter student body, then you're playing with fire. No matter how genteel your means may be, people whose jobs are threatened by academic standards will rise up in fury to demand your ouster. Installing serious entrance standards would anger scores of thousands of parents whose kids would be denied admission for no other reason than that they can't read and have no clear reason for being in college. And think of the catastrophic effect on faculty employment.

Or suppose some reformer proposed to reverse the prevailing grade inflation, or restore a substantive core curriculum, or replace a faculty that is now dominated by adjuncts – badly paid part-timers and temps – with one that has terminal degrees and is full-time and professional. All of this would require a shakeup in resources and employment; and the fact that this might be all to the public good would be deemed totally irrelevant. Such proposals instill dread because the campuses are not just places of education, they are also places of employment; and when improving education threatens jobs and familiar routines, as it surely does, ferocious opposition is certain.

One of Shirvani's proposals would have raised admissions standards, at least for the two flagship campuses where whole departments would have faced devastation. Teacher-training programs, for instance, draw their majors mostly from the bottom half of college-bound high school graduates. These also enter with the lowest ACT scores of any academic major and then, through the magic of grade inflation and easy courses, graduate with very high-grade point averages. Currently, Mississippi's Governor Phil Bryant wants to refuse admission to any applicant with ACT scores below 21, and panicked ed school administrators immediately warned that even so modest a rise would cut their enrollments, and more importantly their faculties, by half.

Standards would also prove fatal to many other feeble departments, including those whose names end in "studies," that is, programs whose students are recruited not according to their academic merits but by their status as members of victim groups. But across the campuses generally, hundreds of Mickey Mouse courses exist only to attract badly prepared students bearing tuition money and ending them would have disastrous effects.

Another reform, long overdue, is Shirvani's proposal for a feedback system between the colleges and the high schools. The latter blissfully delude themselves that academically, their college-bound graduates are well prepared. That claim, however, draws hysterical laughter from virtually every professor in the respectable disciplines. Blunt talk might present the high schools with a dose of reality and spur some badly needed soul-searching on their part. Yet this too would disrupt entrenched practices in high schools, damage reputations, and inspire resistance.

Shirvani also proposed a three-layered campus system, with the University of North Dakota and North Dakota State University at the top, the four-year colleges in the middle, and community colleges at the base. Avoiding redundancy by clarifying the individual missions of each is undeniably a good idea (the education courses offered by the several 4-year campuses numbers in the hundreds), but even this is resisted by those fearing a loss of status. The Minot *Daily News* has complained that Minot State would be "lumped into a tier" with the likes of Dickinson, Valley City, and Mayville and be unable to "attract top-notch students."

So, the state will spend close to a million bucks to buy off Shirvani and his reforms. This means that the campuses won't have to worry about significant change for the foreseeable future. The buyout will put a sign in the window that says in bold letters, "Chancellor Wanted: No Reformers Need Apply." Henceforth, applicants for the job will play it safe. They'll praise the *excellence* of the status quo and resume rhapsodizing about the wonders of growth.

But let's not lay all the blame on the educational establishment, uncaring though it may be. Something much deeper is wrong, which is the mass culture's indifference to education and its contentment with mediocrity. If the citizenry gave a damn, we would not have these endless scandals about failing schools.

We should be grateful to Dr. Shirvani for having challenged our contentment, if only for a brief period. And we should all take a long, soulful look in the mirror.

America's Favorite Alibi
for School Failure

The Pew Trust's annual assessment of public education announces some very old news, which is that our schools are failing, that they have been for generations, and that nothing of any consequence is being done about it.

Why not? Well, apart from the idiosyncratic problems of the 50 states, what the Pew researchers heard from school authorities everywhere was complaints about under funding. Improving education costs money and the money simply isn't there. This was thought to be especially true in North Dakota, to which Pew awarded a D+ for adequacy of funding and poor grades as well for its failure to adopt clear standards in core subjects like English and Math.

The link between low funding and low student performance is taken for granted both by the Pew Staff and by the former president of the North Dakota Education Association, Max Laird, who has nevertheless defended the state's honor by asserting that a) these grades don't mean much and b) it's urgent that the legislature provide more money in order to raise them. The dualism is so fetching that one imagines Laird's NEA counterparts in exactly 49 other states reflexively making exactly the same argument.

That our schools are under funded is something that "everyone knows."

But are they? Consider:

Between 1970 and today, per-pupil expenditures (measured in today's dollars) have more than doubled, from $6,012 to $12,401. During this same period, composite scores on the Scholastic Aptitude Test (as it was formerly called) *dropped* 76 points despite a couple of revisions intended to make the test easier. Much of the decline is due to a sharp drop at the top ranks of the SATs, meaning that the schools are under challenging their most talented students. In 1970 the average SAT score in reading was 537, while by 2015 it had fallen to 495.

The ACTs show a similar history. Controlling for the proportions of test takers, state-by-state comparisons show little positive correlation between funding levels and scores. In 1970, average composite scores for math and English were 19.9, and by 2015 they had fallen to 18.6. *Education Next* (from which these figures are taken) concluded that "a large body of empirical evidence … overwhelmingly shows that … increases in resources generally do not raise educational performance."

In international comparisons too we find no real correspondence between funding and student performance. The US ranks near the top of the world in per-pupil spending K-12 but ranks near the bottom in student achievement. While our 4th graders perform fairly well among their foreign peers in math and science, by the 8th grade they have fallen below the middle and by the 12th grade they are invariably at or near the bottom, at least among the developed nations. This shows that after the 4th grade (where student potential is lower), our schools do not challenge their students as rigorously as most other advanced nations.

In a 2012 survey by PISA (Program for International Student Assessment), American high school graduates placed 22nd among 24 nations in math, having been outclassed by countries in which per-pupil spending is far lower. The only countries below the US were Estonia and Cyprus. In science, American students placed 27th out of 35 participating nations. The countries the US managed to beat were mostly in the Third World. Pascal D. Forgione, US Commissioner of Education statistics, says that "people have a tendency to think this picture is bleak, but it doesn't apply to their own school. Chances are, even if your school compares well in SAT scores, it will still be a lightweight on an international scale."

All six contestants at the top of the PISA survey were Asians (Hong Kong, Taiwan, Singapore, Macao, South Korea, and Shanghai) whose per-pupil expenditures are a small fraction of our own, and we were also outscored by countries such as Estonia, Poland, Vietnam, Slovenia, Latvia, and Slovakia. Only 2% of American students reached the highest scores in math, compared with 31% of students in Shanghai.

In the latest survey by TIMSS (Trends in International Math and Science Study) our 12th graders scored 15th out of 16 participating countries in advanced math, and in advanced science the US was 20th out of 22 countries, beating only Cyprus and South Africa.

Still more shamefully, the US has one of the highest rates of illiteracy in the developed world. The National Assessment of Adult Illiteracy has found that 14% (32 million) of American adults can't read, and another 21% read at the 5th grade level. Among high school graduates, nineteen percent left school without ever having learned to read. This has gone unchanged over the past ten years.

Why does higher funding fail to produce higher academic performance?

Mainly, it's because cultural factors are more important than money. America's per-pupil spending is about $11,100, while Shanghai's is $1,593. Although under funding is the education establishment's favorite alibi for school failure, researchers find that success is inspired less by high spending than by households in which self-discipline and achievement are taken seriously. *Education Week* observes that "students who are in stable communities and in higher income families [tend to] have greater success later on. Such values seem to be far more common in Asian household than in Western ones.

But the worst handicap out kids' face is that infamous smorgasbord curriculum that is a curse upon American schools everywhere. The Fargo District's program of studies is bloated with cotton candy electives like "Relationships," "Sewing and Fashion," "Social Inclusion," and so on. Otherwise, the curriculum is heavily weighted toward business (12 courses), consumerism (14), health (6), marketing (5) and other nonacademic subjects. Except for English, the liberal arts are nearly absent, with just 2 credits required in history, ½ credit in economics, and ½ in government. One course in "humanities" and one in philosophy are offered as electives. A handful of academic subjects survive only as relics of the past.

So exactly what is it about this chaos that more money is supposed to improve? Will throwing more money into the course in "Bachelor Living" remedy our kids' near-total ignorance of math and science, of history and government, economics, and literature?

We are already spending more than enough to provide the best schools in the world, should we ever take it into our heads to do so. Right now, we have a hugely wasteful school establishment that lurches from generation to generation with no detectable purpose, few real standards, and an unshakeable faith that that the next round of spending will produce different results.

But at some point, we might ask whether it is just possible that school failure might have less to do with funding than with faulty assumptions. If we want our kids to become more proficient readers, then perhaps we should consider the mind-boggling possibility that it may be necessary to actually teach them how to *read* rather than how to weave baskets and decorate cakes.

How Local Chauvinism
Blocks School Reform

With a note of righteous indignation, *The Forum* inveighs against a gaffe (i.e., a blurting out of the truth) by a member of the North Dakota legislature, Mr. Joe Satrom, who is denounced for having described the state's schools as "mediocre." It then pontificates, for the thousandth time, on the state's "record of excellence" in graduation rates, college matriculation, and scores in math and English that are "among the nation's best." It tacks on, inevitably, the obligatory addendum that of course the schools still need more money.

Duly chastened, Mr. Satrom promptly submitted a revised view. He now affirms that the educational status quo is, after all, tops: "teachers in North Dakota are second to none and our students consistently perform well on standardized tests."

Thus, the taboo against truth-telling in education remains inviolate. Indeed, the power of local chauvinism is such that reform is effectively banned as a topic of public debate, at least locally. Former Assistant Secretary of Education Chester Finn, Jr. calls this syndrome "retail complacency" — the flattering delusion that while schools are awful everywhere else, in our back yard they're just fine. The result is that a nation chock full of substandard schools can't muster a constituency anywhere for reform.

Indeed, Mr. Satrom was far too kind in saying that the state's schools are mediocre. Mediocre means middling, or average; and our educational system, even by American standards, is in many respects close to the bottom of the pack. So occasionally it's healthy to put aside our vanity and try to see ourselves as others see us. Here's a sampling.

~	*Education Week,* a journal which monitors school quality in the 50 states, routinely ranks North Dakota near the bottom for its academic standards and accountability. This year, though, it awarded the state a "C-" which lifted us up to 45th place. We also get a "D" for efforts to improve teacher quality, putting us in 48th place. Only 24% of our 8th graders are judged to be proficient in writing (i.e., able to give coherent responses to questions in clear language), well below the national average. In reading, just 38% are judged proficient, and in math just 36%.

~	The US Department of Education says that we have the highest college dropout rate in the nation. That's the flip side of having the nation's highest enrollment rate, which is accomplished when we take in thousands of hopelessly unqualified people in a desperate effort to keep enrollments up. Also, a third of our college freshmen require remediation because, despite spending twelve years in our *excellent* public schools they somehow never grasped the basics of such things as math and grammar.

~	The Fordham Foundation this year gives the state another "F" for its social science standards.

~   The Heritage Foundation ranks the state 44th out of 50 for a climate that's hostile to school choice.

~   The National Institute for Literacy reports that 15% of adult North Dakotans are functionally illiterate.

And so on. Even when our students beat the national average, they're beating a standard that is itself abysmal; in international comparisons (most prominently in math and science) American 12th graders reliably wind up at or near the bottom, being stiffed even by a good number of impoverished Third World countries.

"Everyone knows" that the schools are under-funded. So: Will more money fix things? Recall Einstein's definition of insanity: doing the same thing over and over and each time expecting a different result. Currently America spends, in inflation-adjusted dollars, nearly three times as much per student as it did in 1970, but student achievement has remained flat. Why shouldn't it? What counts is not how much money we randomly throw at the schools, but the purposes for which they spend it; and they have no clear purposes. A rational citizenry will not, therefore, go on sinking more and more money into a burgeoning bureaucracy, sports facilities, educationist fads, and an intellectually barren curriculum in the pathetic belief that *this* time, *somehow*, our kids will suddenly start learning English and history.

Our schools fail to educate because they are enthralled by a pedagogical doctrine (called progressivism) which says that all subjects are of equal value, so that education cannot establish priorities among them. Dysfunctional ideas, not inadequate funding, is the chief cause of school failure. One day, surely, a political leadership will emerge with the imagination to challenge ideas that are now deemed too normal to be wrong. Until then, even mediocrity will remain out of reach.

A False Idea
of Progress

According to the established wisdom, President Joseph Chapman's tenure at North Dakota State University has been a fabulous success. He's the fellow who made everything grow – enrollments, sports, construction, research, and graduate programs to suit the most esoteric of tastes. The expansion of virtually everything was so extravagantly admired that to ask whether any of it had anything to do with education would have seemed rude.

Indeed, over the past eleven years Dr. Chapman himself has never, so far as I know, uttered a single word about issues that *are* related to education, such as the indiscriminate admission of students without reference to their qualifications, the disintegration of the core curriculum, the replacement of the career faculty by adjuncts (teachers who are part-time and temporary), and so on. That didn't seem odd because no one else ever talks about them, either – not the governor, not the legislature, not the State Board of Higher Education, not the trustees, and not the leaders of other institutions.

It isn't entirely their fault, because the anti-intellectualism that has always been part of American history makes a serious discussion of the nature and purpose of education reform so hazardous that, except for some badly mannered denizens of contrarian think tanks, hardly anyone in public life is willing to acknowledge its failings or examine the assumptions which underlie it. So, what passes for a reform proposal usually boils down to a half-hearted request for more money.

Much, perhaps most, of the public expects education to yield an immediate and material payoff of some kind, and when it doesn't there are mutterings about public resources being wasted on something that is plainly useless. And of course, true education really *is* useless, at least in the immediate sense. Reading poetry is unlikely to get you a lucrative career, and learning to love the classics probably won't elevate your social status. Nor will a strong philosophy program increase the local population – a terribly, terribly important goal in this area – or bring in new businesses or create new jobs. Art, too, seems ill-suited to securing higher ends. Altogether, it's hard to explain the value of a liberal education to those who are themselves uneducated and regard the idea of knowledge for its own sake as mind-boggling.

On the other hand, the very word "growth" has an aura that inspires all kinds of warm-fuzzies and visions of impending well-being. A growing population is believed by many to be an antidote to the subliminal specter of loneliness. Growth is virtually synonymous with human progress, and the great thing about it is that you can even measure it with numbers. On the other hand, you can't put numbers on a student's joy about having discovered poetry or a new-found excitement about physics. So, the universities talk constantly about growth and never about the enlightenment of students.

Though most academicians instinctively hate this sort of philistinism, campus authorities everywhere feel they must defer to the educational opinions of the masses. Hence the various bread-

and-circus distractions proliferate, and academic substance is displaced by sports, job training and froth courses intended to increase the enrollment of students whose most important goal is to party for two or three years before venturing into the adult world. The campuses, which once marched to their own drummers, have become junior partners in the university-industrial complex, and the commercialism that has always been ruinous to higher education is what now defines its success.

It is for these things that Dr. Chapman is so greatly admired, perhaps most of all, by the students on his own campus. They admire him because with the new corporate standard of success – making everything grow– he enhances the prestige of the institution they attend. For them it's all a free ride. The institution's growing prominence does not require more talent, homework, or achievement (except perhaps in athletics) on the part of the students themselves.

What is to be done? Perhaps, as Prof. Stanley Fish has said, it's time for academics to speak truth to power – that is, to stop patronizing those who have never experienced the liberal education they are so quick to criticize, and to do some criticizing in return. From public officials, Fish says, "we should allow no false statement to pass uncriticized and unrebuked." Instead of sheepishly trying to explain education in their "vocabulary of business or venture capitalism," we might try "to stand up for ourselves unapologetically, and to comport ourselves as if we were formidable adversaries rather than easy marks."

But standing up to hubristic officials won't be enough if their views merely reflect the anti-intellectualism of the underlying culture, which they surely do. The challenge for reformers, therefore, is to confront the public itself. It would be good if responsible people, whether in academia or in public authority, would break some taboos and begin piquing not just officials, but a culture which keeps floating blissfully along on assumptions that are never challenged and are disastrously wrong.

Can Marshmallows
Make Kids Smarter?

For generations, educational researchers have weighed the factors associated with student achievement, factors like I.Q., curricular standards, teacher training, class, and school size and so on. Sometimes the research surprises, as it did in 1966 when Prof. James S. Coleman reported that successful schooling depends more on the quality of students' households than on the schools themselves. Today it's widely agreed that achievement is strongly leveraged by childhood circumstances, such as a home in which books outnumber TV sets. But now an essay in *The New Yorker* argues that the most powerful predictor of success in school, and in life, may be … marshmallows?

In a 1960s study designed by Stanford psychologist Walter Mischel, a researcher places a marshmallow in front of a 4-year-old and explains the rules: Wait 15 minutes before eating the marshmallow and you will earn a second; eat it before then, and you won't get another. Watching through one-way glass, the researchers typically find that a few kids devour the treat immediately, while most others struggle but yield within 3 minutes, and just 30 percent hold out to the end.

Years later, Mischel checked the same kids to see if the marshmallow test correlated with success in high school. It did. Those who had held out for the full 15 minutes were getting better grades and had SAT scores averaging 210 points higher than those who had succumbed within 30 seconds. The will power demonstrated by delayed gratification benefited kids in several other ways as well, such as having fewer behavioral problems and a greater ability to save money, avoid obesity, and resist drugs.

Though psychologists have generally regarded intelligence as the most important variable in academic success, Mischel believes that I.Q. itself is to a large extent a byproduct of willpower. Mastering algebra requires not just intelligence but also an ability to stay with something that isn't immediately rewarding.

What accounts for differences in will power? Mostly, Mischel says, it's a question of the "strategic allocation of attention" – i.e., of controlling distractions and blocking out temptation. Indeed, the high-delaying kids figured this out for themselves: Instead of obsessing over the marshmallow in front of them, they covered their eyes, sang songs, played hide-and-seek under their desks, or pretended it wasn't really there. The low delayers, by contrast, simply stared at the marshmallow until it conquered them.

If Mischel is right, then the salient point here is not just the primacy of self-control over I.Q., but that self-control can be taught. When the low delayers were coached with various tricks (for example, pretending the marshmallow is only a picture) their power to delay gratification improved dramatically. "Once you realize that will power is just a matter of learning how to control our attention and thoughts," Mischel writes, "you can really begin to increase it."

So Mischel's team is now collaborating with schools in several cities to see how self-control might be taught on a normal, daily basis by incorporating it into school routines. (Already, kids in the KIPP charter schools wear T-shirts that read, "Don't Eat the

Marshmallow.") They plan to develop videos which praise delayed gratification, and to offer new strategies which schools and households might "ritualize" until they become ingrained.

What to make of all this? Mischel himself cautions against utopian expectations. It's still uncertain whether new traits, once introduced, will persist over time, or fade as the early successes of the Head Start schooling program seem to do.

Still, the question intrigues: Have we been missing something important, something that was always right under our noses? After all, taming passions has been a theme of social betterment ever since the time of Plato's *Republic*. In B.F. Skinner's utopian novel, *Walden II*, hungry children must stand five minutes in front of "forbidden soup" before consuming it. And "culture of poverty" theorists has long said that in explaining intergenerational welfare dependence we habitually misdirect our focus to economic factors when the root cause is usually poor impulse control.

Is our present focus in education also off-center? Maybe it's time to rethink what really counts.

Marshmallows, anyone?

Two Cheers For
the Common Core

Over 2 centuries ago, the founders of the Republic – radicals in their day but conservatives in ours – favored the idea of "common schools," that is, schools in which all students, regardless of social class, religion, or geographic region should receive (as Thomas Jefferson put it) a "general diffusion of knowledge," meaning that the same basic subjects should be taught all over the land. Jefferson thought history was especially important for a people who are "guardians of their own liberty," because it equipped them to assess their rulers and arm themselves against demagogues.

But for a hundred years our colleges of education – the teachers of our teachers – have been locked into a thoughtworld known as "progressivism," an ideology which says that few, if any, subjects need to be taught in common because none has any particular importance.

In the 18th Century J.J. Rousseau proclaimed, against Christian teaching, that "man is a being naturally good … that there is not any original perversity in the human heart and that the first movements of nature are always right." If that is so, then education should proceed not by formal instruction from adults but spontaneously, according to the students' own impulses. Rousseau's American heir, John Dewey, added that because "there is no such thing as degrees or order of value, we cannot establish a hierarchy of values among studies." Charles Prosser, who was part of the progressive tradition in American education, said that "business arithmetic is superior to plane or solid geometry; learning ways of keeping physically fit, to the study of French; learning the technique of selecting an occupation, to the study of algebra; simple science of everyday life to geology; simple business English to Elizabethan classics."

Believing that reason cannot determine educational priorities, our modern progressives have abandoned schooling to the judgments of children themselves. The material expression of progressivism is the "smorgasbord" curriculum that has displaced most of the academic subjects in virtually every public school. The smorgasbord includes few academic courses and invites students themselves to complete their studies by choosing from hundreds of cotton candy electives reflecting transient whims.

When our schools confess their inability to establish priorities, we should not be shocked by surveys that consistently place American students among the most poorly educated in the developed world. Last month the Educational Testing Service surveyed "millennials" (those born after 1980) in 22 countries and ranked Americans 16th in literacy, while in both math and problem-solving they were tied for last.

With equal consistency, Asian students dominate these competitions because, in defiance of progressivism's contempt for "rote learning" and "mere facts," their schools teach substantive knowledge and require rigorous standards. E.D. Hirsch, in *The Schools We Need and Why We Don't Have Them, says* "schoolwork that (progressivism) has called 'developmentally inappropriate' has proved to be highly appropriate to millions of students the world over."

Might the proposed Common Core restore some sanity to public education? Its purpose is to require the same substantive topics (initially English and math) in schools everywhere, and to assess students' progress with uniform tests at each grade.

The word "uniform" scares us. But in *Left Back*, education historian Diane Ravitch tells us that in its earliest days "the American public school was remarkably similar across regions," and that local control coexisted comfortably with broader American values. This was due in part to publishers of school texts who sought nationwide markets; the McGuffey Readers, which first appeared in 1836, were in such wide use that they were a national text in all but name. But subjects taught in common also reflected a national consensus on the purposes of schooling that has mostly disappeared. The *Nation at Risk* report in 1983 recommended that all high school students' study "the new basics," which included four years of English, three of math, science, and social sciences, all of which combined suggests a national core curriculum.

If local school districts can accept the national monopoly of progressivism, the ideology that has for a century ruled American education without ever sparking a backlash, surely, they can accommodate a serious national curriculum.

Let's remember too, that American families are highly mobile, so that a sixth of our students move across state lines each year. Kids who have to change schools several times during their school careers complain of having to read *Mockingbird* and *Charlotte's*

Web over and over as they leave one school and enter another. A uniformly scheduled national curriculum would end this waste.

Nor should we fear national testing and reporting because we already have them. When the No Child Left Behind act required the 50 states to self-report their annual progress, the result was that, with the honorable exception of Massachusetts, every state engaged in inflating their students' scores. Citizens received an honest assessment of each state's real performance corrected only after a respected federal agency, the National Assessment of Educational Progress, conducted its own study. Neutral appraisals, whether governmental or private, are essential to getting an honest picture of student progress.

Federal usurpation should concern us, but in principle a common curriculum should not. Math is not one thing in Iowa or something else in Ohio. A meaningful core curriculum should include not just math and English, but a broad range of arts, sciences, and humanities.

Inviting students to design their own education is crazy. Those who take substantive courses (usually because their parents are serious about education) acquire intellectual capital and the habits of self-education, while those abandoned to the smorgasbord will be handicapped socially, financially, and by a lower capacity for enjoying life. Instead of reinforcing social class divisions, we should insist that a first-rate education is a civil right for every student. Local control is important for many reasons, but the freedom to substitute cake decorating for history cannot be among them.

Isn't it time we picked our schools off the floor? The Common Core proposal isn't perfect, but at worst it's the devil we don't know. The devil we do know – schools distorted by progressive ideology – have failed us for a hundred years.

A Tax of the Best Kind

Congress enacted the Corporate Average Fuel Efficiency mandates for the auto industry in 1975, just after the OPEC oil boycott, in order to reduce the country's dependence upon foreign oil. Currently, CAFE requires automakers to meet a fleet average of 29 mpg, and by 2025 this will rise to 54.5 mpg. That may be achievable. But even if it is, don't expect a corresponding drop in gas consumption because mandates are foiled by a paradox known as the "rebound effect."

As automobiles become more fuel-efficient, drivers tend to respond by purchasing bigger vehicles and driving more miles simply because they can do so at little or no extra cost. In 1970, when motor vehicles were less efficient, pickups, vans, and SUVs were a mere 3 percent of sales. Today they are more than half. Since 1980, the fuel efficiency of passenger cars has risen by 60 percent. But because today's vehicles are heavier and more than twice as powerful, the improvement in average mpg is slight, going from 23 to just 27.

Now that fuel prices are falling, the rebound effect is happening again. In 2015 motor vehicle sales increased overall by 6 percent over the previous year, and most of the increase comes from gas-guzzling pickups and SUVs whose sales have shot up by 16 percent. Forget about reducing fuel consumption with mandates.

Mandates also distort markets by forcing automakers to produce vehicles that consumers may not like. Even now, buyers are mostly ignoring compact hybrids and plug-ins: The CEO of Fiat-Chrysler is begging buyers not to purchase its all-electric car, which loses $14,000 with every copy, and the Chevrolet Volt which, though priced at an astounding $40,000 below production cost, isn't selling either.

A far better means of reducing gas consumption is with – dare I say it? – a tax increase. The federal gas tax was last raised in 1993 and has remained at a ridiculous 18.4 cents per gallon ever since, even though it has lost a third of its purchasing power from inflation. Our roads and bridges are crumbling because the Highway Trust Fund, which is financed by fuel taxes, is too broke to keep up with needed repairs.

Federal and state taxes combined add an average of 49 cents to the price at the pump. By contrast, gasoline in Europe is as high as $8 per gallon, with taxes often making up half or more of the pump price. Europeans complain, but they also respond by driving sensibly sized cars (half of which are efficient, clean-burning diesels) that get far higher mpg than those sold in America, as well as by using alternative means of transit.

A serious gas tax improves consumer behavior while preserving consumer choice, so that those who "need" a 9,000-pound Ford Excursion to visit the corner grocery could keep driving them. It can also raise some serious revenues. Currently, each penny of the federal tax yields $1 billion to the Treasury annually. Isn't that a nice ratio? As North Dakota's oil revenues decline, the state would surely benefit from an increase in gas taxes, which stand now at an anemic 23 cents per gallon.

But since 1993 a federal tax rise hasn't been seriously considered. Congress prefers mandates because their costs are hidden (even though they add $1,900 to the average price of a new vehicle) while taxes are dangerously visible.

That may change. Reps. Tom Petri and Earl Blumenauer are pushing a US House bill to raise the gas tax by 15 cents over a 3-year period, and index it to inflation. Bob Corker and Chris Murphy have proposed a similar bill in the Senate. The amounts are much too timid, but at least they are starting a conversation. If there was ever a time to act it's now, when falling gas prices would cushion even a large increase.

Energy independence is not, for the moment, a pressing issue. But improving infrastructure and reducing atmospheric pollution remain urgent concerns. So is highway safety.

Low gas taxes inspire a host of problems that can be resolved very simply, given only the will to do so. Right now, we have one of those rare windows of opportunity for enacting a policy that is clearly in everyone's interest.

"Demosclerosis" – Why Washington Doesn't Work

At the start of Lyndon Johnson's Great Society 50 years ago, polls showed that 76% of Americans trusted government to "do the right thing …most of the time." Today just 19% do. The difference is not that the government has suddenly started doing bad things; it's that in domestic policy at least, it can't seem to do anything, period.

During the Great Depression, Franklin Roosevelt enacted radical new programs expeditiously and, in a spirit of experimentation, kept some and discarded others. Lyndon Johnson, with supermajorities in Congress, enacted a swath of culture-changing programs like Medicare and Medicaid, the Civil Rights Act, the war on poverty, and many others within months of his first inauguration. Some of these programs were in turn dismantled by his successor, Richard Nixon, with equal dispatch. Throughout the 1960s, the government had the flexibility both to add new programs and to terminate those that weren't working.

But by the Clinton era progressive government was choking on its own success. Declaring that "the era of big government is over," President Clinton hoped to modernize government by trimming its obsolete and useless agencies; yet during his tenure of eight years he was unable to eliminate a single major program. His own National Performance Review observed that "the federal government seems unable to abandon the obsolete. It knows how to add, but not how to subtract."

Washington's paralysis is now a permanent affliction. Today's inter-party gridlock masks a deeper malady, one that Jonathan Rausch, in *Government's End*, calls "demosclerosis" – a political system so paralyzed by a vast regime of rent-seeking interest groups that it can't respond to changing conditions.

Government programs that outlive their original purposes no longer die a natural death but are simply repurposed to serve the interests of a new clientele. In 2013 some 11,000 D.C. lobbyists spent $3.2 billion buying influence, mostly from Congressional cronies, and a large share of it was devoted to defending obsolete or redundant programs which serve no national interests, just those of private interest groups. So much money is spent on obsolete programs that both sides of the political spectrum lose Funding isn't available for progressives to try new ideas, and conservatives can't reduce government bloat.

The poster boy for zombie government is the Commerce Department. Created in 1903, its original purpose was to operate lighthouses. But today its 43,000 bureaucrats mostly dispense welfare to corporate clients and protect them from competition. Otherwise, its current mission is so obscure that former Commerce Secretary Robert Mosbacher says the agency is "nothing more than a hall closets where you throw in everything that you don't know what to do with."

Another federal agency, the Export-Import Bank, has been reauthorized 16 times since its creation during the New Deal, despite determined attempts on both the left and the right to kill it. Most of its funds go into loan guarantees for foreign customers of American businesses, most importantly Boeing Aircraft. In effect these guarantees are an indirect subsidy for Boeing to cushion its competition with foreign aircraft manufacturers who are subsidized by *their* governments. This, however, handicaps Boeing's domestic rivals, who don't get subsidies, by effectively making their products more expensive than Boeing's. The Ex-Im bank itself (commonly known as "Boeing's Bank") stays alive only by patronizing many smaller businesses that are strategically located in key Congressional districts.

So, it is with countless other programs among the living dead. Farm subsidies, enacted in 1933 for poor rural folk, are now devoted to making rich landowners richer. The REA, TVA and other agencies designed during the Great Depression now serve wholly different interests that do not need government help. Tobacco is still subsidized, and ethanol is still mandated. Just recently, Congress renewed the National Flood Insurance Program, which has so far transferred $40 billion in insurance subsidies to affluent homeowners who keep rebuilding in flood-prone areas.

These antediluvian entities persist because of the "problem of the indifferent majority." When $1 billion is distributed among one thousand members of an interest group, its recipients will be far more impassioned about defending the program than 100 million taxpayers will be about ending it. Further, the lobbyists' right to manipulate the system is enshrined in the First Amendment's guarantee of free association, as well as the Supreme Court's holding that lobbyists' spending obscene amounts of money on their Congressional cronies is protected as a form of free speech.

So, can anything be done to make government more responsive?

Maybe. Term limits, for example, might weaken the bonds between lobbyists and legislators. If Congressmen know they will not have lifetime careers, interest group support will be less important to them, at least in their later years, and may induce them to become more nation-regarding. Even that old cynic LBJ once allowed that his own behavior would have been better had he known that he could not succeed himself.

Campaign finance reform may also be possible. Sen. John Sarbanes (D-Md) wants to wean Congress from PAC bribery – that is what it is – with federal matching funds of 9 to 1 for candidates who agree to accept no more than $150 from private donors. A third of Congress has signed on so far.

And corruption-fatigued voters can help. Economist J. K. Galbraith, who was well-seasoned in government, observed that power doesn't "tend" to corrupt – it invariably corrupts. He advised citizens to vote consistently against incumbents to prevent their entrenchment.

Don't expect dramatic change. Jonathan Rausch counsels a strategy of "radical incrementalism" – that is, bypassing the Congress-PAC axis with piecemeal state and local activism. Initiatives from businesses, non-governmental organizations, volunteerism, and combinations thereof can bring substantive change over time. So will the unpredictable imperatives of technology.

We need fresh thinking about government. Americans are a creative people who needn't be locked forever into a moribund system predicated on greed and the fear of change.

Why Does College Cost So Much?

Over the past 2 decades college tuition has risen in real terms almost 300 percent nationwide, faster than any major consumer item except tobacco. In some states a year of college now equals a third of the average family income. It's about 25 percent in North Dakota, where the typical student borrows almost $3,000 annually to stay in school.

What's behind these soaring costs? Supply and demand, for one thing. It is now scripture that everyone, regardless of interest or ability, *must* enroll in college. Then, when everyone does, we are shocked – *shocked!* – to find that the price of college has been driven up. And as we scrape ever deeper into the talent barrel, we find – *another shock!* – that students take longer and longer to graduate, if they ever do. Even after six years, 43 percent of American college students still haven't finished their degrees. Those who dropped out and others who are still hanging around have helped to waste scarce resources and push tuition costs upward.

Financial aid, intended to offset rising tuition, simply compounds the problem. In *Going Broke by Degree,* economist Richard Vedder points out that aid is usually self-defeating because giving money to students allows "universities to raise their charges – and to use the increased incomes for [purposes] which have relatively little to do with enhancing the undergraduate learning experience." Indeed, the National Center for Public Policy and Higher Education reports that in 36 states the aid-tuition spiral has left students worse off than they would have been in the absence of aid. In North Dakota, rising tuition costs have outrun family income by nearly a third over the last decade.

Rising tuition also raises questions of fairness. By age 24, seventy-one percent of students from the top quartile of household incomes have earned college degrees, as opposed to just ten percent from the lowest quartile. Elite schools routinely solicit surplus applications in order to cherry pick the top students who can pay full tuition while culling equally talented students who can't. This assures the best of both worlds – a high quality student body and high revenues. Harvard, which has an endowment of $25 billion and weeps over the plight of the poor, enrolls just 8 percent of its undergraduates from households with incomes below $50,000.

Where does the money go? Prof. Vedder estimates that of each new tuition dollar going to the public colleges, only 21 cents go into actual classroom learning. Most of the rest goes to the permanent staff. For example, during the 1980s and 1990s faculties typically got hefty pay hikes, lighter course loads, more travel, and a shorter academic year, none of which translates into better education.

And bureaucracy keeps growing inexorably (what else is new?) as Chief Diversity Officers, Vice Provosts for Inclusion, Deans for Green Construction, and a river of stylish new posts is dreamed up. Vedder notes that in 1976 there were 3 administrators per 100 students, while today there are 6. In 1929, for every dollar spent on instruction, 19 cents went to administration; by 1996 it was 48 cents.

Students aren't all living like monks, either. Chester Finn, a former Assistant Secretary of Education, once toured several campuses with his daughter and was greeted everywhere with the "Chivas Regal strategy" (as one dean called it), which lures students with such amenities as posh apartments, fancy food courts, and gyms with indoor climbing walls. Finn's daughter said it was "like comparing resort hotels." There being no free lunch, such frills add up to higher tuition.

Then there is that ferocious status race. Universities don't really have a "bottom line," an output that can be expressed in hard numbers and used for comparison with rival schools, so the academic status seekers flaunt inputs instead. Student achievement goes unnoticed at *US News and World Report* – a newsweekly with absurd leverage in academe – but if you spend enough money, they'll call you a Major University. Spend it on labs and you may be a Research Institution – *very cool.* Spend millions on sports and you'll be familiar in taverns throughout the land – *wow!* Spending even modest amounts on undergraduate teaching may achieve great results, but those results can't be measured with certainty. Status is impressively visible, so that's where the money goes. History or literature, by contrast, seem so … rustic.

Though the schools habitually plead poverty, their spending is far in excess of a mission that, once upon a time, focused on the cultivation of intellect. It may be futile to point out fat in higher education when everyone *knows,* or is supposed to know, that in education fat does not, cannot, exist. Yet it may be inevitable that the traditional campuses will be forced to slim themselves down as markets and modernity confront them with lean, no-frills competition. Enrollments and tuition may begin to fall as voucher-bearing students forsake the traditional campuses in favor of community colleges, vo-techs, the for-profits, and Laptop U.

That can be a good thing. The 4-year brick-and-mortar campuses are overrun with partying malingerers who would do better almost anywhere else. They were admitted because of a secular religion that says growth of enrollments – and growth of any kind – is progress. But in higher education less is more. Serious students who need it should get serious aid. The hordes of mediocrities who drive costs up and educational quality down should be referred elsewhere.

The Cowardice
of Academia

On the campuses it's commencement season once again, time for inviting eminent people who will get honorary doctorates and hefty fees for addressing this year's crop of college graduates. It's also the season for disinviting them. Currently a slew of speakers is being turned away by universities out of fear that something these luminaries might have said, or or have been associated with, might be offensive to someone, somewhere, somehow.

At one time universities could boast of being bastions of free speech, arsenals of liberty, places where unpopular ideas could get a respectful hearing. But that noble image has not survived the age of multiculturalism. Speakers representing every field of thought are now confronted by campus bullies who claim a right to veto any speaker they don't like, no matter how many others might want to hear from them.

Today's multicultural heresy is the deadliest assault on academic freedom since the McCarthy inquisitions of the 1950s. The difference is that while McCarthyism threatened the campuses from the outside, today's threats come from the *inside*, with academicians imposing a similar reign of terror upon themselves, proudly and with a pious sense of duty. That's because multiculturalism claims to serve a higher cause than that of academic freedom, which is that of heroically defending an assortment of identity groups that are supposedly still smarting from the ravages of racism, classism, ableism, and a dozen other recently-discovered -isms that Western civilization, inherently oppressive, has inflicted upon them. One of the movement's most sacred tasks is to shield such victims from any possibility of further offense that might come from too much freedom of expression.

One of the first casualties of this season's purge was Ayaan Hirsi Ali, who was to be honored by Brandeis University for her work in promoting women's rights in Africa. Her credentials should have been impeccable. A native of Somalia, she was raised in an Islamic household where she was subjected to genital mutilation, beatings, shrouding, and a forced marriage which she avoided only by fleeing to the Netherlands. Once there, she wrote a screenplay that was critical of Islam's treatment of women and for which her partner, filmmaker Theo Van Gogh, was murdered by an Islamic immigrant whose assimilation into Western culture appears to have been unsuccessful. Elected to the Dutch Parliament, Ali was denied police protection and then deported by a government unwilling to risk more Islamist displeasure. She now lives in the United States, but as an apostate from Islam she remains fair game for assassination, anywhere, by true believers who don't take kindly to criticism.

Shortly before commencement day, some Islamic students and a few faculty members were indignant to learn that Ali was a critic of Islam, and upon learning this, they circulated a petition demanding that the university rescind its invitation. They didn't want to hear from Ali, and they thought no one else should either. So, Brandeis – horrified of *offending* a minority group – instantly obeyed.

Yet Brandeis says that its honorary degrees acknowledge "outstanding accomplishments" and that it "does not select degree recipients on the basis of their political beliefs or opinions." So how did it justify booting Ali, who was previously cited by *Time* Magazine as one of the planet's 100 most influential people? Well, it claimed that her beliefs were "inconsistent with Brandeis University's core values." Indeed, its president claimed to have been shocked – *shocked!* – by recent revelations of Ali's criticisms of Islam, even though her best-selling memoir, *Infidel*, published years earlier, had already laid out in gruesome detail her case against the treatment of women in Islamic countries.

Nor did Brandeis, a Jewish institution, have any qualms about awarding honorary degrees to anti-Semites like playwright Tony Kushner ("supporters of Israel are the most repulsive members of the Jewish community") and Desmond Tutu ("gas chambers were a neater death than apartheid"). But then, according to the multicultural creed, some victim groups are more equal than others.

Shortly after Ali received her pink slip, former Secretary of State Condoleeza Rice met the same fate at Rutgers. It seems that some faculty members were *offended* by her association with the Bush Administration – known, card-carrying Republicans! Rutgers solved its problem by replacing Rice with a safe choice, Eric LeGrand, a retired football player.

Others booted in quick succession included Ann Coulter for having conservative political views "inconsistent" with those of Fordham University; the NY City police commissioner Ray Kelley, who was rejected by Brown University for being a cop; Jason Mattera, the conservative editor of *Human Events*, who was scheduled to follow the Marxist writer Francis Fox Piven (who spoke for 2 hours), at Messiah College but was turned away because his ideas were "too controversial." Conservative writer/actor Ben Stein was given the heave-ho by the University of Vermont for his skepticism about the theory of evolution and was replaced by liberal Howard Dean. Neurosurgeon Ben Carson was repulsed from Johns Hopkins for his criticism of gay marriage and Obamacare. Azusa Pacific University bounced Charles Murray for having co-written *The Bell Curve*." Christine Lagarde, a French leftist who is the first woman to head the International Monetary Fund, was rejected at Smith College for running a "neocolonialist organization." Even novelist Alice Walker was turned away from the University of Michigan for holding incorrect views on the Israeli-Palestinian conflict.

It's now an established rule: If just one member of a group claiming a history of victimhood disapproves of a speaker, or pretends to, then that's the end of it. The thousands of others who wanted to hear her will be overruled without any pretense of debate. The reform group Foundation for Individual Rights in Education has compiled a list of 120 speakers who have been disinvited because of opposition from faculty, students, or outside pressure groups. The campuses boast of teaching critical thinking, but they are, according to FIRE spokesman Robert Shipley, "teaching students to think like a censor."

Students have been punished for distributing copies of the US Constitution – really! – on Constitution Day. How long until possessing a copy of J. S. Mill's blasphemous book, *On Liberty* will get students be banned from the campuses?

How did higher education come to embrace a doctrine that is utterly hostile to Western civilization and to the very soul of education – one that regards censorship as unimportant, but sees the possibility of *offense* – a normal aspect of everyday life – as tragic?

Several things account for this. In good measure, it's because many academicians live in an environment of mistrust. Their careers, which were attained at great cost, depend upon being a "good colleague," meaning that they need the continued good will of their peers to survive. They are not about to risk their hard-won professions by bucking the prevailing fashion. When the diversity bandwagon rolls by, you jump aboard – or else.

Also, many academics love to pose as heroic champions of the oppressed and being in the camp of the saints. And there is more than a whiff of anti-American sentiment among intellectuals who see themselves as an aristocracy of talent but who, in liberal societies, are excluded from the ruling class. Perhaps white guilt is also a factor, along with a masochistic pleasure in loathing the culture that made them what they are.

But ultimately, multiculturalism maintains its iron grip on the campuses simply because the forces needed to loosen it do not exist. Higher education is intensely politicized, but its ideological spectrum is so narrow that it includes no faction to the right of center, at least none large enough to form an effective opposition. Boards of regents and alumni associations typically indulge even the most outrageous violations of their schools' missions rather than rock the boat. Lacking even the slightest counterforce, higher education is left mired in a group thinking so powerful that opposing views cannot get a serious hearing.

But debate is always necessary, not just for the good of the minority but for the intolerant majority too. The evil of silencing an opinion, said J.S. Mill (who isn't much cited on the campuses these days) "is that it is robbing the human race; … those who dissent from the opinion, still more than those who hold it. If the opinion is right, they are deprived of the opportunity of exchanging error for truth: if wrong, they lose, what is almost as great a benefit, the clearer perception and livelier impression of truth, produced by its collision with error."

Just so. In suppressing the most basic ideals of academic freedom, our closed-minded multiculturalists are robbing themselves, their overprotected victim groups, and the surrounding community of the armament of truth. Until multiculturalism is somehow defeated, everyone will go on losing.

Some final thoughts:

> Commencement speakers are supposedly chosen in recognition of their outstanding achievements in science, literature, or some other important field. Their personal political views should therefore be deemed irrelevant to the purposes of the graduation ceremony.

> There is a paucity of backbone among the campus leadership. Where are today's John Silbers and R.M. Hutchinses, legendary presidents willing to defend higher education's ideals against faculty bullies, student mobs and multiculturalism's thought police?

> Black conservatives are not supposed to exist. "There is a disgraceful double standard," says black journalist Juan Williams, "among academic liberals, in the hatred they direct at black conservatives … [who] don't fit into the role carved out for black persons in America." Prominent blacks like Clarence Thomas, Walter Williams, Shelby Steele, John McWhorter, Ward Connerly, Ben Carson, Sen. Tim Scott and many others are denounced as Uncle Toms because they refuse to see themselves as helpless victims of "the system."

> It's futile to look for speakers who are without sin. The history of every prominent person is today preserved on the Internet like a fly in amber, and it stays there without any statute of limitations. It's so easy to find blemishes, whether real or not, and to use them as pretexts for discrediting anyone you want, that even naughty children shouldn't find it sporting.

> Lastly, we might disabuse ourselves of the fantasy that there is a basic human right not to be offended. Universities do not have a duty to protect their constituents from the normal vexations of life or to provide therapy for the thin-skinned and those who find prestige in proclaiming themselves victims. Thieves may pick your pocket or break your bones, but unfashionable ideas won't harm you. If anything, confronting them will only make you stronger. The best response to offense is a shrug of the shoulder and a willingness to proffer, with civil discourse, ideas of your own.

Saving the World through Thought Control

Is there any place in this free land of ours so hostile to free thought as our university campuses?

The latest assault on the mind comes from the University of Minnesota, whose College of Education recently floated a Mao-style proposal to screen its students for incorrect social views and then reeducate them in something called "cultural competence."

Though UM has now disavowed the program (after condemnation by civil rights watchers), the idea was to sensitize future teachers who would face an ever-growing list of identity groups by immersing them in courses whose "overarching framework," as the proposal put it, would be race, class, and gender. Students would also write forced confessions – "autoethnographies" – to confront them with their own stereotypes and bigotries. After graduation, tests and workshops would continue to harass them on the job in order to detect unbelievers and recidivists who somehow managed to infiltrate the workplace. Those who failed to understand that America (in the words of the proposal) is a ghastly broth of "white privilege, hegemonic masculinity, heteronormativity, and internalized oppression" would be deemed unfit to continue as teachers.

Like most campus crackdowns, this one was inspired by the multiculturalist dogma which romanticizes weakness and proclaims a duty to squelch any idea, or any word, that some ultra-sensitive member of some allegedly oppressed group may claim to find offensive.

But shameful as it is, multiculturalism with its culture of censorship is only one aspect of a related malady, which is the campuses' endless fixation with political causes. These days, they're tilting against every windmill from Wal-Mart to American imperialism. They're boycotting Israel, the military, sweatshops, polluters, and a host of other evildoers. They're installing campus bureaucracies for diversity, green construction, grieving, and whatnot. They're pressuring American firms here and abroad to pay higher wages and to abandon child labor in Third World countries even if the kids' families are starving. Lincoln University in Oxford, Pa. even proposes to combat obesity by denying diplomas to seniors who are overweight.

Read the universities' mission statements and you'll find the same messiah complex everywhere. A typical case is my alma mater (the University of North Dakota) whose social work department claims a duty "to empower vulnerable, oppressed, and disadvantaged populations," to "promote … respect for diversity," and to "act on social justice issues." Whether these ambitions are worthy in themselves is not the point. The question is whether they are the proper concerns of academic institutions.

Most certainly, they are not. In his book, *Save the World on Your Own Time*, Prof. Stanley Fish argues that when campuses devote academic resources to political goals, they "deform … the true task of academic work: the search for truth and the dissemination of it through teaching." Elsewhere, Fish adds that "it does not seem to me that we academics do [our] job so well that we can now take it upon ourselves to do everyone else's job too. We should look to … our own shop … before we set out to alter the entire world by forming moral character … or combating globalization … or anything else."

How is "social justice" to be achieved? Plato famously answered: By minding your own business. Do what you do best and don't presume to do what others do better. When we mind our own business, society reaps the advantages of specialization and division of labor. Academics are very good at teaching and research, but they are not equipped to conduct statecraft any more than diplomats are equipped to teach math. The surest way for higher education to improve the world is by cultivating students who are thoughtful rather than programmed. Doing this requires a certain distance from the here and now.

Indeed, in an address at Columbia University during the Great Depression, the legendary philosopher-journalist Walter Lippmann wondered whether the scholar "can do a greater work for his nation in this grave moment … than to [refuse] to let himself be absorbed by its distractions." The world, he said, "will go on somehow, and more crises will follow. It will go on best, however, if among us there are men who have stood apart, who refused to be too anxious or too much concerned, who were cool and inquiring, and had their eyes on a longer past and a longer future."

Sad to say, higher education these days isn't much use for scholars who are cool and inquiring. On the campuses, self-glorification by saving the world continues to be all the rage.

What Separates Heroism
from Narcissism

Every president's worst fear is that of being roused at 3 a.m. to be informed of some horrific act of war or terrorism in progress. So, while they are charged with finding a balance between liberty and national security, leaders will err, if err they must, on the side of security; and executive organizations like the National Security Agency will reflect this bias in policies that may compromise personal freedom.

The NSA data leaked by Edward Snowden, Bradley Manning, and Julian Assange reveal locations of American nuclear sites, names of intelligence operatives, and other information that governments legitimately keep secret. But they also reveal a surveillance operation so broad as to include spying on foreign allies, domestic businesses and even charities. Most jarring are the accounts of the NSA's massive stores of data and its Orwellian potential for spying on every citizen in the land. Currently, the NSA tracks every cell phone call made in America.

Governments seldom volunteer for their own misdeeds, and internal checks on intelligence agencies usually have little credibility. So, what should we make of those who take it upon themselves to break loyalty oaths and laws in order to expose government secrets, at least when the scope of government surveillance may seem unjustified?

When Socrates was tried for impiety, he acknowledged the majesty of law (if not of every law) by defending himself before a jury and then accepting the legitimacy of its sentence, which was death. When Henry David Thoreau refused to pay taxes for a war he regarded as unjust, he submitted to arrest and went to jail rather than pay them. M.K. Gandhi, an admirer of Thoreau, defied colonial rules and then marched to the magistrate's office where, to show his respect for the law, he invariably asked for the maximum sentence. Martin Luther King, a disciple of Gandhi, likewise manned up and went to jail as a means of making a statement about unjust racial laws.

And when Daniel Ellsberg in 1971 leaked the "Pentagon Papers" to the *New York Times*, he did so believing that the war policies pursued by a succession of presidents were unconstitutional and had to be brought to the public's attention. He too made no effort to evade the judgment of the law. Each man knew that the willingness to accept responsibility was what distinguished the civil disobedient from the common criminal.

The NSA leakers, however, have exempted themselves from this venerable tradition. Private Manning resolved his difficulties with the law by striking a plea bargain. Assange and Snowden fled, respectively, to Ecuadorean and Russian soil – hardly symbols of the openness they claimed to champion. Snowden even tried to blackmail the government by threatening to reveal an additional "doomsday cache" of secrets unless he received amnesty.

What inspired these three? Patriotism? A desire for reform? Or was it something else, perhaps a desire for fame, or even a strain of anti-Americanism?

Critics and supporters alike use similar words in describing them: "arrogant," "narcissistic," "self-promoters," and "paranoiacs." Writer Heather Brooke calls Assange a "predatory narcissistic fantasist" whose arrogance and "pretensions of infallibility" had earlier alienated his own co-conspirators at Wikileaks. She quotes the sense of self-importance he exhibited at his headquarters: "I am the heart and soul of [Wikileaks], its founder, philosopher, spokesperson, original coder, organizer, financier and all the rest." In short, something of a universal genius.

The *New Yorker's* Jeffrey Toobin describes Snowden as a "grandiose narcissist who deserves to be in prison." He fled the US and went to Hong Kong, Moscow, and Ecuador, dropping secrets all along his path as if flaunting his hostility to his home country. And even Manning's defense psychiatrist found him "narcissistic" and "lacking in empathy," as well as sexually confused. Acquaintances described him as a misfit in both school and military life; one said that he was "permanently frustrated with the world."

An act's legitimacy will be judged in large measure by its perceived motivation. If it seems inspired by neurosis or by grandstanding, then the act, however benign its social effects might prove to be, will seem more like an egotistical prank than an act of patriotism. So, while the leakers have – we may hope – sparked a long-needed debate over government hubris and the proper scope of federal surveillance, they have also compromised the majesty of their cause by ducking personal responsibility for their acts. Had they forthrightly accepted responsibility, their statement about government abuses would have resonated far more powerfully.

President Obama says that snooping on citizens is only a temporary thing. But so long as unhappy people have access to technology, governments will always have to watch for terrorists; and just so, citizens will always have to watch their government, sometimes to the point of breaking its laws. When such law-breaking becomes necessary, it deserves to be undertaken by a class of people who are motivated by something higher than fame and narcissism.

In the meantime, the leaks have already yielded one interesting result, which is that some progressives are finally beginning to ask whether their core political faith – a trust in the benevolence of the ubiquitous State – is really warranted.

An Idea So Stupid that
Only an Intellectual
Could Believe It

Prof. Jean Baudrillard, the famed postmodernist who wrote books like *The Gulf War Did Not Take Place*, who denied that 9/11 was a "real event," and who inspired "The Matrix," a film about people who inhabit a fake world, died last month. At least he *appears* to have – one can't be sure. Appearance, postmodernists say, is about all there is, and even *that* is manipulated by elites who profit from mass delusion. So perhaps Baudrillard will return; as he himself insisted, time, causation, and, indeed, "any [physical) law can be reversed."

Usually, proclaiming this sort of thing lands you in the max ward, but in academia these days it wins prizes for Advanced Thought. Postmodernism is a movement of the Left with roots in Marxism and Freudianism as well as German nihilism (whose pantheon of heroes has included full-blown Nazis like Paul De Man and Heidegger) and it specializes in "deconstructing" what naïve persons take to be common-sense reality.

What is its attraction? Biologist Paul R. Gross says in his *Higher Superstition: The Academic Left and Its Quarrels With Science*, that knowledge of the doctrine bestows, as Marxism did in its day, the "illusion of membership in a secular priesthood, an inner circle of initiates privileged to understand, by means of esoteric doctrine, the secret inner working of the world, a coven of hierophants signaling to each other in arcane jargon impenetrable to outsiders."

Its Newspeak also serves to discourage inconvenient questions. Thus, in one of his books Baudrilliard observed, about something or other, that "our complex, metastatic, viral systems, condemned to the exponential dimension alone (be it that of exponential stability or instability), to eccentricity and indefinite fractal scissiparity, can no longer come to an end." Now, who could question a genius like that?

First favored by literature professors who don't like literature ("culture theory" says that it's meaningless), postmodernism has since ballooned into a theory of everything: With stunning boldness, its prophets dissect ("transgress" is the favored word) all fields of knowledge with the certainty of omniscience; indeed, they claim to have mastered all aspects of reality – because postmodernism's central insight is that, well, there *isn't* any reality apart from what is inside your own head.

The postmodernist movement, though still a recent fashion, has already achieved an iron grip in higher education. Those seeking a career in certain academic fields must convince their prospective employers that they have not only mastered the doctrine of deconstructionism, but also that they accept it without question. "If you want to make it in the [literary] criticism racket," say Jeremy Stangroom and Ophelia Benson (*Why Truth Matters*), "you have to be a deconstructionist or a Marxist or a feminist. Otherwise, you don't stand a chance."

When Benno Schmidt left the presidency of Yale to become commissioner of baseball, he was asked why anyone would leave one of the world's premier universities for a job in sports. His answer was that in baseball you get to work with a better class of people.

He was right. Today large sectors of the academy are controlled by people who, under the spell of postmodernism, are openly hostile to intellect. They preside over the various "studies" (cultural, multicultural, feminist, whiteness, gay and lesbian, fat, etc., etc.) programs that make up the grievance industry, all of them in departments where factuality is deemed inconsistent with their missions. But even serious departments, notably English, are said to be closed to unbelievers. Campus liberals make no issue of the Left's anti-intellectualism, perhaps because it undermines their cherished view that anti-intellectualism is the defining characteristic of the Right.

In such bastions students may learn that there is no Truth, just "truths" that are determined by ethnic, gender, and class interests; that reason is merely a Western prejudice and is inherently repressive; that classic literature – indeed, all communication – is "radically indeterminate," i.e., meaningless; that historical facts are subordinate to ethnic legends; that gender is a social invention; that Western civilization is no higher than that of any jungle clan, and that (as Saul Bellow wryly observed) putting men on the moon is no greater an achievement than putting a bone through one's nose.

The essence of deconstructionism is that "reality" is a mass delusion, mostly psychological experience manipulated by elites who profit from bad trips. Just so, the essence of liberation lies in swapping their ugly reality for the postmodernists' beautiful one.

Postmodernism's war against reality is most vivid in its portrayal of physical science as a "mythical construct." In 1996 a prominent journal of "culture studies" called *Social Text*, ran an essay by physicist Alan Sokal which, employing the language of deconstructionism, boasted of shredding the entire "Western intellectual outlook" and its premise "that there exists an external world, whose properties are independent of any individual human being and indeed of humanity as a whole." Sokal argued that "physical reality … is at bottom a social and linguistic construct" that "postmodern science" has finally demystified. Armed with this revolutionary knowledge, Sokal delivered such revolutionary insights as these:

- Gravity is not a law of nature but only a "social convention."

- Quantum gravity (a theory dealing with space and time on scales of a millionth of a billionth of a billionth of a billionth of a centimeter), has "profound political implications."

- Quantum field theory confirms postmodernist theories of psychoanalysis.

- Political change requires a "profound revision of the canon of mathematics."

Well, some things, as George Orwell observed, are so stupid that only an intellectual can believe them. And in fact, as soon as Sokal's essay was safely in print (and widely acclaimed by the postmodern Left as a major breakthrough) he announced to the journal's readership that – *gotcha!* – it was all an elaborate hoax. Its purpose was to expose the stupidity of intellectuals who will swallow any idea that identifies them as *avant-garde* and as deep,

deep, deep thinkers. Sokal's hoax may be the most spectacular of the 20th Century.

In accepting it uncritically (*Social Text* showcased the piece in a special issue without even subjecting it to a standard peer review), the journal's editors and a good part of the Left revealed their obsession with a profane fantasy that endows intellectuals with a godlike power – the power to mould universes with words: "*Let there be …*" whatever the wordsmiths choose. One devotee boasted triumphantly that, with publication of Sokal's essay, postmodern science is now "free from any dependence on the concept of objective truth."

(Adding insult to injury, Sokal invited anyone wishing to demonstrate deconstructionism's power to repeal the laws of nature to do so by jumping from his 19th floor apartment in New York. So far there have been no takers.)

Science tries to understand physical nature. But what if there *is* no physical nature? In the Silly Putty world of postmodernism, liberated from facts and armed with a do-it-yourself epistemology, science has nothing to do and is necessarily abolished. But "theorizing about 'the social construction of reality,'" says Sokal, "won't help us to find an effective treatment for AIDs or devise strategies for global warming. Nor can we combat false ideas in history, sociology, economics, or politics if we reject the notions of truth and falsity."

It is not even possible to function as a civilization if everyone lives in his own universe where facts and reason have no connection with anything outside our own skins. Without membership in a common reality a vacuum opens up that can only be filled by the use of force. "Justice is the interest of the stronger," Thrasymachus instructed Socrates.

Seventy years ago, Bertrand Russell wrote that "the concept of 'truth' as something dependent on facts largely outside human control" serves to check "a certain kind of madness – the intoxication of power which invaded philosophy with Fichte … and to which modern men, whether philosophers or not, are prone. I am persuaded that this intoxication is the greatest danger of our time, and that any philosophy which … contributes to it is increasing the danger of a vast social disaster."

Postmodernism contributes to this madness and to nothing else. It persists on our politicized campuses solely because it wears the protective coloration of the Left and because there is no substantial presence on the Right to challenge it.

And yet: Will the majority of sober academics forever tolerate a scam that mocks the whole idea of education, that even ridicules *thinking* as "repressive?" Without internal restraints on this "certain kind of madness," eventually there will be external ones.

How to Destroy
Western Civilization
without Firing a Shot

Multiculturalism is an anti-Western ideology and a child of the political Left which claims guardianship of approved minority groups that are allegedly damaged by Western values and white oppression. Such guardianship includes a responsibility for shielding the movement's clientele against all possibility of still more "offense." In higher education this requires a regime of benevolent authoritarianism that includes racial favoritism, reeducation programs for whites, political correctness with its endless taboos, revisionist histories, the abolition of due process, censorship, and of course a corps of language police to block any communications that might upset one or more members of the favored identity groups.

But multiculturalism is not confined to the campuses. Today it presides as a sort of collective superego that determines what is, or isn't, appropriate in social relations throughout the entire Western world. Its guilt-inducing power is such that it has led to a loss of confidence especially among Western peoples when they deal with Third World inhabitants who, being poor and generally dark-skinned, are presumed to be morally superior to decadent, oppressive whites. But in its zeal for purifying the West, multiculturalism has created new injustices far greater than those it presumes to correct.

A few weeks ago in Rotherham, England it was revealed that some 1,400 young girls, many as young as 11, were gang-raped and tortured between 1997 and 2013. These were daily occurrences that the *NY Times* has called a "16-year reign of terror and impunity" in which the girls were subjected to beatings, mock executions, and trafficking; one girl was raped by more than 200 men, and another was doused with gasoline with the threat of immolation if she ever told anyone. Still another said that rape was a normal part of growing up in her neighborhood. Their families were also terrorized and were not even offered counseling.

The authorities were repeatedly informed of all this but they did nothing. Well, almost nothing. Parents and social workers who reported the crimes were fined, arrested, or sent to classes in diversity training. Only one case was ever prosecuted.

Why wasn't this horror taken seriously? Because, for one thing, the victims were all slum-dwelling whites, which allowed the police to label them as "white trash" and "tarts" whose claims of abuse could be dismissed as a lifestyle choice.

But as virtually everyone now admits, the real problem was the intimidating power of multiculturalism. The rapists were a gang of cab drivers, mostly of Pakistani heritage who – dark-skinned, Islamic, and Third World – were well aware of the taboo against judging them by the same standards that apply to Christians and affluent whites. Fearing to blame the gangsters for rape, the Brits instead blamed *themselves* for what they have come to believe is their own innate bigotry. In 1999 a government report stated that any law enforcement officer who had not undergone diversity training must be presumed a bigot.

So, a conspiracy of silence prevailed among government officials, the press, and the police, all of whom feared to offend Britain's growing Muslim population. Reports detailing the abuse back to 2002 were ignored. Alexis Jay (the investigator who finally got the public's attention) reported that virtually everyone who knew of the abuses turned a blind eye "for fear of being accused of racism." According to the *NY Times*, some officials were even ordered "to withhold information on the origins of the abusers."

Police investigations are now in progress in other cities across the country where similar revelations are beginning to emerge. A spokesman for Britain's Association of Chief Police Officers warned of "many more Rotherhams to come."

Multiculturalism, with its theology of white guilt and the superior virtue of the oppressed, has succeeded brilliantly in turning the West against its own core values. It has produced a culture so uncertain of itself that it shrinks from making the most basic judgments about right and wrong, lest some member of the grievance industry might yell "racist!" Columnist Ross Douthat, an anomaly at the *NY Times* (he is an out-of-the-closet conservative) says of Britain that it is "too committed to 'diversity' to act appropriately," and that it is "so open-minded that both its brain and its conscience have fallen out."

Does multiculturalism have any redeeming value? Despite its lofty claims of raising minority self-esteem and enriching social interaction, the most extensive research efforts say that its effect is exactly the opposite. "The more ethnically diverse the people we live around," reports political scientist Robert Putnam, "the less we trust them …. In colloquial language, people living in ethnically diverse settings appear to "hunker down" – that is, to pull in like a turtle."

The academic research confirms the experience which has led the leaders of Germany, France, and Britain finally, after decades of immigrants' failure to assimilate into the cultures of the host countries, to denounce it as a threat to national unity. Masses of immigrants who insist upon retaining their own national and religious identities while condemning the values of their host countries could hardly be otherwise.

Sooner or later our fashionable progressives must put an end to their tiresome self-flagellation and stop hating the civilization that produced them. And everyone should quit the pretense that "offenses" are abnormal to life and can be abolished by the thought police. Until we stop being sheep and recover our common sense and our backbones, we'll go on having more Rotherhams.

In School Size,
Less is More

After much agonizing, the Los Angeles School Board has ended construction on its Belmont Learning Complex, a high school which, had it been completed, would have been one of the largest in America. Designed for 5,300 students and described as the district's "crown jewel," it was aborted because the proposed site contained toxic residues from an old oilfield. One hundred and seventy million dollars went down the drain.

The interesting question, though, is not how the site could have been so carelessly chosen, but: Why was such a grandiose project ever conceived in the first place? Why do we persist in building schools of such colossal scale?

Apart from our unthinking admiration for bigness as a value in itself, the pat answer is that economies of scale allow big schools to offer a wide range of programs and facilities at a lower per-student cost.

In 1940 America had 200,000 K-12 schools, and today, with a much larger population, these have been consolidated into 62,000. The average school today has five times as many students, and a quarter of high schools have enrollments of over 1,000. But in light of education's failure to respond to reform efforts (and spurred also by mass killings by alienated students in large schools such as Columbine in Colorado), some reformers are asking whether bigness is itself an impediment to learning. They are aided by a body of research which, as William Fowler (a US Department of Education official) has noted, overwhelmingly "confirms beneficial effects for small high school size." In plain language, it seems that kids do better in small schools.

How do we know? One clue is in rates of student socialization and participation. In an early study *(Big School, Small School)*, Roger Barker observed that while big schools can offer more extracurricular activities, small-school kids reported "more satisfactions relating to the development of competence, to being challenged, to engaging in important actions," and were far more likely to bond with other students.

Big schools, with their anonymity, have more discipline problems, more vandalism and violence, more antisocial attitudes. "Behavior problems are so much greater in larger schools," one recent study concludes, "that any possible virtue of larger size is canceled out by the difficulties of maintaining an orderly learning environment." By contrast, teachers and administrators in small schools are more likely to enjoy their jobs and to be closer to their students. Parents are more involved because small scale makes them feel more influential.

Size also affects academic achievement, as James S. Coleman and his colleagues reported in their 1966 standard work, *Equality of Educational Opportunity.* One of their many counter-intuitive findings was that the school's formal assets (quality of teachers, facilities, equipment, etc.) are less important to classroom success than "attitudes of student interest in school, self-concept, and sense of environmental control," all more typical of small schools. Small-school students have better attendance, are more likely to graduate and to graduate sooner. Size is a particularly sensitive factor in the success of minority and disadvantaged students.

Okay, but what about course offerings? Doesn't it take big schools to offer the specialized and often exotic electives necessary for enriching the curriculum?

Maybe so, but unless you swallow the progressivist dogma whole, the real problem here is quite the opposite: It's the basics that aren't being taught, anywhere. Electives don't "enrich" education, they displace it. Where is the report that doesn't trace the school crisis to the flea market curriculum of careerism, hobbies and feel-good psychobabble which everywhere crowds out courses with academic substance?

Though Fargo's high schools offer multitudes of courses (220 at my count}, most are unrelated to anything that could reasonably be called education. The Family and Consumer Sciences Department, for instance, offers 17 courses with titles like "Kits and Crafts," "Relationships," "Fit and Fast Foods," "Fashion Trends," "Living Skills" and "Sewing for Fun." Anyone who thinks that small schools are handicapped by an inability to offer this sort of "enrichment" should have his head examined. (By the way: Care to guess how many courses are offered by the History Department? Sorry, just kidding. The Fargo schools don't have a history department.)

Finally, what about those economies of scale? If big schools have no other virtues, aren't they at least cheaper to operate?

Maybe not. Consolidated schools do have advantages (one bigger swimming pool is likely to be cheaper than two or three smaller ones), but they also have economic drawbacks. Transportation is one. Big schools draw more kids from distant homes, meaning higher per student costs for buses, drivers, garages, and upkeep. Smaller, decentralized schools allow students to bike or walk. Administration is another; in big schools it displaces the sense of communality, so that schools that might have been governed by a principal-faculty consensus now require new layers of bureaucracy.

What's the best size overall? The Cross City Campaign for Urban School Reform recommends a limit of 350 for elementary schools and 500 for high schools. Other studies, including surveys of principals, yield similar ballpark figures. Don't look for exact numbers. The important thing is our schools are already too big, and building still bigger ones is likely to be a false economy. Large school size is another of those fashionable assumptions about education that needs to be freshly examined.

Where Have You Gone,
Ma and Pa Kettle?

Farm subsidies, enacted during the Great Depression as "temporary" relief for poverty-stricken rural folk, are now in their 80th year. They've been around so long that hardly anyone recalls what their purpose was, or is; they've just … *always* been there, like air and water, and they've long since passed into the realm of entitlements for rich and poor alike. Currently they run about $17 billion annually (even as farm incomes soar) and the new farm bill, due any day, may include more billions for a "permanent disaster fund" intended to make farming totally risk-free.

In 1933, 20 percent of Americans were farmers, typically Ma and Pa Kettle homesteaders with mixed crops, draft horses, a few cows and pigs, chickens scratching in the back yard. Today the farm population is less than 2 percent and its practitioners are typically high-tech people running extensive enterprises that are more industrial than agrarian. Yet the farm lobby and its career-obsessed Congressional cronies go on pretending that over the past century nothing much has changed, that today the "small family farm" is still prevalent, poor, and eternally dependent.

But in an influential *Time* essay, Michael Grunwald has detailed how subsidies wreak environmental devastation, violate trade agreements, exacerbate Third World poverty, and yes – in mockery of all the syrupy rhetoric about preserving an idyllic way of life – promote "industrial mega-farms and the depopulation of rural America."

Far from keeping the Kettles on the land, subsidies make it easier for their wealthier neighbors to buy them out. Grunwald cites research by the Federal Reserve System showing that the most heavily subsidized counties suffer the highest population losses. This happens, in part, because highly mechanized, consolidated farms have little need for non-family labor or for nearby villages. The last village enterprise to disappear is usually the tavern. During the 1990s, North Dakota, the most heavily subsidized (on a per-capita basis) of all states, lost population in all but 3 counties. It has more land under cultivation than at any time since 1954, yet there are fewer farms than at any time since 1910.

By pushing up cropland prices – the US average is now $4,130 per acre – subsidies put farming careers beyond the reach of almost all potential entrants unless they inherit farms from their parents. Just 6 percent of current farmers are under the age of 35.

Them as has, gits. Only a third of farmers actually receive subsidies, and of these the top tenth gets three-fourths of the swag (for an average of $34,000 each), while the bottom 80 percent average just $700 annually. That's right: In this fast shuffle the "small family farm" – whose image of poverty and heroic struggle is cynically employed to legitimize the whole case for subsidies – gets stiffed. So do the taxpayers: The median net worth of subsidized farms is five times that of the non-farm households that are forced to pay the bill. Yet none dare call the farm lobby a "special interest."

Just what is a "small family farm" anyway? The Kettles would be shocked to learn that farms with yearly sales of $250,000 now fit that label, and that just bearing the label of "farm" may by itself qualify any landowner for assistance. "Small" has gotten so big that a proposal to cap subsidy payments at $2 million annual gross income is considered radical. Sen. Kent Conrad wants this pared to $750,000, while populist Sen. Byron Dorgan thinks the Kettles might squeeze by with annual subsidies of *only* a quarter million.

But why should *any* farm be insulated from risk? Every year a million Main Street businesses fail and as many new businesses spring up to replace them. That's considered normal, so bailouts aren't necessary. But if the Kettles should fail, *that's* a national tragedy. The difference, as we are constantly told, is that farming is spiritual. "In today's fast-paced, interconnected world," explains Rep. Jerry Moran (D-Kansas), "there are few industries where sons and daughters can work side-by-side with moms and dads, grandmas, and grandpas. But we still find that in agriculture…. It is a celebration of … an endangered way of life that we must work each and every day to preserve."

Got it? The *wholesomeness* of 2 percent of the population is what saves the other 98 percent from debauchery. Farm subsidies preserve the national character. The case for giving billions to the planter class rests on *that*.

But myths won't always prevail. Resistance to this madness is growing in Congress, and many farmers themselves have come to resent subsidies as an insult to their competence. Rising crop prices too will deconstruct the fond myth of agrarian poverty. Ma and Pa Kettle really don't live here anymore.

So, it's not unthinkable that the coming pork fest might be the last. In a parting salute to a matured industry, retiring Agriculture Secretary Mike Johanns said, "Congratulations! We celebrate your success. You don't need subsidies anymore!"

How Harvard Welcomes
Unpopular Ideas

Harvard president Larry Summers recently asked whether the dearth of women in math and science might be due in part to "intrinsic aptitudes," and faculty mobs instantly began howling for his scalp. Never mind that gender differences are a legitimate topic of scientific inquiry, and that Summers himself posed the question in order to invite debate. The problem is that the academic Left has assumed a more or less global responsibility for the protection of persons at risk of being offended, including women, and now it feels duty-bound to savage any idea that might possibly offend someone, even those as privileged as female Ivy League professors.

Feminists are offended by "intrinsics" because they threaten to displace the preferred explanation of women's victimization, which is male prejudice, and thereby weaken the case for quotas and federal regulation. Summers' apostasy did, of course, end the only way it could. After a lengthy period of groveling, he was forced to resign; and everyone else got a useful reminder, if another one was needed, that a university is no longer an appropriate place to debate ideas, at least not political ones.

Harvard had other issues with Summers, including his belief that professors should actually teach classes. Many of Harvard's star professors found this to be outrageous. Cornel West, for instance, indignantly resigned his professorship in philosophy to transfer to Princeton where he might better concentrate on his more lucrative interest in producing rap lyrics and videos.

Why do the mobs have such an easy time of it, everywhere? A university is supposed to be a marketplace of ideas, after all – so when the campus Left subverts its very reason for being, why doesn't the opposition spring to its defense?

It's because in higher education in general, and in the Ivy Leagues in particular, there *is* no opposition. Campus pluralism is long gone, a casualty not of some wicked design but of its suffocation by the sheer numerical crush of an entrenched faction. What remains is less a marketplace than a political monopoly of the Left with few internal or external checks. In place of debate there is at best an occasional family quarrel among liberals. This leaves the Left free to do whatever it wants.

Nationally, faculties on the Left (mostly Democrat) outnumber those on the Right (mostly Republicans) at least in the social sciences and humanities, by a ratio of 8 to 1. (Among the general population the ratio is about 1:1.) The closest thing to parity among large campuses is Houston University where the Left predominates by a modest 3:1. Elsewhere it reaches totalitarian proportions. At Harvard, Syracuse and Colorado-Boulder the Left-Right ratio is over 20:1. At Denver College it was 35:1. Williams College, with a faculty of more than 200, boasts exactly 4 Republicans. A few years ago, Colorado-Boulder hired a prominent conservative, a political scientist named Steven Hayward, and the event was so shocking that it made national news.

Whole departments are tight little islands. The history departments at Brown, Cornell and Denver are Republican-free. So are the English Departments at Brown, Santa Clara, and Colorado. Eight of the sociology departments surveyed are totally cleansed. Women's studies? Forget it.

In a forthcoming issue of *Academic Questions*, Professors Daniel Klein and Charlotta Stern examine the voting patterns of members of six professional associations in the social sciences and humanities. Here the Left-Right ratio averages about 10:1, though it varies between disciplines (from 3:1 in economics to 30:1 in anthropology.) And despite the Left's large numbers, the authors say, its internal range of political opinion is very narrow.

In a separate study of Stanford and UCLA, Prof. Klein found Left-Right ratios of 8:1 and 10:1 respectively. Here as elsewhere, science and engineering were the most GOP-friendly, though all 23 departments surveyed were lopsidedly Democratic.

In a 2005 national research project by Stanley Rothman *et al*, of 22 departments, liberal dominance ranged from a ratio of 88-3 in English departments to 49-39 in the most conservative department, business. Not one academic discipline had anything close to parity between Left and Right.

"The most serious problems of freedom of expression in our society today exist on our campuses," said former Yale president Benno Schmidt.

It should be obvious why. Some reformers are pushing an "Academic Bill of Rights" devised by David Horowitz of the Center for the Study of Popular Culture. Among other things, it pledges universities not to discriminate against applicants on the basis of political belief.

Maybe Larry Summers could have used one of these. Maybe all of us could. Surely "diversity" ought to mean something more than skin color and should include such esoteric things as, say, ideas.

Academia's Most Famous Confidence Man

Ward Churchill is best known as the University of Colorado professor who several years ago wrote an essay comparing the 2,700 victims of the 9/11 attacks to Nazi bureaucrats ("little Eichmanns," in his words) who, because they were in the service of a wicked imperialistic regime, deserved their fate. In the ensuing furor, Churchill was dropped from the college speaking circuit and was later fired by his home campus. He then sued, claiming that UC caved to local pressure and punished him in violation of his First Amendment right of free speech. UC replied that it dismissed him because an investigation turned up a history of plagiarism in his published works. The contentious point was that UC investigated Churchill only *after* his off-campus remarks had gotten the university in hot water and threatened its funding from both public and private sources.

In April of 2009, a Colorado jury agreed with Churchill, sort of, and awarded him damages of $1. In July a state judge upheld UC's refusal to reinstate him to his old job. Similar refusals were upheld by two higher state courts and were confirmed by the state's highest court. Finally, his case made its way to the U.S. Supreme Court.

Colorado hired Churchill in 1991 as a teacher of ethnic studies, a pseudo-field designed less to educate students than to assure them that they are victims of Western civilization and its myriad evils, and to provide therapy in the form of low expectations, easy grades, and immersion in ethnic chauvinism. Churchill arrived with only a master's degree from an obscure state college and a few publications in obscure journals. The most compelling item on his vitae was his claim to be of Native American heritage, which he fortified by regularly wearing a costume of waist-length hair, a headband, and sunglasses. He also cultivated a warrior image by claiming a military history as a sniper, paratrooper, and point man on patrols in Vietnam. There is a widely circulated photo of him in a leather jacket cradling an assault rifle in a pose reminiscent of a Che Guevara tee shirt.

Once in place, UC gave him a career that most Ivy League Ph.D.s could only dream about. Hired as an associate professor, he was tenured for just one year and then awarded, in short order, a full professorship, a six-figure salary and a forum for pop stardom with a built-in radical following. So (as Churchill would later argue) if the university really cared about academic integrity, why hadn't it vetted him *before* lavishing all these perks? They even took his word that he was a Native American, which turned out to be as bogus as his scholarship. Also bogus was his depiction of his military career, which was in fact spent safely indoors as a film projectionist.

According to UC's website, the mission of the Ethnic Studies Department is to move students "beyond existing social, cultural and economic paradigms to more inclusive paradigms in which they are the subjects of their own reality." And indeed, reality is exactly the issue in contemporary education. If the current paradigm of Western civilization – with its "privileged" notions like reason, science, and objective truth – is horribly oppressive, then the multicultural studies programs over which Churchill presided open up a much more agreeable reality in which truth and falsehood are whatever you choose them to be.

Multiculturalism's interest in history, for instance, is not that of an honest intellectual enterprise but, as A.M. Schlesinger says in *The Disuniting of America*, "rather a social and psychological therapy whose primary purpose is to raise the self-esteem of children from minority groups." So, minority students are taught revisionist histories which say that art and architecture, science, philosophy, mathematics, and medicine were not originated by Europeans but were the work of ancient civilizations in Africa and elsewhere, whose golden ages, now suppressed, were plundered by the classical European civilizations.

In this Silly Putty world, plagiarism and misrepresentation are meaningless and the teachings of self-promoting confidence men are as valid as those of the most revered scholars. So, believing that Churchill would suffice as a reasonable facsimile of a Native American with whom his students could identify, UC could treat his academic qualifications, or lack thereof, as excess baggage.

That's because at UC and at ethnic studies programs everywhere, what matters is that teachers must faithfully mirror the ethnic characteristics of their students. The Church of Multiculturalism says that black students can only relate to black teachers, Native American students to Native American teachers, and so on. No authority outside the pertinent identity group, however intellectually distinguished, can be authentic. There is no transcendent intellectual tradition to command respect and no common moral or esthetic traditions to be shared; there are just ethnic compartments, each with its own peculiar world view. In the

Orwellian tradition of doublethink, students get segregation in the name of inclusion.

Churchill is the inevitable product of a system of higher education that has lost its compass. When education no longer has the faintest idea of what it is about, it becomes fair game for any confidence man who seems to be certain of what he's up to.

The happy ending here is that just the other day the US Supreme Court announced its refusal to hear Churchill's last appeal. Mercifully, the drama of a shameless self-promoter who became America's most famous professor is finally over. Justice has been done, satisfyingly, deliciously, as in this fallen world it almost never is. But the multicultural madness that created him, with its historical and moral relativism is, unfortunately, still in place.

Will Machines
Replace Humanity?

"The world of 2014 will have few routine jobs that cannot be done better by some machine than by any human being. Mankind will therefore have become a race of machine tenders…. Mankind will suffer badly from the disease of boredom, a disease spreading more widely each year and growing in intensity. This will have serious mental, emotional and sociological consequences…. The lucky few who can be involved in creative work of any kind will be the true elite of mankind, for they alone will do more than serve a machine."

This prophecy, penned by science fiction writer Isaac Asimov fifty years ago, will haunt us from now on.

Six years after the Great Recession officially ended, unemployment remains stuck at 5.5 percent, though among 18- to 24-year-olds it is 18 percent. These figures don't include the millions of others who have given up looking for work and the millions more who are stuck in jobs that are part-time or temporary and poorly paid. The New York Federal Reserve Bank reports that about 44 percent of recent college graduates are doing work that that makes no use of a degree. The previous decade was the first since the 1930s in which there was no net job creation. In most of Europe the situation is even worse.

Employment is usually the last thing to recover, so some economists say that jobs will eventually come back in due course. Others say that the current stagnation is structural and that major adjustments to infrastructure will be needed before the jobs will return.

But a third view is gaining traction. This one claim that today's unemployment is due mainly to automation – machines replacing human labor – and that things will get steadily worse as this New Industrial Revolution creates far more disruption than did the previous revolution wrought by steam engines and electricity.

Two MIT professors, Erik Brynjolfsson, and Andrew McAfee, say in their new book, *Race against the Machine,* that while automation expands overall wealth, it also creates losers who may not comprise "some small segment … like buggy whip manufacturers," but, "in principle … a majority or even 90 percent of the population."

Can human labor survive in competition with a technology that advances at an exponential rate?

Consider: According to Moore's Law, Artificial Intelligence doubles in power every 18 to 24 months. So far, this law has held up pretty well. Already, AI beats the sharpest contestants on *Jeopardy!* and outthinks every grandmaster at chess. Software can analyze legal documents far faster and more accurately than a platoon of lawyers and at one-tenth the cost. And robots these days don't just assemble things on production lines, they also play soccer, prowl rugged battlefields, and perform delicate surgery. Soon technology may mimic not only the intelligence of the human brain but even its emotional and moral sensitivity in caring for invalids and the elderly. Extend Moore's Law a few decades hence and ask: Will there be anything left for humans to do?

In 1900 farming employed 40 percent of the US workers. But mechanization and other technological advances have reduced today's employment in agriculture to less than 2 percent of the labor force. Similar histories show up wherever technology gets a foothold. In 1980 22 percent of workers were in the manufacturing sector and today it's just 9 percent – though some of this loss is due to global trade. Automated factories, warehouses and offices today operate efficiently with only a single human tender.

Jobs are disappearing in the services sector too, and even in the arts. We already have driverless cars and pilotless airplanes. Drones may soon deliver packages to our doors. Computers are writing novels and composing music, synthesizers are replacing orchestras, and film makers are able to cast long-dead actors in new roles. Dexterous robots can navigate rugged battlefields and may one day replace human soldiers. Eventually, artificial intelligence will generate scientific theories beyond the comprehension of any human scientist.

The previous industrial revolution, based on steam power and electricity, displaced masses of workers, but in the process, they opened up new jobs in other sectors. The new digital revolution, though, almost certainly won't repeat that history and even if it did, few humans would qualify for them. Despite soothing assurances from many economists that continuous retraining will keep workers abreast of machines, the sophistication of technology grows exponentially while human ability advances hardly at all. And even if humans had inexhaustible intellectual reserves, they would soon be spiritually exhausted by the pressures of unrelenting change. "It is naïve," says Jeremy Rifkin in his book *The End of Work,* "to believe that large numbers of unskilled and skilled workers will be retrained to be physicists, computer scientists, and high-level technicians" in the new knowledge sector.

Many economists have come to agree. Eventually, says Cornell professor Hod Lipson, "all jobs will be gone, including creative ones."

Yes, *all jobs*. Then what?

Plainly, a radical new social contract will have to be fashioned in order to assure economic security for all, one that will bridge the severed connection between income and work. At first, this might include a steady resurrection of New Deal-like programs to maintain infrastructure and beautify public spaces, government support for volunteer work and so on. But eventually, as technology eliminates most, and then all, jobs, the new contract will require a full-blown guaranteed annual income for everyone. Since material wealth will be generated solely by machines, there would be no justification for anything like the extreme income inequality that we have today.

More imponderable is Asimov's point about the spiritual effects of unrelenting leisure, which will impact masses of people who may be unable to find meaning or self-definition in a world that excludes them from work. What will they do with themselves? Will they take up art and good works as utopian thinkers have always said they would? Without careers to prepare for, will they nevertheless continue to learn and to challenge themselves?

Or will the Devil find work for idle hands? Debauchery, war, and troublemaking have always served to relieve boredom. Will statesmen figure out a livable solution of some sort, or will they let things slide until the human race erupts with a backlash of some kind, perhaps another Luddite movement, this time on an apocalyptic scale?

There is surely no principle of nature that says the march of technology must come to an end or even slow its pace. And yet, apart from a few scholars, hardly anyone seems to be taking notice of a crisis unfolding on a global scale that will surely prove the greatest challenge humanity has ever faced. The political class, as always, sticks safely to its quotidian tasks and avoids looking past the horizon.

But it's a specter that demands debate today. Tomorrow may arrive sooner than we expect.

Corruption In
the Oil Patch?

North Dakota has a reputation for honest politics and, therewith, a citizenry that has confidence in its leaders, or at least one that defers to them. But two in-depth reports running 11,000 words, by Deborah Sontag of the *NY Times* (Nov 23-24, 2014), portray an unseemly *modus vivendi* that has apparently developed between members of the oil industry and the state officials who are responsible for regulating it. It's an account of crony capitalism which raises suspicions that state regulatory agencies have been captured by corporate interests.

The oil boom has been accompanied by train derailments, spills, explosions, toxic dumping, tainted water, dead birds, and "development" of scenic and historic places. By virtue of clever contractual arrangements, mineral rights have been leveraged against the owners of surface lands to allow oil companies and the BNSF railroad to run roughshod over farms and ranches virtually without restraint; owners of the mineral rights below simply do what they want. All this has been followed by corporate and government cover-ups and harassment aimed at those who might protest. A Tioga grandmother, whose refrigerator contains jars of blackened tap water that gushed out during the fracking process, tells the *Times* that protests are futile because "we're outnumbered, outgunned, and outsuited."

A good portion of the state's residents are also unsympathetic to the protesters, who are seen as standing in the way of progress. "North Dakotans," says the *Times*, "do not like to make a fuss. Until recently, those few who dared to challenge the brisk pace of oil development, the perceived laxity of government oversight or the despoliation of farmland were treated as killjoys. They were ignored, ridiculed, threatened, and paid settlements in exchange for silence." Many in both the general population and in the state government seem less concerned with protecting people and places than with extracting petroleum at the fastest rate possible.

Citizens have also been denied access to timely information, something which should be a public entitlement. Regulatory agencies commonly meet without announcing either their meeting times or their agendas and then, with no pretense of debate, simply issue decisions as accomplished facts. The North Dakota Industrial Commission, which regulates oil, conducts its monthly meetings with little or no discussion and its decisions are usually unanimous, as if everything were prearranged. Wayne Schafer, a representative of the conservationist Sierra Club, says that "you feel as if the meetings are a performance, that everything's sort of done under the table, with a lot of back-room deals."

Where we find sudden wealth, we should also expect to find corruption. What is most unsettling is the corporate money accepted by state politicians, and especially by officials who are directly responsible for overseeing the petroleum industry. During his 2012 election campaign, Governor Jack Dalrymple received some $550,000 from oil-related executives and PACs representing Exxon Mobil, Marathon Oil, Denbury Resources, and Continental Petroleum, whose CEO, Harold G. Hamm, gave Dalrymple $20,000.

The governor's office refused the *Times'* request for an interview and would not respond to questions about conflicts of interest.

Such questions are especially pertinent to Dalrymple because of his chairmanship of the North Dakota Industrial Commission, which oversees oil production. The governor and his wife also own petroleum shares, including those of Exxon Mobile, which has ongoing business with the Commission. There appears to be no legal requirement that state officials recuse themselves when deciding issues that appear to involve conflicts of interest, and few if any do so voluntarily. This would appear to conflict with a state bribery statute, which makes it a felony for public official to accept "a thing of pecuniary value" from anyone presiding over an imminent or ongoing public action.

And that old revolving door keeps spinning smoothly too: Former governor Ed Schafer, who lobbied for tax reductions for oil companies, was duly appointed to the board of Continental Resources and given a $700,000 share of the company's stocks.

Public-spirited lawyers, injured landowners, and some Democrats (the regulators are predominantly Republicans) have tried to speak out against derelict regulators but to date they have turned up neither an interested public nor a sympathetic judge to hear their cause.

What is most puzzling is that until just now the state's news media have expressed almost no interest in examining these apparent conflicts of interest. Why does a distant east coast newspaper have to break a story about corruption that should have been of consuming interest locally? Perhaps our "North Dakota nice" makes us pushovers when it comes to malfeasance. "We North Dakotans trust our politicians – even when they sell us out," said a seemingly embittered ex-business partner of Dalrymple's.

We're not as clean as we'd like to think. Our regulatory efforts must be accompanied by a clear mission, transparency, and teeth. Should we tolerate a government that has hidden agendas and divided loyalties? If not, maybe we should stop being nice and start asking some tough questions.

Margaret Mary, RIP

Although fashionable academicians embrace scores of non-academic causes in the name of "social justice," proclaim themselves champions of the downtrodden, and wear their idealism on their sleeves, no American institution treats its workers as shabbily as the academy itself. Its callous exploitation of its contingent faculty – "adjuncts" – who now make up 70 percent of US teachers in higher education – is legendary.

At the bottom of the academic caste system, adjuncts are faculty fill-ins who normally work part-time for meager wages with no benefits, no job security, and little chance for advancement; they are lucky even to get office space to meet with their students. They are assigned the largest classes and perform drudgery the senior profs won't touch, and they are generally excluded from participation in departmental affairs, committees, campus governance and the faculty culture in general. Despite their majority status, they have virtually no influence in campus affairs, and they are commonly ignored, often pointedly so, by their more aristocratic colleagues.

Administrators like adjuncts because they are cheap, and they permit curricular flexibility. They are easily procured from local sources (even from day labor agencies – seriously!) and the throngs of underemployed people with advanced degrees will assure that many will fit whatever specialties the campuses may wish to fill. Better still, the campuses have no obligations toward them, so that the instant they cease to be useful they can be unceremoniously disposed of. It's like throwing out the leftovers after dinner.

And for their part, adjuncts tend to accept their lot because the higher education bubble that began in the late 1960s has flooded the country with so many college graduates that even graduate degrees have lost their purchasing power. At the moment, some 115,000 people with baccalaureate degrees are working as janitors and another 323,000 are working as waiters. Hundreds of thousands more have settled into careers as bartenders, truck drivers and other blue-collar jobs. According to the Berkeley Center for Labor Studies, 22 percent of the part-time college faculty falls below the poverty line.

That same bubble also created a proletarian army of wannabe professors with advanced degrees who are afflicted by foot-in-the-door syndrome – the delusion that if they hang around long enough in some wretched academic niche, their on-the-scene visibility will give them an edge should a full-time job one day open up. That seldom happens, but the prospect of an academic career is so enticing that even the smallest hope goes a very long way. Anyway, even an adjunct's thankless routine may beat pushing a broom.

The recent tragedy of Margaret Mary Votjko illustrates how utterly surreal the situation is. Votjko was an adjunct at Duquesne University where she taught French (she was fluent in five languages besides English) and died penniless at the age of 83, after 25 years of service. Her salary ranged from $2,556 to $3,500 per semester course and in her final year she earned a grand total of $10,000. Burdened with costly treatments for cancer, she was unceremoniously terminated with no pension and no severance pay. When she died, she was buried in a cardboard box.

What did Duquesne do to ease her hardships? When friends described her plight and appealed for help, the university referred them to local social service agencies.

Though Duquesne charged students $31,385 per year in tuition and paid its president a salary of $675, 471, it defended its treatment of adjuncts by saying it had to pinch pennies. When asked about its shabby treatment of Votjko in particular, Duquesne's provost replied that every university treats its adjuncts in much the same way: "My response to all the frenetic email and blogging traffic," a spokesman said, "is that I find it a little puzzling that it is being directed toward one institution, as if somehow other institutions were not confronting exactly the same issue." In other words, if every school exploits the bejeezus out of its adjuncts, it must be okay.

Though many outside of academic life were shocked that this could happen to a university professor, poverty among adjuncts is so commonplace that in higher education it has come to seem normal. According to the American Association of University Professors, the average salary for a full professor in 2012 was $123,000, while for adjuncts it was just $16,200 for those lucky enough to teach full time. In that same year, according to ABC News, 33,665 holders of Ph.D.s and 293,029holders of master's degrees were on welfare. In 2015 the University of California-Berkeley Center for Labor Research reported that 25 percent of part-time faculty members nationwide were receiving at least one form of public assistance.

Invariably, the campuses claim that they haven't the money to support a full-time professional faculty. But money isn't really scarce. It's just that much of it goes into higher priorities such as sports palaces and athletic circuses, gyms with Olympic-sized swimming pools and indoor climbing walls, sumptuous student centers, spacious student apartments in place of yesteryear's monastic dorms, coaches who get multi-million-dollar salaries, and star professors who never teach.

Since 1975, the real cost of campus administration has tripled. Professor Benjamin Ginsberg of Johns Hopkins finds that the numbers of students and professors have both increased by 51 percent while the number of administrators has increased by 85 percent. Members of lower support staffs – "deanlets" and "deanlings" – have risen by an incredible 240 percent. Today, the campuses have more bureaucrats than full-time professors. What most of these people do is anyone's guess.

And research being cooler than teaching, money goes heavily into labs and technology and redundant research projects. Where is the rinky-dink community college that doesn't have a nano research laboratory? Most of this is intended not to fortify the school's educational capacity but merely to burnish institutional status, which may impress donors and local boosters.

You may say that if adjuncts are exploited, it's their own choice. But apart from the injustice of their treatment, a faculty of part-timers and temporaries diminishes the entire educational enterprise. While many adjuncts are outstanding teachers, most don't have terminal degrees, and the haphazard nature of their employment disrupts both their professional development and the careers of students who depend on them.

Adjuncts are often indispensable as pinch-hitters in providing short-term continuity and curricular flexibility. But a faculty heavily dominated by transient, low-status outsiders who have no influence over the institutions in which they serve and who are kept in a state of permanent amateurism, is simply incapable of providing students the quality of education to which they are entitled.

The faculty is the soul of the university, yet it is being systematically degraded everywhere. It would be good if higher education could finally abandon its obsession with its frills, its causes, fashions, and status-seeking, and return to the proven traditions of education. There could be no more productive way to invest campus resources than in restoring professionalism to the faculty. And it would be refreshing if academicians would put an end to nauseating pretenses of moral superiority, which as the Votjko case demonstrates, is an outrageous hypocrisy.

The Injustice of
Racial Preferences

Affirmative Action began in 1964 as a temporary program intended to increase the presence of people who, in higher education and elsewhere, are members of ethnic groups thought to be underrepresented in colleges and workplaces due to histories of discrimination. Its purpose was unabashedly egalitarian: "We seek equality not just as a right and a theory," President Lyndon Johnson said, "but equality as a fact and result." On the campuses, a priority was to build a "critical mass" of each minority group, meaning numbers large enough to make everyone feel at home; and to speed things up, racial quotas would be employed in creating a student body until a level playing field was secured for all.

But in an early challenge to affirmative action, *Bakke v California* (1978) the US Supreme Court ruled that overt quotas for racial minorities violated the14[th] Amendment's equal protection clause. The universities responded with inventive new admissions practices that conformed to the letter of the law if not always to its spirit, for example, with "holistic" recruiting strategies that targeted related factors like poverty, personal histories, and neighborhoods which might serve as tip-offs to the applicants' race.

In *Grutter v Bollinger* (2003) the Court further narrowed the use of race when it forbade the University of Michigan's law school from adding points to minority applications. But because society had (in the Court's view) a "compelling interest" in the "benefits that flow from a diverse society," the school was allowed to continue its consideration of race, though only as one factor among others.

On the same day the Court ruled (in *Gratz v Bollinger*) that race could not be the decisive factor in undergraduate admissions. In short, it's okay to use race so long as it is indirect.

Texas finessed the racial quota problem by guaranteeing that all students finishing in the top tenth of their high school class, anywhere in the state, would be admitted to any state-supported university of their choice. Those missing the cut, however, might get reconsideration in a backup holistic pool where other factors would be considered, though race would not be excluded.

Abigail Fisher, who is white, just missed the cut and was refused admission to the University of Texas at Austin. She sued, claiming that race was unconstitutionally applied against her in the holistic pool, where she had outscored minority students who had succeeded in gaining admission. Her case was heard by a federal district court and then a circuit court, both of which ruled against her.

In hearing her case, the US Supreme Court made no decision on the propriety of using race in a holistic context, but simply remanded Fisher's case to the Fifth Circuit Court on the grounds that it had failed to apply "strict scrutiny" to a matter involving the sensitive issue of race. The Fifth Circuit Court then split 2-1 in favor of the University of Texas, affirming its original decision on the grounds that "it is ... settled that universities may use race as part of a holistic admission program where it cannot otherwise achieve diversity." Fisher then sought an *en banc* hearing from the full 15-member court, but she was denied by a vote of ten to five.

These precedents have greatly narrowed the use of racial preferences as a remedy for past racial inequities. The chief remaining issue the courts face now is: Will race-conscious admission policies create a diversity of backgrounds that will be conducive to students learning from each other?

At this writing, Fisher has been granted a new hearing by The Supreme Court, which has already heard oral arguments on the forthcoming case. The Court is scheduled to render its decision in the summer of 2016. When it does, it could put a final end to litigation on the issue of racial preferences. In the meantime, it seems likely that, barring a change in the Court's membership, affirmative action, assuming that it survives at all, will survive in a much-diminished form since its inception in 1964. Sentiment in the federal courts is clearly one of increasing skepticism about the efficacy of racial preferences in affecting social reform.

One problem is that some research since *Grutter* has cast doubt upon whether there really a "compelling interest" in is promoting diversity. Some surveys have reported that most minority students say they already feel welcome on the campuses, even short of a supposed "critical mass" to comfort them, thanks.

Another problem is that even when racial diversity is firmly established on the campuses, the results are not necessarily what its supporters have hoped for. Since racial preferences apply only to selective colleges, blacks and Hispanic enrollments enabled by preferences are small, Numbering between 10,000 and 15,000 each year. This, sociologist Thomas Espenshade says, is only "about 1 percent of the entering freshman class nationwide and just 1 percent of all black and Hispanic 18-year-olds." This means that diversity's impact upon the national culture is likely to add up to something less than a compelling national interest.

Ethnic diversity is also supposed to improve academic achievement for everyone, though it seems not to do so. Espenshade says that in elite schools' half of all blacks and a third of Hispanics graduate in the bottom 20 percent of their classes. Further, the public aim of ethnic assimilation is being undercut by students who practice private segregation. Only half of students reported having a roommate or a close friend of a different race during their college years.

Preferences are losing favor among voters too. Against fierce establishment opposition, voters in large several states (including Michigan after the *Gutter* decision) have passed initiatives outlawing racial preferences; the list otherwise includes California, Washington, Nebraska, Arizona, Oklahoma, Florida, and New Hampshire, whose combined populations comprise over a quarter of the US population. A 2013 Rasmussen poll found that only 14 percent of respondents nationwide favor using race as an admissions factor, that 55 percent oppose it, with the rest undecided.

Most of those who oppose preferences do so on grounds of fairness. Is it morally right to block one person's ambitions in order to boost those of another person whose only claim to advancement is an acceptable skin color? Before Michiganders outlawed preferences, blacks and Hispanics applying to the University of Michigan with SAT scores of 1240 had a 90 percent change of admission, while whites and Asians with the same score had only a ten percent chance.

Previous research by Espenshade found that to have an equal chance of getting into elite colleges, Asians must outscore blacks on the SATs by 450 points and whites must exceed blacks by 150 points.

Although in the elite universities Asians and Jews are Already represented in proportions far out of their numbers in the general population, they are still, more than any other group, held down by glass ceilings which in effect punish them for being members of out-of-favor ethnic groups.

This, it seems to me, is the fatal flaw in the case for affirmative action. Spin it as you will, racial preferences are contrary to the American tradition. In whichever direction they apply, and whichever constituency they are intended to benefit, they are simply unjust.

Whatever the Supreme Court decides, it may be an anti-climax because even now what survives of affirmative action is likely to be too weak to inspire passion among either its supporters or its opponents. What began as a heroic effort to further social equality has been boiled down to something more like a tempest in a teapot.

Professor Espenshade, writing in the *New York Times*, says that affirmative action "treats the symptoms but not the root causes of an underlying social problem." Some other means, he says, such as early childhood education, peer-to-peer mentoring, looking into sleep routines and other interventions may do more good for low-income families trying to encourage learning among disadvantaged children.

Do College Graduates Make More Money?

Each year the American Council on Education asks freshmen why they are in college and consistently the top answers are, "to get a better job" and "to make more money." We drill it into them: In the "new economy" (whatever that is) everyone, like it or not, *must* go to college; those with degrees will have fulfilling, lucrative careers, while those who don't will wind up in an underclass consigned to day labor and sweeping the streets.

As you would expect, the campuses are not about to contradict this college-or-the gutter fatalism because most of them were dangerously overextended in the bonanza 'sixties and 'seventies and now they are desperately trying to avoid empty dorms. Limiting admissions to serious students is not an option; why, historic Antioch College went belly up just the other day.

Now it is certainly true that college grads earn more than high school grads, currently estimated to be 62 percent more over a lifetime. But many skeptics warn that the economic advantages of a degree have been oversold and that for many students, perhaps most, college is a poor investment.

Here's why:

First, incomes of college graduates reflect several factors besides the fact of a diploma. These include parental education and income (with their attendant social connections and ability to offer financial help), and also personal traits like verbal skills, intelligence, and the persistence needed to endure several years of study. What students take out of college often matters less than what they bring to it. According to Edwin Rubinstein of the Hudson Institute, studies controlling for these factors indicate that the value of college itself accounts for only about 15 percent of the high school-college income gap. When higher education's boosters attribute the income gap solely to the possession of college-earned skills they are giving the rooster credit for the dawn.

Mostly, what college does is to screen for personal strengths. Harvard graduates command high salaries not because they've had four years of superior instruction, but because just getting into a highly selective school tells employers they have unusual ability. High scores on standardized tests like the SAT and the IQ tests do the same thing. Talented people tend to do well with or without college; for them, actually getting a degree is often nothing more than icing on the cake.

Second, a college degree has very high opportunity costs. The time you spend in college is time you *won't* spend gaining work experience and earning money. Over 4 or 5 years, how much would that come to? The tuition you spend might have more productive uses elsewhere too. At Harvard, tuition is about $160,000 over 4 years: Put that sum into municipal bonds at 5 percent, and in 30 years you'd have over $500,000 – more than the average college grad accumulates in the same time.

Third, many degrees are in oversupply and will never pay off. The *Current Population Survey* reports that 20 percent of college grads hold jobs that anyone could do. Right now, 80,000 college grads people are working as bartenders, 19,000 as parking lot attendants, and 300,000 as waiters and waitresses. Anne Mathews, in her book *Bright College Years,* notes that in Washington, D.C. a third of Domino's Pizza deliverers have college degrees. The glut is partially disguised by a "credential inflation" in which employers tack on irrelevant requirements for unskilled jobs just because they know they can get them. Mathews tellingly cites an ad for a warehouse-supervisor job at The Gap: "Bachelor's Degree required, and the ability to lift fifty pounds."

It shouldn't be surprising, therefore, that most college incomes have been flat for decades. The *New York Times* reports that while women's earnings have risen marginally, those of "male college graduates have failed to keep pace with economy-wide gains in productivity." Gains also go disproportionately to the top of the income scale, where just 1 percent of Americans receive 22 percent of all income. A few super-earners distort the high school-college gap by pulling up the average income for all degreed people. Average out Bill Gates' wealth and mine and I am worth $20 billion.

Ultimately, what that celebrated 62-point gap shows is not that college graduates are doing well but that, as economist Robert Samuelson has put it, "high school graduates are doing miserably." Over the 1980s, for example, real college earnings rose an anemic 4 percent, while earnings for high school grads *fell* a disastrous 14 percent. As high school grads must now share unskilled jobs with college grads, their wages fall still further, and they become stigmatized as unfit even for simple work. Amazingly, this is said to clinch the argument that the declining fortunes of high school graduates is due to their lack of a college degree, so that the remedy for a degree glut is - more degrees! We have rigged society so that the young are railroaded into years of college and indebtedness just to have a shot at an ordinary job.

But decent jobs don't necessarily require a college degree. Most can be mastered with on-the-job learning, on-line schooling, vocational school, military training, and other traditional means. Skilled tradesmen such as plumbers, electricians, pipe fitters and elevator repairmen earn as much as most people with recent college degrees. Ignore the uninformed snobs who think blue collar work is demeaning – it isn't; and there are satisfactions in manual labor that are not to be had by staring at a monitor.

Should you go to college? If you are bright and ideas turn you on -absolutely! Take up history, literature, philosophy, or some major that is worth pursuing for its own sake and let the economic chips fall where they may. But if all you want is a job, don't let the myth-mongers scare you into wasting years of your life.

Charlie Hebdo and the West's Loss of Confidence

London's radical cleric Anjem Chaudary justified the January attacks on the Charlie Hebdo cartoonists in Paris with these words: "If freedom of expression can be sacrificed for criminalizing incitement and hatred, why not for insulting Allah or the Prophet?" He was referring to those ubiquitous hate speech laws which even "enlightened" European countries use to intimidate journalists and bloggers whose reportage might possibly be offensive to someone. Even Canada has them. On American college campuses too, you damn well better watch your mouth. Chaudary finds this hypocritical, and he's right: If Westerners don't value their own traditions of free speech, why should jihadists? What's sauce for the goose, you know....

So, let's not lay all the blame for the Paris massacre on the Islamic terrorists, because they've had plenty of moral support from Western countries, or at least from elites who appear to be contemptuous of the publics they lead and, one suspects, of themselves as well. The terrorists' "war against civilization," says journalist Andrew McCarthy, "has essential support: Islamist leaders who vow to conquer us, and Western leaders who don't think we are worth defending."

Credit this to a form of self-hatred known as multiculturalism. Its mission, as Samuel Huntington says in his book, *Who Are We?,* is to "weaken (Western) cultural and creedal identity" while strengthening different "racial, ethnic, cultural and other subnational identities." Multiculturalism teaches Westerners to romanticize Third World cultures, no matter how miserable, and to despise their own; and it says something terrifying about the power of ideas that the West's repudiation of its own core values like free speech, national unity, and patriotism – painfully won over the course of millennia – should have been accomplished within a period of a single generation. Naturally, the West's loss of self-confidence has not gone unnoticed by its enemies.

The impresarios of multiculturalism are mostly denationalized elites in business, government, the media, and the universities. There is in most developed countries a growing gulf between these elites and the national majorities who reject the elitist worldview, especially its enthusiasm for masses of immigrants who resist assimilation and threaten national identity.

In America, the elites in Congress, journalism, academia, and major interest groups polled by the Center for Immigration studies found that 60 percent favored increased immigration, while only 14 percent of the general public did. Elite-mass sentiment in Europe, especially in its northern regions, shows similar proportions. This divergence has led to the rise of extremist parties in several European countries and speculation about an impending culture war. If Europe's leaders won't defend their own nations' cultural identity, then perhaps the neo-Nazis will.

Why is there a gap between elites and masses? The simplest explanation is that elites, who are better educated and more experienced than the masses they govern, believe themselves to be better qualified to judge cultural questions than are the masses. The ruling classes could do *brilliant* things … but the talents of this would-be aristocracy are thwarted when their powers are limited by a divided mass public. How does it get its revenge? Easy: Import Third World immigrants who, by their refusal to assimilate, will cause the host cultures endless trouble.

If Western governments are too confused to face down their enemies, maybe private citizens and non-governmental organizations can do something. For their part, the surviving satirists at Charlie Hebdo responded to the attack on them with a resolute resumption of defiance. Their first post-attack edition, with *another* cartoon of the Prophet on the cover, sold 5 million copies.

But maybe they could use some help.

Every September 30th an organization called the "Center for Inquiry" sponsors an event known as "Blasphemy Day," which marks the day in 2009 when a cartoon displeasing to Islamists led to the bombing of a Danish embassy and riots that led to over 100 deaths. The Center is a network of skeptics (well, okay – atheists) that strives to challenge taboos against religious criticism and to repeal hate speech laws with satire, ridicule, and other means that are not necessarily in good taste.

Today the event has celebrants around the world. Its purpose is to be militantly offensive – to force the public's attention with abrasive criticism and to make religion and religion-sponsored suppression of speech, subject to normal debate like any other topic. "There is no human right not to be offended," they rightly say.

What if this idea went global? What if newspapers, magazines, and social media all over the world agreed to publish satirical cartoons and criticism of religious zealotry all on the same day, and to do so periodically? This would be a collective middle finger upraised against terrorists, who might then reconsider whether their target populations really are guilt-ridden pushovers after all. With many participants acting in concert, terrorists would have no unique targets for retaliation.

The best way to legitimize blasphemous speech is to normalize it. Iterated often enough, blasphemy might persuade even the fanatics – and our own Western thought police – that criticism of everything is permissible and is here to stay.

For decades, Europe's leaders have flaunted their superior "tolerance" by encouraging the immigration of cultures whose worldviews are incompatible with those of the host country, as if tolerance were the highest of all possible values, higher than national unity, security, and human rights. But now that extremist right-wing parties are threatening their rule, the Left's chickens are coming home to roost. Will the diversity-mongers admit error?

No, never. They are either blind to the social problems they have created, or else they positively welcome them.

Computers Don't Improve
Student Performance

North Dakota has $12 million in surplus educational funds and a debate is brewing about what to do with it. The North Dakota Education Association wants the bulk of it for a teacher's bonus - *surprise!* - and some legislators want it turned over to the school districts for whatever they may choose to do with it. The governor, however, wants to earmark most of it for "technology" (read: computers). The first two proposals are probably harmless. The third isn't. Spending more money on computers will only compound the miseducation of our kids.

I know, I know - this is blasphemy of the worst sort. For years we have heard the most beautiful claims about how computers are about to revolutionize education - how a blizzard of raw data from the information superhighway will trigger quantum leaps in student achievement, release an explosion of creative talent, make life-long scholars out of kids who don't even read newspapers, and so on. And these claims have come from the most authoritative sources in government, business, and, of course, the teacher-training colleges.

Nevertheless, these claims have no basis in fact. Not only are computers not turning kids into Einsteins, but a growing body of research shows no real evidence that they boost student achievement *at all*.

They may even lower it. In a summary of the research published in *Atlantic Monthly*, Todd Oppenheimer finds that the contorted world of computer imagery thwarts the developing child's need for physical and social experience, stunts the imagination, dulls causality (the sense of being able to affect changes in the physical world), and blurs the distinctions between canned images and reality. Teachers complain of passive students who can't deal with open-ended questions, can't see relationships between ideas and can't even establish rapport with their peers. Oppenheimer sums up computerized schooling as "educational malpractice."

But technology is revolutionizing the schools, no doubt about it. As students take up computers, they stop reading books. Teachers, who once molded intellect and character, are being demoted to "facilitators" - pathetic, cardboard figures who render advice on student-driven projects and otherwise stay meekly on the sidelines. And resources once devoted to teacher salaries or building repairs are now thrown into the technology chase as if nothing else mattered.

But computers have had no greater impact than on the way we think of education itself. Costly and prestigious, they have acquired more gravity than the subject matter they are supposed to serve. And for good reason. The schools can hardly spend millions on computers and then put them in the closet along with the microscopes and dissection kits, pending some future opportunity for their use; no, at that price they must be used to their full value, which is to say constantly and conspicuously. New uses will have to be invented for them, and the traditional curriculum, which doesn't cost nearly as much, and isn't flashy at all, will have to give way.

Thus, schools across the country are dropping subjects like music and art in order to make room for more computer labs. And a widely-cited poll by Public Agenda shows teachers and the general public in agreement, by an appalling 3-to-1 ratio, that it is more important to teach "computer skills and media technology" than the works of classic writers like Plato and Shakespeare, Hemingway, and Steinbeck. If anything is more anti-education than that, I can't imagine what it is.

And that's why it's so sad that North Dakota Governor Ed Schafer and so many others are still beguiled by the computer mystique. Policymakers never, never mandate funds for a traditional liberal education, but only for things that serve to compromise it.

But okay. If money must be spent on prestigious "technology," then I propose some benign sabotage - a sabotage of the sabotage, if you will. What if we stopped pretending that "technology" means "computers" and little else? What if we spent those mandated funds on technologies that really are educational?

At the Smithsonian Institution, one of the most interesting exhibits is Foucault's Pendulum, a massive blade which descends from the ceiling and sweeps over the floor to topple a circle of blocks in a dramatic representation of the earth's rotation on its axis. It always has a crowd sitting by it in silent fascination. Why not put one into a school? It's technology, after all, and it's so visually impressive that it might inspire lots of kids to take an interest in science. It would surely become a community attraction as well.

Or why not an aviary, an aquarium, or a garden of exotic plants to kindle an interest in the life sciences? Or a working model showing the principles and possibilities of solar power? Or a scale model illustrating an important principle of architecture and structural engineering? Or a planetarium? Or a replica of a landmark experiment like the Michelson-Morley measurement of the velocity of light, or one of those bizarre experiments in quantum physics?

Why not a historical display of technology itself, depicting man's earliest tools, metallurgy, hieroglyphs, telescopes, compasses, calculators, engines and a hundred other devices which represent milestones in the history of discovery and tangibly bring home a key principle of science?

The point is, we don't have to make a mad dash to the computer shop every time we hear that hackneyed phrase about bringing technology into the classroom. Technology has its rightful place but it's stupid to reduce it all to computers or insist that the entire curriculum must be revamped in order to accommodate it to computers.

The schools are under attack by techno-mystics who believe liberal education to be excess baggage for the coming "new age" - though they never seem able to explain why – and by an educational establishment uncontrollably addicted to fads. But teaching Plato and Shakespeare is a timelessly good idea. Silicon snake oil is not.

The Great Ph.D. Swindle

In the year 1900, about 500 Ph.D. degrees were awarded in the United States. Last year 55,000 were. Nearly two million Americans have doctorates, about 2 per cent of the entire workforce. Our small state offers them in over 60 fields and students are flying into them like moths to a flame. President Charles Kupchella of the University of North Dakota thinks we might offer 50 more. And why not? Since we're already tossing out Ph.D.s like Tootsie Rolls, why not 500?

The teaching market, of, course, crashed over 40 years ago, and ever since then tens of thousands of Ph.D.s have scratched out a living in "temporary" blue collar and clerical jobs because the professional class careers they expected to have are hopelessly glutted.

So, what, apart from an Orwellian sadism, accounts for the universities' zeal for dangling still more doctoral programs? Plain old self-interest. Though they profit from the cheap labor of graduate students, their main concern is with their image and with how the public perceives and rewards them. As with other public agencies, universities are expected to carry out their mission effectively; yet when they have programs in flying airplanes, horse racing, and processing beef (as our state's universities do), you have to wonder: Just what is their mission? The sad truth is that we no longer have a consensus on the meaning of education. So how do they show that they are performing effectively? Why, by growing. Getting bigger.

As education descends into formlessness, sheer, physical growth has, by default, come to define its mission and to serve as its standard of performance. Even the best administrators know that it is solid, provable expansion, not the unmeasurable vagaries of student achievement, by which their own performance will be judged.

Are students better versed in history, literature, and math than ever before? Who knows. Are more of them turned on to an enthusiasm for poetry? That's hard to say. Well then, are the campuses growing? Absolutely! Enrollments are up five percent from last year and we have the numbers to prove it!

It is within this context that the president of North Dakota State University appears to understand his mandate. In a newspaper op-ed piece he recalls how, newly installed, he intuitited the campus' "tremendous potential for growth." He then recounts a heroic record of subsequent growth in enrollments, construction, research expenditures, campus payrolls, Carnegie rankings, and so on. Believing passionately in the universities' duty to serve as instruments of state policy, he also extols his campus' "entrepreneurial spirit" in attracting industry, creating new jobs, and boosting the local population. So much for the ancient ideal of scholarly independence.

The point at hand is that a comprehensive strategy of growth should include scads of new Ph.D. programs whether there is a genuine need for them or not. Can they stand on their own feet? Clearly, NDSU's president doesn't think so. For while he claims a "proven demand' for them, he stops short of claiming that this demand reflects a *public* need for the services of more Ph.D.s. That is the usual meaning of "demand," but being a clever man, he knows that such a claim would be preposterous. So, read him closely and you'll find that "demand" refers instead to the *personal* desires of students who, for God knows what reasons, might like to have a Ph.D. diploma to hang on the wall.

So, by sleight of hand, private wants and public needs are equated and are said to lay equal claim to the public purse. In this agnostic age, a demand is a demand.

But that too is preposterous. With no roots in any sort of public need, these degrees become mere ornaments and status symbols; the universities may as well turn up students who "need" Rolex watches and then inform the public of its duty to pay for them.

In short, the Ph.D. industry rests upon a hoax. What is to be done? The "obvious thing' as Jordan Ellenberg observes in *The Great Ph.D. Scam)*, is simply to shut it down. It's madness and the legislature ought to put an end to it.

Forget the growth psychosis that plagues the local culture. Forget the tempest over how the two major universities might divvy up the next batch of Mickey Mouse Ph.D. programs. Forget local chauvinism and our place in the nation's academic status race too. When the country is crawling with half-starved Ph.D.s. the question must be not how many more doctoral programs does the state need, but: Does it need any such programs *at all?*

If it does, then damned few. The test should be whether the state has a genuine need for more expertise in some particular field, and if so, whether it is cheaper to home grow it or buy it elsewhere. With mobs of Ivy Leaguers beating a path to our doors looking for any kind of work in academia, it makes about as much sense for us to grow our own Ph.D.s as it does for Harvard to grow its own wheat.

Is the Republican
Party Finished?

Republicans have lost the popular vote in five of the last six presidential elections and their hold on Congress owes much to House gerrymandering and the overrepresentation of senators from small red states. A swath of states from Florida through California, once securely red, is turning purple, leaving the GOP at risk of becoming a minor party centered in the plains states.

The GOP's greatest problem is demographics. California, which until recently had a sharply competitive 2 party system, is now an invincible one-party state in which Democrats hold supermajorities in both houses of the legislature and a monopoly on all statewide offices. California, Texas, Nevada, and Hawaii are already majority-minority states with 7 more expected within 15 years. According to the American Enterprise Institute, the white population, which was 80 percent in 1980, is now 63 percent and by 2060 will fall below 44 percent.

The upshot is that the GOP – supposedly the party of small government – now faces growing blocs of voters who love big government. Hispanics for instance: Ronald Reagan famously said that Hispanics are "natural Republicans – they just don't know it yet." Against the facts, some Republicans still see Hispanics as latent Republicans, in part because emigrating to a strange land shows an entrepreneurial spirit, especially if it's illegal.

But in 2012 Hispanics voted 71 percent Democratic. Why? Well, most are poorer and less educated than the indigenous population, and disadvantaged people tend to prefer a generous government over a frugal one. Also, a priority for many Hispanics is family reunification, and most Republicans lack enthusiasm for importing millions of additional Democrats. As it is, the Hispanic population is growing 4 times faster than the general public and by 2050 they will form nearly one-third of the US population.

Single women, another rapidly growing group, aren't starry-eyed about small government either. Though in 2012 married women voted 53 percent for Romney, singles voted 67 – 31 for Obama. They too are disproportionately low-income and concerned about economic security and health care, especially if they have kids. "Women without husbands," the *New Republic* recently observed, "decide elections." It used to be said that a diamond is a girl's best friend. Today the welfare state is.

Asians are America's fastest-growing ethnic group. Educationally and financially, they are also its most successful, and if anyone qualifies as "natural Republicans," it should be they. But the Asian vote is, well, inscrutable. Once strongly GOP, it has swung sharply leftward; in 1992 Bill Clinton received just 31 percent of the Asian vote, but in 2012 it went 73 percent for Obama. Asians currently favor (55 to 36 percent) more government services, and they also claim to be repelled by the GOP's image of being religious, anti-intellectual, and racially insensitive.

And if the GOP needed still more bad news, a recent Pew Trust survey says that "millennials" (aged 18-33) are indifferent to cultural issues like religion and marriage and, unlike previous generations, they become more liberal as they age. Most support expanded government services. In 2012, they voted just 37 percent GOP.

Can the GOP win back a majority without losing its soul – by defending limited government and not pandering to identity politics?

Maybe. A GOP faction called "Reformicons" believes the party can appeal to low-income and middle-class voters with ideas that don't require a Leviathan government. In the 1960s and 1970s, for instance, the GOP introduced such ideas as a guaranteed annual income, revenue sharing, block grants to states, and expanded child tax credits to streamline the welfare system and reduce bureaucracy.

Nor are minority voting patterns immutable. A key factor in elections is candidate likeability. In 2012, avuncular Chris Christie won reelection in Democratic New Jersey with 51 percent of the Hispanic vote, 21 percent of blacks, and 57 percent of women, all far surpassing Romney's vote in the same state.

The GOP might also court millennials through greater use of internet social media, which attracts them more than TV ads. The GOP also needs to shed its image of Tea-party anti-intellectualism and recapture a respect for new ideas and experimentation.

That said, the GOP still faces long odds and probably will for a long time. Nationally, we may see a generation or more of uninterrupted Democratic dominance, at least in the presidency. As immigration continues to bring in impoverished people from Third World cultures, and as domestic illegitimacy rates rise, it may well be that traditional American conservatism will simply become extinct.

Why Sports Do Not Belong
in Higher Education

The University of North Dakota's president, Charles Kupchella, was just kidding - wasn't he? - when he told Ralph Engelstad, the angel of UND's $100 million hockey arena, that "my job is to make certain the hockey team has a university it can be proud of." After all, the remark was ominously close to one made long ago, by a president of the University of Oklahoma who said, *without* kidding, that he hoped to develop a university of which the football team could be proud.

Kidding or not, such remarks affirm the lopsided presence of sports in higher education. And it's a presence that nearly everyone finds agreeable, especially when it's housed in magnificent structures financed by generous donors. The *Forum,* infallibly boosterish, even gushes that the "arena's spill-over effect will strengthen the university's academic programs in ways we can't imagine." But in truth, the effects of such programs are quite predictable, and they are seldom benign.

That's because, as Robert M. Hutchins once observed, in higher education as elsewhere, the love of money is the root of all evil. To attract money, universities must please non-academic audiences, and that usually means compromising the integrity of academic standards, and even of their traditional mission. Money received in lumps for pet projects often creates centrifugal forces that weaken the unity of purpose that a university must have. "Few restricted gifts," Hutchins noted, meaning gifts that are spent only on the donor's intentions, "have ever been given to a university that paid the expense of receiving them."

And few gifts exact a higher price than those devoted to sports. That is a point forcefully made by former Assistant Secretary of Education Chester Finn, Jr., who, in *Commentary*, examines a spate of surveys on the college sports industry and its insatiable appetite for more resources. Indeed, the professional mourners for underfunded colleges may find comfort in the fact that construction costs for sports stadiums are now soaring along at $4 billion annually. They may be reassured as well by coaching salaries that commonly exceed those of university presidents and even state governors. At last count, some 30 coaches around the country were drawing annual salaries of $1 million or more and some go as high as $12 million.

The annual cost of a football team frequently exceeds $100,000 per player. At Vanderbilt athletic programs cost out at $4,000 for every student enrolled, money that (as its president has noted) is not going into teaching and research. Chester Finn describes sports and recreational facilities at Arizona State as "lavish" while its library, located in an underground cavern, is "a dark forbidding place."

But despite the riches lavished upon them in the form of athletic scholarships, remediation, endless tutoring, and bogus courses like "Philosophy of Storing Badminton Supplies 301," the jocks don't do nearly as well academically as their relatively impoverished classmates. Barely half of football players graduate within six years, and only 40 percent of basketball players do. Women may fare even worse. Title IX, which demands equal athletic opportunities with men, has tilted recruitment from academically talented women to those with athletic prowess. The result is that female athletes score 60 points lower in SATs than their non-athletic sisters. Where sports assume higher importance, as in Division 1-A universities, the deficit is nearly 100 points.

Worse, the prestige accorded to sports legitimizes a false idea of what is important in higher education. It should not be surprising that male students spend far more time watching televised sports and engaging in athletic activities than they do in homework and in reading for pleasure; or that college-bound kids have distorted ideas of what they are supposed to do once they get there. "Why," Chester Finn asks, "should any student conceive of his college experience as being primarily about learning?"

Off-campus too, the sports mystique - "beer and circuses"- masks sloppy academic standards and confusion about the purpose of college. Why worry that the university is degenerating into a trade school, so long as the football team is doing well?

Now don't get me wrong. I'm not a sour puritan, a spoil sport, an ingrate. It's just that our perennial visions of limitless benefits flowing from sports palaces aren't supported by the evidence. I truly appreciate Ralph Engelstad's generosity, and I'll even concede that he could have spent it on projects of a far more destructive nature. Imagine the horrors that might have ensued had that $100 million wound up, say, in the School of Education, or in Multicultural Studies.

But the central point remains, which is that feeding the sports industry does nothing to nourish higher education. It merely crowds out resources and reverses the relationship between sports and learning. A. Bart Giammatti, former president of Yale, has said that "What was allowed to become a circus – college sports – threatens to become the means by which the public believes the entire enterprise [higher education] is a sideshow."

Scholarship and sports are utterly unrelated. The real question is not why the sports industry has so large a presence in higher education, but why it should have any presence there at all.

A Forgotten Crisis

On the first Earth Day in 1970, America's population had just passed 200 million, an event that greatly alarmed environmentalists who believed that nothing so seriously threatened the country, and the planet, as too many people. It was widely feared that the current level was not sustainable and that both the natural world and the social order would be irreversibly damaged if it were not reduced. The mood was one of crisis and radical ideas were flying about.

Kenneth Boulding, a must-read economist at the time, opined that America's optimal population was somewhere between 50 million and 100 million. Biologist Paul Ehrlich's doomsday book, *The Population Bomb,* was a national sensation, and dystopian films like "Soylent Green" portrayed a world of a standing-room-only population crush that necessitated cannibalism. Memberships in organizations like Zero Population Growth and Negative Population Growth were growing explosively. And at the time it was noted that half of America's population growth came from immigration.

Today our population is 320 million. The Pew Research Center projects 438 million by 2050, with 82 percent of the increase coming from immigration. At that rate, we will reach 438 million by 2050 – just about what India's population was in 1975.

Yet hardly anyone now talks about overpopulation. The subject appears to have become taboo for polite people. And environmentalism has been decoupled from demographics, that is, immigration and ethnic birthrates. What has happened?

Well, much of the doomsaying of the 1970s was oversold. In the U.S., at least, the gloomiest prophecies haven't materialized – so far – and some threats, such as acid rain and the decline of certain endangered animal species, have even been reversed.

But political realities have also changed. Because most of today's population increase is due to immigration, complaints about the evils of overpopulation may seem to imply racial hostility toward immigrants, most of whom have been Hispanics and Asians. The newly arrived have been historically defensive about their place in the culture; and since the foreign-born are now 14 percent of the US population and can easily swing elections, political elites may deem it prudent to avoid talking about overpopulation.

But more broadly, public debate on anything touching upon ethnicity raises suspicions of racism. Though liberals have been in the forefront of the environmental movement, they, like everyone else, are cowed into silence from the terror that multiculturalism, a busybody movement that claims a monopoly of virtue in protecting selected minority groups – victims all – from every possibility of offense whether the victims like it or not. Ultimately the two movements must collide: environmentalism and limitations on population growth imply restricted immigration, while multiculturalism, always in search of new ethnic groups to champion, demands "celebrating" it.

Nevertheless, immigration-fueled growth remains a threat, not just to the physical environment but to American national identity. This is not lost on our multiculturalists who see very little that is good in the American tradition anyway, and who are pleased to use immigrants, especially the least assimilable among them, as instruments for its dilution.

The resulting ethnic diversity promotes not tolerance but resentment and separatism. Though Miami is an interesting city, its heavily Hispanic population has little identification with Western norms, so that it a commonplace to say that it is no longer an American city; it is said by many of its residents to be the capital city of Latin America. And according to Mario Obledo, president of the League of United Latin American Citizens, it is a virtual certainty that "California is going to be a Mexican state." He adds that if Americans "don't like it they should leave." The Latino student organization MECHa, which has chapters on 4,000 campuses across the country, has stated, "We declare the independence of our mestizo nation. We are bronze people with a bronze agenda." Its slogan, reminiscent of Mussolini's fascism, is "For our race, everything; for those outside our race, nothing."

This goes unchallenged by the politically correct Left, which hasn't the stomach to speak up against what it seems to regard as the legitimate demands of noble savages. Thus, multiculturalism and mass immigration alter the country's character not by debate and democratic consensus but by the tyranny of the accomplished fact.

But overpopulation remains a threat. It has not gone away, it is growing. An exploding population worldwide means more pollution and future wars over water, land, and living space. Immigrants, whether they arrive legally or not, quickly establish roots which can't be pulled no matter how many indigenous Americans might resent the growing influence of foreign cultures. If responsible elites – academics, journalists, politicians, and others – can't shed their paralytic guilt and their terror of being called racists, then irresponsible people will. Inevitably, we shall have a violent backlash among people who, in rebellion against the multicultural creed, do not agree that they have a duty to "celebrate" the destruction of their own culture.

The Oldest Profession
Faces New Competition

April 2015 saw the creation of 223,000 new jobs, which lowered the official rate of unemployment to 5.4 percent. Is this great news?

Nope. It's mostly government hype because the true extent of joblessness is far higher than that although it is disguised by creative accounting. Something like three-fourths of the new jobs is part-time, poorly paid and offer neither a decent salary nor benefits nor a secure future. Also, the official rate doesn't include people who, because of discouragement, have dropped out of the labor market; or those who have gone back to school, hoping to wait out the bad job market until an upturn in jobs might eventually appear.

Another escape from a bad labor market is disability payments, resort to which has quadrupled since 1970 even though Americans are healthier than ever. And the new job figures don't account for the 22 million Americans who have been *under*employed for many years, such as college graduates working as waiters and bartenders. But the telling fact is that the full-time labor force has shrunk to its smallest size in decades and that average wages have remained flat since the 1980s.

This dismal picture is due increasingly to automation – to machines replacing human labor – and it will only get worse.

Moore's Law, formulated in 1965, says that the power of computers doubles every 18 to 24 months, and to date the law has held firm. Because of the ever-increasing adaptability of machines, many prognosticators are pessimistic about the future of human labor. Cornell University's Hod Lipson, a robotics engineer, says that one day "all jobs will be gone, including creative ones." Yes, *all*.

This is apparently not taken seriously by most economists, who persist in believing that technology will create as many new jobs as it destroys, just as it always has. But even if jobs were created in new sectors, what would stop machines from claiming *them* as well?

What is different about the digital revolution is that its machines seem capable of doing literally everything more efficiently than humans, including services. A case in point is machines designed to comfort humans. For a good many years, the Japanese, who have been leaders in artificial intelligence, have owned *aibos*, robotic pets such as mechanical dogs that wag their tails and display friendship. Many are thought of as family members. When they wear out and can't be repaired, funerals are held for them. Robots are blending into human culture as if they were fellow creatures of nature.

The oldest profession makes for an interesting illustration of how far this can go: According to May's edition of *Reason* magazine, life-sized, anatomically correct dolls – "sexbots" with "skin" virtually indistinguishable from human flesh – are already plying their trade in Japanese brothels. Gerhard Fettweis, a professor of communications at Dresden University, believes that within 20 years, sexbots will mimic humans' biochemical signaling system corresponding to arousal and tenderness when appropriate. Two

New Zealand researchers predict that robot prostitutes will put their human colleagues out of business by 2050.

If hookers can be replaced, what profession is secure? What are the prospects for humans in any line of work? Our social contract has always said that education and hard work would get you the American dream. But as jobs of every description disappear, it will eventually become clear to all of us that a new social contract is needed to guarantee economic security for everyone who, through no fault of their own, becomes jobless.

There is ample precedent for this. A guaranteed annual income has been favored by prominent economists on both the Left and the Right, including James Tobin, Paul Samuelson, J.K. Galbraith, Milton Friedman, and Friedrich Hayek. In 1968, 1,200 economists signed a letter to Congress promoting the idea. Alaska has used a Permanent Fund since 1977 to distribute billions to its residents from oil wealth without any preconditions except residency.

In 1969, President Nixon proposed a "Family Assistance Plan" intended to guarantee a basic income for every family. The plan was eventually dropped because of opposition (from caseworkers and welfare administrators, among others, whose careers were threatened), and also because a pilot program found that income guarantees reduced incentives to work. But in a world devoid of jobs, such objections will be moot.

There are several approaches to a guaranteed income, and all are simpler than the chaotic welfare system and crony capitalism that now supports tens of millions. And since wealth will be generated by machines, everyone would get equal payments and there would be no justification for the grotesque inequalities we have now.

In *The Second Industrial Revolution*, authors Erik Brynjolfsson and Andrew McAfee offer a startling image of how suddenly exponential change may overwhelm us: Put a grain of rice on the first square of a chess board, then two on the second, four on the third, and so on. Through most of the board, the numbers rise unimpressively. But in the last rows, they rise at an unbelievable rate: at the last square we find a pile of rice bigger than Mount Everest.

This is how the loss of jobs is likely to proceed: with deceptive slowness at first, then with brutal speed. Rampant technology will disrupt every aspect of life. The time to begin facing up to the march of machines is now rather than later. Whatever we may think about the guaranteed income, it is simply inevitable. Providing security for millions of people who won't have jobs is something we shouldn't be putting off.

Must we "Celebrate" New Americans?

The local newspaper demands that we "celebrate" the influx of Third World immigrants into the Fargo area and says, without offering evidence of any sort, that they do not burden the taxpayers and that ethnic diversity enriches us all. It adds that "every wave of refugees, starting in the 1940s … has added to the color and richness of society's tapestry."

Ah, those were the good old days. Up until the 1980s, jobs of all kinds were plentiful. Today they're being steadily lost to globalization and to automation. Three-quarters of the jobs being created today are part-time, temporary, poorly paid and with no security and no benefits. Careers are mostly a thing of the past, and wages in general have been flat since the 1980s. Bringing immigrants into this uncertain environment is reckless.

Lutheran Social Services is helping to resettle Somalis who arrive mostly poor and uneducated, with a resettlement package that includes air transportation, food stamps, housing subsidies, Medicaid, job training, cash payments extending for several years, and education for each of their kids – Somalis typically have six – that runs about $11, 000 per year. That's not a burden to taxpayers? The *Minneapolis Star-Tribune* reports that $1.6 billion per year is remitted to their connections back in Somalia, and that some of it winds up in the hands of Al Shabab, a terrorist organization.

"Immigrants have assimilated into their communities while preserving the heritage of their ethnic and religious roots," *The Forum* says." Exactly. These days, immigrants don't blend into American life but sequester themselves into "*their* communities." Although Jefferson, Franklin and other founders of the republic wanted immigrants "dispersed" all over the land, we have something like 30,000 Somalis (Somali spokesmen say it's far higher) concentrated in an enclave near Minneapolis called "Little Mogadishu."

Why do so many come to Minnesota? Because, as reported by the US State Department, Minnesota's welfare system, along with Maine's, is the most generous in the nation. The State Department also admits that some 20,000-30,000 Somalis got into the US by lying about family connections already here, and that most are not refugees but are seeking a more affluent life.

Somali culture includes the "richness" of female circumcision, forced marriages, polygamy, male dominance, and sharia law. Self-segregated from the broader Anglo culture, will they voluntarily give up such practices? If not, will America's leaders have the backbone to insist on real assimilation? And for their part, will devout Muslims want to assimilate into a shallow pop culture that is devoted chiefly to electronic toys, celebrity worship and rap?

Minneapolis has Somali gangs that engage in sex trafficking, and friction between Somalis and indigenous students in the public schools is commonplace. It's pointless to ask who is at fault when the problem is a clash of cultures that have radically different world views. In Europe, marginalized Muslims commonly inhabit urban ghettoes that have no-go zones where non-Muslims fear to tread. Of course, that couldn't happen here. Could it?

Neither are Hispanic immigrants and their progeny evenly dispersed throughout the land. They are heavily concentrated in California (where nearly half the population is of Hispanic origin) and the southwest, often in totally self-sufficient communities with their own Spanish-language newspapers, radio, and TV. Miami is said to be an interesting city, but it is no longer an American city. It has come to be known as the "Capital of Latin America," and some residents of Miami-Dade County are talking about secession. So is La Raza, an organization of disaffected and ambitious Mexicans who want to reclaim California from what they deem an inferior Anglo culture.

Yet those who presume to question the wisdom of mass immigration are, according to the Forum, nativists, xenophobes, racists, liars, and dolts.

Well, count me in. My question is admittedly impertinent: How does America benefit by importing uneducated and impoverished people, especially when there is no serious attempt at assimilating them? Of course, the received answer is that protecting American interests is selfish and that we must prove our nobility by sacrificing our own interests to the world's less fortunate.

At one time our schools, churches, and businesses sought to turn foreigners into Americans because everyone thought that assimilation was important for all concerned. But today's multicultural elites relish the idea of a balkanized America without a dominant cultural tradition. So, as Samuel Huntington has put it in his book, *Who Are We?*, they promote "measures consciously designed to weaken America's cultural and creedal identity and to strengthen racial, ethnic, cultural, and other subnational identities."

He adds that "efforts by a nation's leaders to deconstruct the nation they governed were, quite possibly, without precedent in human history."

In *The Unmaking of America,* A.M. Schlesinger, Jr. warned that what began as an "ethnic upsurge" of resentment against Eurocentrism in the 1960s now threatens to become a "counter-revolution against the original idea of America as 'one people,' a common culture, a single nation." Three centuries of American unity are being trashed in the name of diversity. For our fashionable elites, diversity is simply a power trip and a means to demonstrate their moral superiority.

One of our great national myths is that ethnic diversity makes life richer for everyone. Except that it doesn't. Harvard Prof. Robert Putnam, whose team has conducted the largest survey on the subject to date, says that diversity damages "social capital" – the ability of people to trust each other and work toward common goals. Putnam's research finds that "civic collaboration, altruism, personal friendship, confidence in local institutions, [and even] happiness" are damaged as diversity increases.

"It would be unfortunate," he concludes, "if a politically correct progressivism were to deny the reality of the challenge to social solidarity posed by diversity." Research showing that ethnic diversity is socially disruptive has been extant for years, yet our diversity-mongers go on swearing that they've never heard of it.

So, who are we? What does it mean to be an American? If citizenship is anything, Schlesinger says, "it is membership in a political community with a more or less distinctive political identity

– a set of public values about governance and law that are very widely shared by those within it." But instead of seeking unity, we are recklessly courting a Hobbesian war of all against all, one in which rival identity groups press their own separate claims for power and prestige and have no strong sympathies in common.

Mass immigration changes the character of nations. Yet it is imposed upon us by private organizations and political elites as an accomplished fact, as if the identities and numbers of its immigrants were none of the public's business and required no debate. Thus, three centuries of American unity are being deconstructed by the zealotry of a handful of multiculturalists.

But immigration does require debate, and soon – before our multiculturalists succeed in turning America into a Third World crash pad.

How the Academic Status Race Exploits Students

North Dakota State University's president Dean Bresciani wants to grow his campus' enrollment from 14,516 to 18,000, increase scholarships to $100 million, and expand endowed faculty positions. All this will be done in order to gain membership in the Association of American Universities, an event which, Bresciani says, will confer … status.

Yeah, status.

We might appraise a university's quality by its production of Rhodes Scholars, its Pulitzer Prizes and so on. But no; in higher education, as in corporate life, the ultimate proof of success is unceasing growth.

Mark Hagerott, the state's Chancellor of Higher Education, boasts that NDSU and UND have retention rates of 80 percent. That, however, is true only for the first year; at the University of North Dakota just 54 percent of freshmen graduate within 6 years, while at NDSU only 47 percent ever finish. Both are well below the national average, which is 61 percent. This is an appalling waste of time and resources, and scraping the bottom of the barrel for thousands more marginal students will guarantee an even higher dropout rate.

Students who drop out usually do so because they were never serious about learning in the first place. They enroll in order to socialize, to party, and enjoy a fun interval before deciding what to do with themselves in their adult lives. But even serious students drop out when they see little hope that their investment in college will ever pay off. And for most of them there are few grounds for hope. According to the Center for College Affordability, barely half of new graduates succeed in securing jobs that actually require a degree.

Against what "everyone knows," even the most challenging college skills are in oversupply. The Census Bureau reports that 74 percent of graduates – check it out – with degrees in science, technology, engineering, and math are working outside their fields. The much-publicized "critical shortage" of STEM personnel is a fraud drummed up by businesses hoping that continued surpluses will further depress wages, and by universities hoping to keep enrollments high. Even President Obama is calling for another million STEM graduates over the next decade.

What is NDSU's response to this glut? Why, it's going to open a new $29 million building for STEM training this spring!

In a flooded market, graduates take what they can get. In 2003 the National Science Foundation found that among 122,000 psychology majors, only five percent held jobs in that field. The Atlantic Monthly has reported that 53.6 percent of college graduates under age 25 currently have jobs that don't require a 4-year degree. Fourteen percent of waiters and waitresses – 323,000 people – have degrees, as do 22 percent of cashiers and 17 percent of bartenders, telemarketers, and motel clerks. According to US News, 284,000 college graduates are working for minimum wage, nearly twice the rate of just five years before.

And 36 percent of graduates aged 25-32 are "boomerangers," graduates who have moved back in with their parents because they can't find jobs that allow them to be self-supporting. Among those who manage to live apart from their parents, another 41 percent remain dependent upon them for financial support.

To compound their troubles, new graduates are burdened with an average of $28,950 in debts. In 2011, student indebtedness nationwide was $1.16 trillion. According to the Census Bureau, some 294,000 M.A.s and 33,000 Ph.D.s are on welfare.

The degree glut has been the five-ton elephant in academia's living room for over 40 years. Yet campus administrators everywhere – deeply, deeply absorbed in expanding their enrollments – claim they can't see it.

Our boosters have fuzzy vision too. Mr. Craig Whitney, who is CEO of the local Chamber of Commerce, takes it for granted that universities are handmaids of commerce, and urges President Bresciani to "grow the business" – the business being NDSU – "with an eye toward the economic success of our region." He approvingly quotes Bresciani to the effect that "our state's current job vacancies of 20,000 positions, most of which call for a college education, is estimated to double if not triple by 2020."

Estimated by whom? Whoever it is, should quit smoking opium.

Isn't it unseemly for universities to practice vulgar boosterism as a means of gaining status for campus administrators while creating ruin for their students? Isn't it cynical to keep flooding the country with worthless degrees when most graduates even now are unable to find college-level jobs? What will NDSU do when it becomes plain to everyone that the market for virtually every college skill is saturated? Massive unemployment among college graduates is not an anomaly that will soon pass. By persistently flooding skilled job markets, the campuses are creating a lifetime curse for millions of their graduates.

You'd think that higher education would have the decency to offer honest career counseling to prospective students who seem no longer to read newspapers or watch the evening news. Ignorant of market conditions, generations of graduates are being led like sheep to the slaughter.

It used to be said that growth for the sake of growth is the ideology of the cancer cell. Today, sadly, it's also the ideology of our universities.

A Generational Return to the Womb?

Although indoctrination, censorship and arbitrary punishments have become normal features of higher education, campus authoritarianism has recently taken a curious turn: A good many students, far from chafing under campus thought control, have become comfortable with it, and are even coming to like it. So now we have demands for another round of censorship, this time from students themselves. Getting students to love their own subjugation is one of multiculturalism's greatest achievements.

In just a bit over 30 years, multiculturalism's war against Western values has succeeded brilliantly in stripping students of their self-confidence. "Look at me," they now say – "I'm easily hurt; therefore, you must protect me." From what? Not just unkind words, but also reminders of unpleasant experiences in their own past. Call it fragility chic.

Its language is already mainstream. Examples include "trauma" (emotional distress brought on by words or images); "trigger warnings" (a cautionary preface to information that someone might find upsetting); "microaggressions" (subtle words or body language that might suggest bigotry); "safe spaces" (shelters where students may be shielded from further trauma); and so on.

The *New York Times'* Judith shulevitz finds an "increasingly prevalent" view among students that they should not have to risk hearing ideas that don't flatter their existing prejudices. Observing a debate at Brown University on the role of culture in sexual assault, she quotes a co-ed who fled the event feeling "bombarded by a lot of viewpoints that really go against my dearly and closely held beliefs."

So, she and others repaired to a campus safe space designed to provide refuge from words, ideas, and images they may find injurious. Shulevitz describes it as a "equipped with cookies, coloring books, bubbles, Play-Doh, pillows, calming music, blankets, and a video of frolicking puppies, as well as students and staff members trained to deal with trauma."

At Columbia, students are demanding the removal of Ovid from reading assignments because of his descriptions of rape. At Georgetown and Oberlin, commentator Christiana Hoff Sommers was received with trigger warnings concerning her skepticism about the existence of a campus "rape culture" and the possibility that her presentation might "contain discussions of sexual assault and may deny the experiences of survivors."

Even humor is injurious. Comedians Chris Rock, Bill Maher and Jerry Seinfeld have all abandoned the college circuit because audiences are too easily offended. Seinfeld despairs of the political correctness that has overtaken the campuses and rendered virtually every subject taboo. Professors too, live in fear, knowing that a single verbal slip can end their careers.

College censorship inevitably spills over into the publishing industry as well. *The Adventures of Huckleberry Finn,* arguably America's greatest novel, has been bowdlerized to remove all references to Nigger Jim and Injun Joe, lest sensitive readers expire from shock. Many other books have also been sanitized, often without the knowledge of their living authors. Dianne Ravitch's book, *The Language Police*, contains as a glossary *of* "Banned words, Usages, Stereotypes and Topics" that textbook publishers won't touch. It runs 30 pages, and the list has probably doubled since its publication in 2003.

"How boring," Ravitch says, "for students to be restricted only to stories that flatter their self-esteem or that purge complexity and unpleasant reality from history or current events."

In *Tablet* magazine, Todd Gitlin recounts his experience at age 19 when his history class was shown a film on the holocaust, *Night and Fog*, by Alain Resnais. Gitlin now asks: "Should we have been given a trigger warning?"

"Hell no," he says. "The pedagogic tactic [of the film was] to produce discomfort, to wound us, to crumple our innocence. Discomfort was the crucible for a 'teachable moment.' We ... needed shocking. Had we not been shocked, upended, we would have been deprived of the profundity of the [film]. Jarring was of the essence. A viewer left in comfort would be a viewer left ignorant."

Discomfort and even shock are sometimes necessary to adequately express a point. Gitlin's advice to college students is: "You're in school to be disturbed .... Shall we stop talking about rape, lynching, death camps? Shall we stop reading the annals of civilization which are, among other things, annals of slaughter? .... Whatever happened to, 'you shall know the truth, and the truth shall make you free?"

Colleges are becoming total institutions bent on shielding students from every aspect of life. It's as if a whole generation has just popped into existence with no experience of family, friends, film, television, or newsprint and is so innocent that just one careless word will be put in a padded cell. College, once a passage to adulthood, is becoming a return to the womb.

What has brought on this new infantilism? According to Steven Horwitz, a professor at St. Lawrence University, it's due to the rise of overprotective parents during childrearing. Where children were once expected to settle conflicts among themselves, they are now closely supervised by a third party – parents – who settle disputes for them. As they grow up, the kids' expectation of third party intervention remains with them. Even in their 20s they want intricate rules to prevent conflict and, should it occur, they now expect college administrators to adjudicate it. Horwitz says that the ability to settle disputes without the intervention of outsiders is a "key part of the liberal order," and that the loss of this ability is a threat to liberalism and democracy.

Can anything be more grotesque than academicians presiding gleefully over a regime of censorship?

They do so because there is nothing to stop them. In higher education the political Left, which espouses multiculturalism and its regime of political correctness, enjoys a political monopoly. It's the only game in town and its power goes unchecked. There is no other ideology, no other countervailing force to challenge the Left's agenda.

The impending retirement of the '60s radicals, who for fifty years have been contemptuous of Western values, and who still retain disproportionate influence on the campuses, might help break the monopoly. Otherwise, sanity can only be restored by piecemeal actions from outside the campuses, such as lawsuits by a civil rights organization. Meantime, academia's thought police will go on running wild.

Self-Flattery
Inhibits Reform

In its March 16 editorial, the Forum cites a Gallup survey that says 89% of North Dakotans believe that the state's schools are either excellent or good, and it chortles that this "remarkable result places North Dakota ahead of all other states in positive attitudes about schools." But this is simply a case of local chauvinism and says nothing about actual realities.

Precisely because this feel-good delusion is found nationwide, neither this state nor any other can muster a constituency for the reform that is badly needed everywhere. The more we admire our schools, the less reason we have to improve them. Chester Finn, who was a former assistant secretary of education, calls this syndrome "retail complacency," meaning that while there is general agreement that American schools are generally bad, the ones in – name your state – are excellent.

The Forum attributes North Dakota's alleged excellence to generous funding. But this is also a destructive myth which deflects public attention from the real causes of school failure. Researchers find little connection between funding levels and school performance. What they usually find instead is a strong connection between student achievement and stable home environments in which education is taken seriously. Education Week observes that "students who are in stable communities and in higher income families [tend to] have greater successes later on."

We see this in every international comparison of student achievement, where the top 5 or 6 nations are invariably in south Asia, where both close families and education are valued far more than in the West. In the TIMSS and PISA studies in math, reading, and science the five top participants invariably include Hong Kong, Singapore, Taiwan, Macao, Japan, and South Korea. None has per-pupil funding equal to those of Western states. American students are normally in the middle, if not at the bottom, depending on their grade level and the number of countries involved. Even so, we are normally outscored by relatively impoverished countries like Estonia, Poland, Vietnam, Slovenia, Latvia, and Slovakia.

Still more shamefully, the US has one of the highest rates of illiteracy in the developed world. The National Assessment of Adult illiteracy says that 14% (32 million) of adults can't read, and another 21% read at the 5th grade level. Among high school graduates, 19% left without ever having learned to read. This has gone unchanged over the past ten years.

America's great failure lies in what it fails to teach. For a hundred years reformers have condemned the smorgasbord curriculum which invites students to avoid challenging courses in favor of junk. Check the Fargo School District's program of studies and you'll see that it's packed with shallow electives. This crowds out instruction in math, reading, history and the essentials by which a person is educated.

Occasional complaints about the schools, the Forum says, "are not reflective of the overall positive attitudes revealed in the poll." This is strange reasoning: Do the Forum's editors believe that attitudes trump facts? If 89% of those polled love unicorns, does that bring unicorns into existence?

Complacent people assume, against all common sense, that the experts must know what they are doing. Anyone who observes the ed schools knows that this is nonsense.

False praise like that of the Forum's is of no help in bringing about school reform. By the way: Are the state's schools any better than the American average? It depends on who you ask. North Dakota is ranked 15th by the Wall Street Journal and 48th by US News. Massachusetts and Maryland are normally judged at the top of the nation.